SOME EARLY DYNASTIES
OF
SOUTH INDIA

By the same author:

Early History of North India
The Śakas in India
Social Life in Ancient India
Evolution of Hindu Sects
Traditional Values in Indian Life (Published by India International Centre for Indian National Commission for UNESCO)
The Achaemenids in India
Racial Affinities of Early North Indian Tribes
Dharma O Kusaṁskār (Religion and Superstition) (in Bengali)

SOME EARLY DYNASTIES OF SOUTH INDIA

SUDHAKAR CHATTOPADHYAYA

MOTILAL BANARSIDASS
Delhi :: Varanasi :: Patna

Head Office : BUNGALOW ROAD, JAWAHARNAGAR, DELHI-7
Branches : 1. CHOWK, VARANASI-1 (U.P.)
2. ASHOK RAJPATH, PATNA-4 (BIHAR)

ISBN 0-8426-0618-1

First Edition : *Delhi* 1974

Printed in India
BY SHANTILAL JAIN, AT SHRI JAINENDRA PRESS, BUNGALOW ROAD, JAWAHAR-NAGAR, DELHI-7 AND PUBLISHED BY SUNDARLAL JAIN FOR MOTILAL BANARSIDASS, BUNGALOW ROAD, JAWAHARNAGAR, DELHI-7

To

AJOY

with blessings

PREFACE

In the following pages an attempt has been made to trace the history of the Sātavāhanas and their immediate successors. Two things are to be especially noted in this connection : *first*, I have not included in the list of the *successors*, the Viṣṇu-kuṇḍins or the Kadambas, because they were successors to the successors of the Sātavāhanas ; *secondly*, while dealing with the Vākāṭakas I have not discussed the history of the contemporary dynasties for the same reason.

In the chapters on the Sātavāhanas, I have tried to reconcile the different Purāṇic versions instead of relying dogmatically on this or that Purāṇa in preference to other as has been the case with some modern historians, who follow either the *Matsya* account or the *Vāyu* one. If this reconcilation is fruitful, it will be found that the Purāṇic account tallies to a large extent with the epigraphic and numismatic sources at our disposal. I have discussed afresh the date of Gautamīputra Śātakarṇi which forms the pivot of the later Sātavāhana history.

Among the eastern dynasties that succeeded the Sātavāhanas, I have noted a dynasty of the Guntur kings started by Siṁhavarman separate from the Kāñcī-Pallava dynasty founded by Mahārāja-bappasvāmī.

Of the western successors, I have noted in detail the history of the Ābhīras. The accounts of the *MUḌĀNANDAS* and the *CUṬUS* have been given in Appendix VI and not in the body of the book, because we practically know definitely nothing of them excepting the bare existence of one *MUḌĀNANDA* and one *CUṬU* king.

The genealogy and chronology of the Vākāṭaka dynasty have been discussed afresh and so the account that follows differs materially from that of the early historians dealing with the subject.

In conclusion, I beg to state that after sending the manuscript to the press I became seriously ill and was confined to bed for nearly a year. It became impossible for me to go through the *proof* pages, and it was through the kindness of

Shri Sundarlal Jain, who arranged for the *proof* page corrections, that the book has seen the light to-day. I pay my respectful thanks to my publisher.

I am painfully aware of many mistakes that have crept into the book and for this I crave the indulgence of the readers.

Santiniketan S. Chattopadhyaya

ABBREVIATIONS

ABORI	— *Annals of the Bhandarkar Oriental Research Institute*
AHD	— *Ancient History of the Deccan* by G. J. Dubreuil
Ait. Br	— *Aitareya Brāhmaṇa*
AIU	— *Age of Imperial Unity*, ed. R. C. Majumdar and A. S. Altekar
ANM	— *Age of the Nandas and the Mauryas*, ed. K.A.N. Sastri
ASIR	— *Archaeological Survey of India Reports*
ASWI	— *Archaeological Survey of Western India*
Bomb. Gaz.	— *Bombay Gazetteer*
CHI	— *Cambridge History of India*
CHIN	— *Comprehensive History of India*, ed. K.A.N. Sastri
CIC	— *Catalogue of the Indian Coins*, ed. Rapson
CII and *Corpus*	— *Corpus Inscriptionam Indicarum*
DKA	— *Dynasties of the Kali Age*, Pargiter
EHAC	— *Early History of the Andhra Country* by K. Gopalachari
EHD	— *The Early History of the Deccan*, G. Yazdani
EHI	— *Early History of India* by V. Smith
EHNI	— *Early History of North India* by S. Chattopadhyaya
Ep. Ind.	— *Epigraphia Indica*
Foreign Notices	— *Foreign Notices of South India* by K.A.N. Sastri
GBI	— *The Greeks in Bactria and India* by W. Tarn
Ind. Ant. and *IA*	— *Indian Antiquary*
IHQ	— *Indian Historical Quarterly*
JA	— *Journal Asiatique*
JAHRS	— *Journal of the Andhra Historical Research Society*

JBBRAS	—	*Journal of the Bombay Branch of the Royal Asiatic Society*
JBORS	—	*Journal of the Bihar and Orissa Research Society*
JIH	—	*Journal of Indian History*
JNSI	—	*Journal of the Numismatic Society of India*
JRAS	—	*Journal of the Royal Asiatic Society of Great Britain*
JRASB(L)		*Journal of the Royal Asiatic Society of Bengal : Letters*
Luders	—	*List of Brahmi Inscriptions*
Manu	—	*Manu Samhita*
MASR	—	*Mysore Archaeological Survey Report*
NHIP	—	*New History of the Indian People*, ed. R. C. Majumdar and A. S. Altekar
PHAI	—	*Political History of Ancient India* by H. C. Raychaudhuri
PIHC	—	*Proceedings of the Indian History Congress*
POC	—	*Proceedings of the All-India Oriental Conference*
Racial Elements	—	*Racial Elements in Indian Population* by B. S. Guha
RV.	—	*Ṛgveda*
Sātavāhana Coins	—	*Sātavāhana Coins in the Andhra Pradesh Govt. Museum* by Rama Rao
Select Ins.	—	*Select Inscriptions* by D. C. Sircar
Suc Sat	—	*Successors of the Sātavāhanas* by D. C. Sircar
The Periplus	—	*The Periplus of the Erythraean Sea* by W. H. Schoff
VA	—	*The Vedic Age*, ed. R. C. Majumdar and A. S. Altekar
Vayu	—	*Vāyu Purāṇa*
Yājñavalkya	—	*Yājñavalkya Saṃhitā*

CONTENTS

INTRODUCTORY

Economic Factors in South Indian History

Lying to the south of the Vindhyas, the Peninsular India, known to the ancients as *Dakṣiṇāpatha*, is a triangular block of old rocks reaching at places 'at a height of 8,760 feet but never having the cover of dense forest'. The average soil is not very fertile though the black soil, localised in different areas, is good for many crops, especially cotton, but hard human labour is necessary to make the same cultivable. In such wild localities the life naturally came to be controlled by the local chiefs and, therefore, in the history of the land though we find rise of smaller and greater kingdoms, the tribal chiefs wielded great power and influence. Even a strong emperor like Aśoka had to recognise the Raṭhikas and the Bhojakas of the Maharashtra country, while the Sātavāhanas who came to power through their help had to allow these feudal chiefs enjoy considerable amount of autonomy. The Raṭhikas and the Bhojakas mainly dominated the Marathi speaking Khandesh and Berar, while to the south, extending far into the Kanarese speaking area, were the Cuṭus and in the east the Ikṣvākus and the Pallavas.

The presence of the Ikṣvākus in the eastern Deccan is interesting, for it shows the tribal drifts in South India in that far off age. The Ikṣvākus were of North Indian origin and they evidently carried with them the North Indian tradition and culture.[1]

1. J. Ph. Vogel observes that 'it is interesting to meet with a line of rulers, settled in the Telugu country, which claimed descent from Ikhāku, i.e., Ikkhāku (=Skt. *Ikshvāku*), the mythical progenitor of the famous Solar dynasty of Ayodhyā. It is well-known that not only Rāma belonged to that illustrious house, but the Buddha, too, is called a scion of the race of Ikshāku (Pali *Okkāka*). It is clear, in any case, that these Southern Ikhākus were rulers of some importance, as they formed matrimonial alliances not only with the *Mahārājas* of Vanavāsa, but also with the kings, presumably the descendants of the Satrap Chashṭana, who resided at Ujjayinī in Central India. The nomenclature of these Southern Ikhāku kings, coupling their personal names with metronymics like Māḍhariputa and Vāsiṭhīputa, seems to be a practice bor-

Similarly, the Sātavāhanas, who were of Andhra or Telegu stock, founded an empire in West Maharashtra.[1] What part the economic factors played in such migrations is difficult to determine, but one thing is clear that to the south of the Vindhya as to its north different ethnic elements contributed to the rise of a composite type of culture. It is, however, not unlikely that the central part of the Peninsula being more rugged and rocky, life thrived more easily on the eastern and western coasts,[2] and thus human settlements in the early period developed mainly in these areas. Besides Aśokan edicts, which were inspired by religious *cum* imperialistic motives,[3] it is not an accident of history that the earliest epigraphs come from east and west. Reference may be made to Bhotripolu inscription of Kubiraka,[4] and the Nasik and Nanaghat inscriptions of the Sātavāhanas.

Early classical authors like Megasthenes, and others who utilised the record left by Megasthenes, speak of the kingdoms

rowed from the earlier rulers of the Andhra dynasty. It will hardly be necessary to quote the instance of Vāsiṭhīputa Siri-Pulumāvi and Gotamīputa Sātakaṇṇi. On the other hand, there are in these inscriptions certain expressions which are also found in the Prakrit copper-plate grants of the early Pallavas'. (*Ep. Ind.*, xx, 6)

1. *infra*
2. Even at the present time the population varies from 256 to over 512 per square mile on the coastal regions.
3. Aśoka issued his edicts to be read by the people in general. So their find spots naturally give us a clue to determine the populous areas in the Peninsula. Thus his Rock Edicts have been found at the Peninsula of Kathiawad (Saurashtra), Dhauli and Jaugada in Orissa, Sopara in Maharashtra and at Erragudi on a rock in the Kurnool district, Andhra Pradesh. Two separate Rock Edicts also have been found in Orissa. The minor Rock Edicts are found at Brahmagiri, Siddapura and Jaṭinga-Ramesvara, in Chitaldurg district of Northern Mysore; Maski, in Raichur district, formerly in Nizam's dominion, Hyderabad; Erragudi, in Kurnool district, Andhra Pradesh; Govimath, in Raichur district; Palkigundu, a hill about two miles distant from Govimath; Rajulamandagiri, on a rock near Pattikonda in Kurnool district. From these evidences it appears that the most populous areas in the ancient period in the Peninsular India were Western Maharashtra, Orissa, Andhra Pradesh including Hyderabad and the northern portion of the Mysore State. This account tallies to a great extent with the picture that we get of the present day.
4. *AHD*, 11

lying to the eastern side of the Peninsula only. The western side formed a part of the kingdom of Sandrocottas (Candragupta) and hence evidently it has not been mentioned separately. Thus we are informed that 'Herakles begat a daughter in India whom he called Pandaia. To her he assigned that portion of India which lies southward and extends to the sea, while he distributed the people subject to her rule into 365 villages, giving orders that one village should each day bring to the treasury the royal tribute, so that the queen might always have the assistance of those men whose turn it was to pay the tribute in coercing those who for the time being were defaulters in their payments.'[1] The account shows that the Greek ambassador must have heard of the Pāṇḍya territory, possibly with its capital Madura, which has been described as Dakṣiṇa-Mathurā, South Mathurā, possibly implying that it was a colony of the Yādavas to whose clan Herakles (Vāsudeva) belonged. But the authenticity of such a tradition is very doubtful.

Megasthenes further speaks of two important kingdoms on the eastern coast, the kingdom of Kaliṅga and of Andhra. We are informed that Calingae possessed sixty thousand foot-soldiers, one thousand horsemen and seven thousand elephants, while Andarae or the Andhras had numerous villages and thirty towns defended by walls and towers and they supplied the king with an army of 100,000 infantry, 2000 cavalry and 1000 elephants.[2]

Pliny who died in A.D. 79 and who drew his materials from Megasthenes and others refers not only to the Andhras but also to the *Calingae* proper as well as *Maccokalingae* and the *Modogalingae*. H.C. Raychaudhuri draws our attention to the fact that, 'in the epics, the *Rāmāyaṇa* and the *Mahābhārata*, we find references to the Matsya-Kaliṅgas and the Madra-Kaliṅgas which may represent the two tribes mentioned by the classical writer. It has, however, been suggested by some that Modogaingae should be analysed as *Modaga* (Telugu *Mūḍuga*, three) + linga = Triliṅga or Telugu country, or as Modo – Mudu = three + galiṅga = Kaliṅga, i.e. Trikaliṅga. In other words, the term is taken by these writers to correspond to Triliṅga (Andhra

1. *Foreign Notices*, 41
2. M'Crindle, *Ancient India*, 137-41

country), or to Trikaliṅga (parts of Mahanadi valley and Vizagapatam district), preferably the latter. It is difficult to come to a final conclusion until further evidences are available. The Matsya Kaliṅgas may have occupied the Oḍḍavādi country in the Vizagapatam region mentioned in the Dibbida plates.'[1]

One of the chief reasons why the Peninsular India, especially its highland portions, was sparingly populated was want of good roads connecting different parts of the country, as hinted in the *Periplus of the Erythraean Sea.*[2] W.H. Schoff quotes Tavernier's description of the Deccan to the effect that, 'wheel carriages do not travel, the roads being too much interrupted by high mountains, tanks, and rivers, and there being many narrow and difficult passes. It is with the greatest difficulty that one takes a small cart.'[3] This affected to a great extent the inland trade of the country and the free flow of population. Elsewhere, the *Periplus* further informs us: 'The inland country back from the coast toward the east comprises many desert regions and great mountains; and all kinds of wild beasts—leopards, tigers, elephants, enormous serpents, hyenas, and baboons of many sorts; and many populous nations, as far as the Ganges'.[4]

The Peninsular India is located on the maritime routes from the Mediterranean and Africa to China and thus it developed trade with nations on either side.[5] This had an important effect on the socio-political life of the people as well as the royal dynasties like the Sātavāhanas, Pallavas and others whose coins show that the rulers took particular care in maintaining a strong navy. Long before c. 45 A.D. when the nature of the monsoon in the Arabian Sea and the Indian Ocean was first discovered (*infra*), Egyptian and Greek sailors had been carrying on trade with the western seaboard of India. J. Kennedy maintains that monsoon must have been known to these sailors and to 'all who sailed along the African and the Arabian coast and that the normal trade route from the Persian Gulf to India can never have

1. *EHD*, ed. G. Yazdani, 19-20
2. *The Periplus*, ed. Schoff, 43
3. *ib.*, 196
4. *ib.*, 43
5. K.A.N. Sastri, *A History of South India*, 35

been along the inhospitable source of Gedrosia.'[1] This seems to indicate that the trade between India and the West was not coastal but it followed high sea routes. The establishment of the Sātavāhana empire, and later on the rule of Kṣaharātas (*infra*), brought peace in the Peninsula and so naturally the Indo-Occidental trade ushered in a new life in the land.

As we shall see later on, the Yavana sailors established settlements in the Far South and while they on their part became Indianised and adopted Indian culture the Indians also must have learnt a good deal from them and derived a good deal from their munificence. It is not an accident that the cave monasteries lie on the trade routes running from Kalyan, Thana, Chaul, Kuda and Mahad. The western traders not infrequently traversed this route and their terminus was possibly Junnar which is surrounded by no less than 135 Buddhist caves.

From the middle of the second century A.D. Peninsular India developed gradually her trade with South-East Asia and curiously enough we find that the pendulum of political prowess now moved from the western to the eastern side. The last three Sātavāhana rulers had their citadel in eastern Deccan while they were succeeded by Ikṣvākus, Bṛhatphalāyanas and Pallavas and to their south were the Colas and the Pāṇḍyas. Compared to them, their western contemporaries, the Ābhīras, Cuṭus, Kadambas and Ceras were of lesser importance. Already at the close of the first century A.D. some Greek sailors had explored the Bay of Bengal, though they were nothing more than of adventurous type.[2] The author of the *Periplus* and Pliny knew hardly anything definite about the Far East, while Ptolemy made important contribution to the knowledge of India beyond the Ganges. The coins of Trajan (98-117 A.D.) and Hadrian (117-138 A.D.) have been found on the eastern side though comparatively rare on the West. This shows that the Greek sailors were now gradually drifting themselves to the eastern side, proved more conclusively by the discoveries at Arikamedu near Pondicherry[3] (*infra*).

1. *JRAS*, 1898, 272-3
2. *Foreign Notices*, 7
3. R.E.M. Wheeler, A. Ghosh and Krishna Deva : 'Arikamedu : an Indo-Roman Trading-station on the East Coast of India' (*Ancient India*, No. 2, July, 1946)

As K.A.N. Sastri has pointed out, from Chinese accounts it is clear that from the first century B.C. South India maintained important trade and political relations with China by sea and possibly Kāñcī took the lead in this respect. There is further evidence to show that the Far South maintained 'active touch with the colonies of Indonesia and that these colonies often employed South Indian products in their exchanges with China'.[1]

Lastly we may note the impact of the north. Kauṭilya maintains that the southern trade routes are more valuable to the people of the Ganges-Jumna valley than the northern routes leading to the Himalayan states. No doubt in northern region the merchants could get blankets, skins and horses, but in the south they could secure more valuable objects like conchshells, diamonds, jewels, pearls and gold. From this it is clear that the north used to exert pressure on the south which the latter could exploit to its advantage. During the Kṣaharāta period merchandise from the north used to flow through Ozene or Ujjayinī and Paithan to the port of Barygaza which became the port *par excellence* for trade with the west. This situation, created by the civil strife of the Parthians which blocked the port of Barbarieum at the mouth of the Indus[2] and the unsettled condition due to tribal uprisings in eastern Parthia blocking the land routes to the west, added to the economic advantage of the south though then under the control of a foreign king, Nahapāna. It was only when a strong Gautamīputra Śātakarṇi took up arms successfully and drove out the aliens from the land, the economic life of the northern part of the Peninsula assumed a national form. The popularity of Buddhism as evidenced by the cave monasteries in Western Maharashtra, as we have already noted, was to a great extent influenced by this trade money. In the Far South, on the other hand, 'the city of Puhar had a large colony of foreign merchants from different parts of the world,' and among the articles of trade we hear of the products of the Ganges valley.[3] This would show how North India participated in the trade of the South which fur-

1. *Foreign Notices*, 12
2. *The Periplus*, ed. Schoff, 37
3. K.A.N. Sastri, *The Colas*, 99

ther developed a cosmopolitan character under the influence of foreigners as well.

The Pre-Sātavāhana Age

The great Indian peninsula lying to the south of the Vindhya or the Narmada, known as Dakṣiṇāpatha in ancient Indian literature, may be divided culturally into two distinct zones, the *first*, comprising the areas where Marhathi and Oriya prevail (known popularly as the Outer Band of the Aryan), and the *second* where the Dravidian tongue is in vogue. It is maintained that the Dravidians belong to the Mediterranean ethnic group and entered India through the north-western and western passes becoming ultimately the makers of the Harappan culture in India.[1] Later on under the pressure of the Aryan invasion they had to move into the interior, as proved by 'large Dravidian patches like Gandi, Kui, and Oraon which have been broken up a very great deal by the infiltration of the Aryan dialects'.[2] Under slow but steady Aryan pressure the Dravidians migrated gradually to the extreme south and made their chief habitat on the other side of the Godavari, while the part lying roughly to the north of it passed under the domination of the Aryans, though a narrow wedge of the Outer Band tongue reaches in the west a little south of Goa.[3]

The earliest historical reference to this trans-Vindhyan region is found in the *Aitareya Brāhmaṇa* (c. 800 B.C.) which refers to Bhīma, king of Vidarbha, and also to the Sātvats whose kings were styled as Bhojas.[4] The Sātvats were a branch of the Yādavas who are condemned in the *Ṛgveda* as *dāsa*.[5] In a passage of

1. "This older and more basic stratum of the Mediterranean group must be distinguished from another closely akin to the European type, which entered this country later, and whose remains have been found in large numbers in the Chalcolithic sites of the Indus Valley and further east. It is probable that this was the race responsible for the development of the Indus civilization and subsequently dispersed by the 'Aryan'-speaking Vedic invaders to the Gangetic basin, and, to a smaller extent, beyond the Vindhyas." (*Racial Elements*, 19)
2. *VA*, 155
3. G.A. Grierson, *Linguistic Survey of India*, i (1927), 144
4. *Ait Br*, vii. 34; viii. 14
5. *RV*, x. 62.10

the earliest Aryan document the Yadus along with the Turvaśas are described as being brought to India by Indra through the sea.[1] R.P. Chanda maintains that the Yadus belonging to the Alpine stock came from Western Asia and differed from Nordic Aryans in race and culture.[2] If the Sātvats were of Yādava origin they may also be considered to be *homo Alpinus* who possibly were the makers of the Outer Band Aryan culture.

It is generally believed that the authentic history of India begins in the sixth century B.C. when there arose sixteen mahājanapadas or great kingdoms as evidenced by the *Aṅguttara Nikāya*. Of these Assaka and part of Avanti lay in South India. The commentator Bhaṭṭasvāmin identifies Assaka with Mahārāṣtra. The part of Avanti in South India centred round Māhissatī or Māhiṣmatī, identified with modern Māndhātā on the Narmada. In the *Dīgha Nikāya*, on the other hand, Kaliṅga is mentioned as one of the seven great kingdoms of ancient India. So far thus practically South India had been maintaining its own history independent of the North. A change came when the Nandas came to power. The great Nanda king Mahāpadma, simply described as Nandarāja in the Hathigumpha inscription, appears to have conquered Kaliṅga and his dominion extended upto the river Godavari.[3] Thus for the first time a portion of South India came under the aegis of the North. The tradition of imperialism thus started by the Nanda ruler was carried to its logical extreme by the Mauryas. H.C. Raychaudhuri points out that the date 313 B.C., deducible from the account of Meruttuṅga, as marking the initial year of the rule of Candragupta, really refers to the beginning of his rule in the Avanti region, which constituted a province or state of his empire with headquarter in Ujjayinī.[4] After this conquest Candragupta realised that the *paths* leading to the South, as described in the *Mahābhārata*,[5] lay now under his feet and he at once marched towards the

1. *RV.*, vi. 20.12
2. R.P. Chanda, *Indo-Aryan Races*, 18-20, 40 ff
3. *PHAI*, 189
4. *ANM*, 136; cf. *GBI*, 47 and fn. 1 & 2
5. *Mbh.*, iii. 61.23. 'This road leads to Vidarbha (Berar), that one proceeds towards the land of the Kośalas (the Upper Mahanadi Valley); beyond them in the southern direction lies Dakṣiṇāpatha.'

South through these tracts. There are certain late inscriptions associating Candragupta with Mysore, but they can hardly be used for writing any sober history. The *Mudrārākṣasa* claims that his sway extended upto the southern ocean. Such descriptions are on *par* with the account of the Mandasor record claiming Kumāragupta as ruling over the earth. More important is the evidence furnished by the Tamil authors, assigned to the early centuries of the Christian era, on the achievements of the Moriyar in the far south of the Peninsula, occurring in the *Ahanānūru* and *Puranānūru*. The passages have been translated by V.R. Ramachandra Dikshitar as follows :

1. 'The rock of the sky-kissing high mountain which the Moriyar had cut down for the free passage of their golden chariot-wheels...'
2. 'If he should hear of our unbearable anguish and grief he would not, even for the sake of the immense riches of the Nandas, tarry there amidst the mountain rocks which the new Moriyan had cut down for the smooth passage of their well-adorned chariot wheels when they came down upon the south with an army of horses and elephants because the king of Mohūr had refused to submit when the Kōśar with chariots, swift flying like the winds, routed the enemy's forces on the field of battle with their drums vociferously sounding on the high hoary Podiyil hill.'
3. 'The sky-kissing snow-clapped mountain-rock which the Moriyar had cut down for the free passage of their golden chariot-wheels when they swept down on the south with the Vaḍukar marching before, strong with the strength of their mighty swift-flying arrows.'
4. 'The mountain-rock which the Moriyar with the sky-touching umbrella and the bannered chariot had cut down for the easy passage of their chariot-wheels.'

The mention of the Moriyar along with the Nandas in the above account clearly shows that the Mauryas are meant, though of course, not directly the first Maurya. The idea however seems to be conveyed by other indirect evidences. The army of Candragupta thus appears to have advanced as far as the Podiyil hill.

But it was more an armed intervention on behalf of the Kōśars than an actual conquest.

Candragupta was succeeded by his son Bindusāra. The Tibetan historian Tāranātha, a very late writer, credits Cāṇakya and Bindusāra with the destruction of kings and nobles of sixteen cities and thereby reducing to submission 'all the territories between the western and the eastern seas'. The region thus connoted by the description is rather vague. It may mean the Peninsular India lying between the Bay of Bengal (*Pūrvasamudra*) and the Arabian Sea (*Paścimajalanidhi*). It may also mean the region of North India which is described as Āryāvarta and as extending from the eastern to the western seas (*āsamudrāt tu vai pūrvāt āsamudrāt tu paścimāt*) in the work of Manu (ii. 20).

Thus in order to determine the theatre of Bindusāra's military operations we have to choose between the plains of North India on the one hand and the Deccan plateau on the other. There are of course some difficulties with the second alternative :

(a) We have no evidence whatsoever in associating Bindusāra directly with the Peninsular India; neither the Tamil, Sanskrit, Pali or Prakrit works contain even a faint allusion to it.

(b) Epigraphic records from the Far South or Kaliṅga, which tell so much about the Nandas, Candragupta and Aśoka are conspicuously silent about Bindusāra.

(c) We know that Kaliṅga was outside the empire of the king; similarly the Colas and the Pāṇḍyas. The first was conquered by Aśoka while the last two maintained their independent existence. Now if by the expression 'between the eastern and the western ocean' we take the Peninsula to be signified, then we have to determine how much of the region on the eastern border passed under his sway because already the western part of the Peninsula had been conquered by his father. This would be a narrow strip lying between the Krishna and the Godavari. Under such circumstances can we take the expression to mean the plateau ?

With the accession of Aśoka, India enters into a new epoch of history. He inherited a vast empire from his predecessors to which he himself added the Kaliṅga country in the ninth year of his reign. A critical study of his records reveals some interesting facts about the trans-Vindhyan region, where 'a line drawn from Pulicat near Madras in the east, to Tirupati, Gooty, Kurnool and Chitaldurg right upto the northern point of South Canara district on the west'[1] shows the southern limit of his empire. In this background we may however note the following facts :

1. In R. E. xiii, the *rājaviṣaya* includes the Bhoja-Pitinikas, the Andhras and the Pulindas.
2. In R. E. v, *Aparānta* includes, according to the Girnar text, Rāṣṭrika-Pitinika.
3. Kaliṅga is described as being placed under a prince of the royal family stationed at Tosalī (Dhauli).
4. Mention is made of four independent states lying beyond the border of the empire: Coḍa (Cola), Pāṇḍya, Kerala-putra and Satiyaputra.

The location of Bhoja-Pitinikas is somewhat uncertain. At a later period we find the Bhojas and Mahābhojas living in the Maharashtra country (Berar) and this has tempted a few scholars to locate Pitinika at Pratiṣṭhāna but the identification is phonetically impossible.[2]

As already stated the Raṭhikas occupied the Marathi speaking area of Khandesh. The term Pitinika is once added with Bhoja and again with Raṭhika. It seems to show some political status of which we know nothing at present. D.R. Bhandarkar points out that in the *Aṅguttara Nikāya* the term *pettanika* is used in the sense of one who enjoys property given by his father, from which it may be inferred to mean a subordinate status under a paternal supreme ruler. (cf. '*save manuse pajā mamā*' Kaliṅga Edict, i)

On the eastern frontier of the *rājaviṣaya* lived the Andhras in the valleys of the river Krishna extending in the north upto the Godavari.[3] As in some texts, the Andhras coupled together with the Pulindas, the Parimdas or Palidas of the Aśokan edicts have been identified with the Pulinda tribe and located in the

1. D.R. Bhandarkar, *Aśoka*, 38-45. T.V. Mahalingam thinks that 'it seems probable that the southern boundary of Aśoka's Empire extended farther south and included the Tondai-mandalam region.' *Kanchipuram*, 7-8)
2. *ANM*, 223
3. *Ind Ant*, 1913, 276-8

Vindhyan region. But philologically Par>(or Pal>) and Pul> cannot be taken as the same. Further, the Parindas appear to have been a frontier people. K.A.N. Sastri points out that the Purāṇas know of 'a land of the Pāradas in Eastern India watered by the Ganges and noted for its horse.[1]

Let us now turn to the independent states lying outside the empire :

The Coḍa territory comprised the districts of Trichinopoly and Tanjore and was watered by the Kaveri river. The plural form of the name in the edicts indicates, according to D.R. Bhandarkar, that during Aśoka's time there were two Cola kingdoms, one of which he identifies with Ptolemy's Soretai (Tamil Sora = Cora) with its capital Orthoura (Uraiyur) near Trichinopoly, and the other with Sora with its capital Arkatos or Arcot.[2]

The Pāṇḍya country comprised in the ancient period the modern districts of Madura, Ramnad and Tinnevelly with the Southern parts of Travancore. As it is also mentioned in plural form in the edicts, D. R. Bhandarkar thinks that it was also divided into two states.

Keralaputra is identical with the Cera kingdom and corresponds roughly to South Malabar region extending to Central Mysore.

The identification of Satiyaputra has caused much speculation. Earlier scholars took it to be north Malabar region and the name was supposed to be surviving in the Satyamangalam (taluk) of Coimbatore. K.A.N. Sastri points out that Satiya corresponds not to *Sk.* Satya, but to Tamil Atiya and *putra* is *magan*, later *mān* in Tamil, so that Satiyaputra denoted the territory of the Tamil chieftain Adigaman (of Tagadur)—who was quite prominent in the Sangam period and might have risen into prominence earlier.[3]

To turn now to the empire of Aśoka. While Kaliṅga was very strictly kept under his rule through a viceroy stationed at Tosali (Dhauli), the Raṭhikas, Bhojas, and Andhras possibly enjoyed a considerable measure of autonomy under the control

1. *ANM*, 223, fn. 2
2. D. R. Bhandarkar, Aśoka, 38; *Kanchipuram*, 7
3. *CHIN*, 500; cf. *JRAS*, 1918, 541; 1923, 412

of a viceroy stationed at Suvarṇagiri, possibly present Kanakagiri between Hampi and Maski in Hyderabad. The Maurya emperor died about 132 B.C. and after him we enter into a confused period of Indian history. What happened to South India is a moot question. Did the Sātavāhanas come to power in this period of turmoil? We shall have now to turn to a critical study of the Purāṇic accounts and a medley of theories centring it.

PART I

THE SĀTAVĀHANAS

Chapter I

HOME OF THE SĀTAVĀHANAS

The Purāṇas describe Simuka, who achieved an independent status for the Sātavāhanas, as Āndhra (*Matsya*) or Āndhra-jātīya (*Vāyu* & *Brahmāṇḍa*) and close the account of the dynasty with the broad statement that 'these......Āndhra kings will enjoy the earth.........years'. On the authority of these statements and other evidences of doubtful historical character, earlier scholars generally maintained that Āndhradeśa was the home of the kings. Recently Rama Rao has tried to revive this theory, already challenged by Sukthankar and others, with the following fresh archaeological and literary evidences:[1]

1. Coins of king Sātavāhana and Śātakarṇi (I) have been found at Kondapuram, while coins of Gautamīputra Śātakarṇi come from Guntur, Kondapuram and Pedabankuru in the Warangal District of Telingana.
2. Khāravela's mention of Śātakarṇi in connection with an expedition which he sent to "Musikanagara" on the Kriṣṇā shows the extent of Śātakarṇi I's dominion in the south.

1. *PIHC*, 1953, 37-8; *JNSI*, xviii, 45; for earlier views, *EHD*, 41; J. Burgess, Buddhist Stūpas of Amarāvatī and Jaggayyapeta, 3-4; *EHI*, 217-19; *OHI*, 119; *CHI*, i 519, 599. P. T. Srinivasa Ayyangar thinks that the Andhras were a Vindhyan tribe and that they extended from the west to the east down the Godavari and the Krishna valleys. (*IA*, 1913, 276-78) D. R. Bhandarkar observes: 'The Telugu country lying between the rivers Kistna and Godāvarī is called Andhra-deśa at present. But whether or not it was the original home of the Andhras, has been called in question. One Buddhist Jātaka, however, speaks of two traders going from the Seriva kingdom to a town called Andhapura situated on the Telavāha river. Andhapura certainly corresponds to the Sanskrit Andhrapura, and as *pura* is invariably used in early Pali literature to signify 'a capital town', Andhrapura must mean the capital town of the Andhra kingdom. The river Telavāha is either the modern Tel or Telingiri both not far distant from each other and flowing near the confines of the Madras Presidency and the Central Provinces. This, indeed, locates the original Andhra country which must, therefore, have comprised parts of both these provinces.' (*IA*, 1918, 71)

3. The *Yugapurāṇa* shows that Śātakarṇi II annexed Kaliṅga to the Sātavāhana empire.

4. The Sātavāhana king Hāla is associated with Sapta-Godāvarī-Bhīmam or Draksarama, in the E. Godavari District, in the celebrated Prākṛta work *Līlāvati*.

On the basis of the above, Dr. Rama Rao concludes that 'central and eastern Deccan continued to be under Sātavāhana rule without any break' till the time of Gautamīputra Śātakarṇi whose sway over these regions is proved by his description '*ti-samudatoya-pītavāhana*' and lord of Mahendra, Cakora, Siritana.

For the present we do not like to enter into a discussion whether Gautamīputra's description in the Nasik record is conventional or factual, for if it can be proved that central and eastern Deccan had been under the sway of the Sātavāhanas from the very beginning, then the description certainly cannot be lightly set aside. So let us first examine the four evidences set forth above.

As Rama Rao bases much of his contention on the find-spot of the coins, we may note at the outset the following excellent observations of W.W.Tarn:—'Much use has been made by some writers on the find-spots of coins in determining where this or that king reigned, but it is not a satisfactory form of evidence ....coins travel in trade and almost any other kind of evidence is preferable.......The following rules seem sound. If a king has an abundant coinage which is found in many places over great distances......that is evidence of a widely extended rule, but not evidence that he ruled in all the places where his coins are found. If the coins of a king with a very large coinage are never found in a particular district, that creates a presumption, in the absence of other evidence, that he did not rule there; but if the coinage be small, no presumption is created; and in both cases, large and small coinage, the absence of coins in a district cannot be set up against other evidence that the king in question ruled there. If only a few isolated coins of a king be known, the find-spot affords no real evidence for the locality of his rule. The belief that the find-spots of copper coins are good evidence of rule, because they do not travel from the place of issue, is unfounded; copper coins must have circulated regularly over all the country served by the mint of issue, which might be very extensive, and a good deal more than that can be determined".[1]

If we now study the findings of the Sātavāhana coins in the background of the above observations, we are constrained to remark that the discovery of a few coins of king Śātakarṇi and Sātavāhana at Kondapuram proves practically nothing. Coins found in the coastal Andhra district must be taken into account very carefully because they may have travelled in trade and we know that these coastal districts had been carrying on trade and commerce with the outside world. We are reminded of the statement of the *Periplus* that coins of Apollodotus and Menander were found in the first century A. D. at the port of Barygaza which was never included in the Indo-Greek dominion.

We must use the evidence of the Hathigumpha record very carefully because the epigraph is very much damaged and, of and on, different readings have been suggested by different scholars with different interpretations. The relevant text, as restored by D.C. Sircar, runs as follows:

"*Dutiye ca vase acitayitā Sātakaṃniṃ pachimadisaṃ haya-gaja-nara-radha-vahulam daṃdaṃ paṭhāpayati. Kaṇhaveṃnā-gatāya ca senāya vitāsiti Asikanagaraṃ* (Jayaswal), *Muṣika-nagaraṃ.*[2]

The above account has been interpreted to mean that the Sātavāhana king (Śātakarṇi I or II) had his capital on the river Krishna (Wainganga with its tributary, the Kanhan, according to E.J. Rapson and B.M. Barua); in other words, the Krishna valley was the citadel of the Sātavāhana power.[3]

1. *GBI*, 440-1
2. *Select Ins*, 207
3. On the term Kanha-bemṇā K.P. Jayaswal and R.D. Banerji add the following note: 'the Sanskrit Kṛishṇaveṇī or the modern Kṛishṇā which rises near Dhom in the Sātārā district. The river flows through the Sātārā, Belgaum and Bijāpur districts and the Kolhapur and Hyderabad States into the Bay of Bengal through the Kṛishṇā district of the Madras Presidency. It forms the boundary of the Nizam's State from Alampur near Karnūl to Nandigāma in the Kistna district. The rise of the Kṛishṇā and its particular sanctity are described in the *Pātāla-Khaṇḍa* of the *Padmapurāṇa*. The earliest epigraphical reference is to be found in this inscription and the second in the Nasik-inscription in cave No. 10 of the Pāṇḍuleṇā group where it is called

But if we consider the hyperbolic nature of the inscription and note at the same time the fact that there is no mention of any actual fighting between the armies of Khāravela and those of Śātakarṇi, we are left with the only conclusion that Khāravela's army failed to advance against the dominion of the monarch and then diverted its course, proceeded south and threatened Asikanagara. The description of the whole episode in two different parts is not without significance. It evidently records two separate operations in the second year of the Kaliṅga monarch and proves indirectly that Asikanagara was outside the dominion of the Sātavāhanas.

Let us now turn to the literary sources adduced for the purpose. Does the *Yuga Purāṇa* prove that Śātakarṇi (II) annexed Kaliṅga to the Sātavāhana empire, proving thereby indirectly the early connection of the dynasty with the coastal region? We are quoting below the relevant texts as translated by K.H. Dhruva :

> 'At the close (of the period) that powerful chief of the Śakas, who was wicked and unholy, will invade the country of the Kaliṅgas being actuated by greed. Attempting to siege the territories of the ruler of Kaliṅga belonging to the Śāta (*Kaliṅga-Śāta-rājyārthī*) (that is Sātavāhana family) he will lose his life (in the campaign); and the dense hordes of detestable Śakas will, without fail, be destroyed by volleys of arrows. Then that king who was the flower of the Śāta family (*Śātavaro-rājā*) will with his forces conquer the (Magadha ?) land and at the end of the tenth year (after the conquest) will give up his ghost'.[1]

In the above account, two expressions are of primary importance for our purpose, viz., *Kaliṅga-Śāta-rajyārthī* and *Śātavaro-rājā*. Rama Rao equates Śāta with Śātakarṇi II. But the second expression clearly shows that Śāta is not a personal name; it is

Karabeṇā. In mediaeval inscriptions it is called Kṛishṇā-Verṇṇā. There is no doubt about the fact that Khāravela reached the Kṛishṇā somewhere in the long and erratic course of that river. It is possible that he went westwards because the term *pachhima-disaṁ* is expressly mentioned. But it is uncertain as to where he reached the Kṛishṇā.' (*Ep. Ind*. xx, 83)

1. *JBORS*, xvi, 22 and 26.

the name of a dynasty. It may be argued that the term *varo* should be attached to *rājā* to make *Śāta* a proper name. But the *sandhi* clearly shows that it is a part of *Śāta* and it cannot be a part of the term, *rājā*. The whole account betrays a reminiscence of the Śaka-Sātavāhana struggle that ended in the overthrow of the Śaka-Kṣaharāta king Nahapāna by Gautamīputra Śātakarṇi. But there is no other evidence to show that Nahapāna or any other Śaka king ever attacked or occupied Kaliṅga. On this point, the account of the *Yuga-Purāṇa* is a highly unhistorical one. Such a source can only be taken into consideration when corroborated by other evidences.

The *Līlāvatī*, on the other hand, instead of proving that the coastal Andhra country was included within the empire of the Sātavāhanas, appears to give just a contrary picture. We need not enter into the romantic details of the work of little historical value, but may simply point out that the substratum of the legend is concerned with some sort of military campaign by the Sātavāhana king, Halā, in eastern Deccan and then his marriage with Līlāvatī.[1] Had that region been the original home of the Sātavāhana, what was the necessity, on the part of a Sātavāhana king, to undertake a fresh military campaign there, unless we presume that it was temporarily occupied by some other power, of which we have no evidence at all ? Such works, in fact, can hardly form the basis of sober history by itself, as *Mudrārākṣasa* cannot by itself form the basis of Candragupta Maurya's life.

There is thus no authentic evidence for believing that Andhra-deśa was the home land of the independent Sātavāhanas. This was pointed out long ago by Sukthankar who even challenged the Andhra affinity of the Sātavāhanas on the ground that they are never called as such in any of the epigraphic records and tried to solve the problem by locating the home in the Bellary District on the strength of the expression '*Sātavāhanihāra*' and '*Sātāhaniraṭṭha*' occurring in the Myakadoni and Hirahadagalli records, and pointed out that we often find in history how inhabitants lend their names to the places they

1. 'The substratum of history in all this legendary matter would seem to be certain military campaigns undertaken in Eastern Deccan, a part of which had probably already come under Sātavāhana sway, but some scholars doubt even this.' Gopalachari, *CHIN*, ii, 306

inhabited originally. This conclusion has, however, been totally rejected by later scholars, but it, at any rate, put a temporary halt to the old theory that the independent Sātavāhanas had their home in the Andhradeśa.

Scholars, with a few exceptions, who dealt with the problem after Śukthankar, maintained that Maharashtra was the home of the dynasty on the basis of the fact that the earliest Sātavāhana epigraphs come from Nasik and Nanaghat. The Hathigumpha record shows that the Sātavāhana kingdom lay to the west of Kaliṅga, and that the Sātavāhana records from the Andhradeśa date only from the time of Pulumāyi. Even if we agree with Rama Rao that the eastern Deccan had been under the sway of Gautamīputra, we cannot associate the earlier independent members of the dynasty, as already shown, with that region. The *Suttanipāta* commentary describes Aśmaka and Mūlaka as Āndhra (Sk. Andhraka, i.e., Āndhra) rājya.[1] The commentator of the *Arthaśāstra* locates both the janapadas in 'Mahārāṣṭra'. It may be noted in this connection that in the Nanaghat record, Śātakarṇi I is described as the lord of *Dakṣiṇāpatha* which, though at a later date included the whole of the Deccan, during the time of the early independent Sātavāhanas denoted the tract lying between the Ganges and the Godavari, as proved by the evidence of the *Suttanipāta*[2]. The *Periplus* on the other hand distinguishes Dachinabades from Damirica or Tamilacam and the eastern part of the upper Deccan is called Masalia lying evidently outside the Dachinabades region, as the description shows. Thus it appears that if Śātakarṇi I was the lord of *Dakṣiṇāpatha*, he was practically the ruler of the Maharashtra region.

After Sukthankar challenged the Āndhra affinity of the Sātavāhanas, several scholars followed him in the track. K.P. Jayaswal thinks that they represented the Satiyaputas of the Aśokan records, while according to H.C. Raychaudhuri 'the name Āndhra probably came to be applied to the kings in later times when they lost their northern and western possessions and became a purely Āndhra power governing the territory at the

1. *Paramatthajotika* on the *Suttanipāta*, 581
2. B. C. Law, *Historical Geography of Ancient India*, 14

mouths of the river Krishna'.[1] Such theories arise from the fact, as held by Sukthankar, that the Sātavāhanas are never called Āndhras in the epigraphic records. But here we should note that 'in those days the custom was merely to note the family name in inscriptions, as is demonstrated by the records of the Śālaṅkāyanas, Bṛhatphalāyanas, Viṣṇukuṇḍins, Pallavas, etc.[2] The Purāṇas unanimously call Simuka as belonging to the Āndhra stock and the dynasty as Āndhra while the *Viṣṇu Purāṇa* names the dynasty as *Āndhrabhṛtya*. The term *Āndhrabhṛtya* means evidently the Āndhras who were once servants and tallies with the description of Simuka as the servant of Kāṇva-Suśarman. This distinguishes Simuka and his successors from the earlier kings who were not subordinates and who ruled immediately after the fall of the Mauryas. Though in the Nasik record Gotami Balasiri claims that her son was an '*eka-Bamhana*' or unique Brāhmaṇa,[3] the writers of the sacred texts regard the Sātavāhanas as not of high origin. We may note here the following account of the *Bhāgavata Purāṇa* :[4]

Hatvā Kāṇvaṃ Susarmānaṃ tad-bhṛtyo
vṛṣalo balī,
gāṃ bhokṣyaty Āndhra-jātiyaḥ kañcit
kālam-asattamaḥ.

1. *PHAI*, 343; V.S. Bakhle observes: 'In the Edicts of Aśoka we find a mention of the Satiyaputras who were on the borders of his empire. . . Sir Ramkrishna Bhandarkar suggested that the independent state of Satiyaputra army was situated along the Western Ghats and the Konkan Coast below; and he further pointed out that along the westernmost portion of the Deccan tableland, we have Mārāṭha, Kāyastha, and Brāhman families, bearing the surname Sātpute which seems to be derived from the Satiyaputta of the inscription. The Sātavāhanas, therefore, it would appear, were the Satiyaputras who asserted their independence after the death of Aśoka and founded an empire in Western India. It is true that the identification of Satiyaputras has not been accepted by all scholars; yet the growing tendency among them to locate the Satiyaputra kingdom somewhere in Western India is, indeed, unmistakable.' (*JBBRAS*, iii, 51)
2. *EHD*, ed. G. Yazdani, 75
3. see *infra*, Appendix
4. *DK*.I, 38, fn. 2

Here the Sātavāhanas are called both Āndhra and vṛṣala. In the *Manu-saṁhitā*, iv. 108 and 140, the term Vṛṣala is used in the sense of a Śūdra, as explained by Medhātithi, while in x. 43-5, it is stated that the Kṣatriyas like Drāviḍas, etc., attained the status of a vṛṣala as they failed to perform the prescribed religious duties.

While searching for the home of the Sātavāhanas in the Maharashtra region, we should note especially the dynastic drifts in ancient Deccan. The dynasty of Khāravela is said to be a branch of the Cedis who had their home in the Bundelkhand region. Evidently the Mahāmeghavāhanas migrated to Kaliṅga and founded a dynasty there. The Ikṣvākus of Andhradeśa possibly came from the north. Similarly, the Sātavāhanas who were Āndhras were immigrants to the Maharashtra country which thus became their adopted home.

Chapter II

THE PURĀṆIC ACCOUNT OF THE SĀTAVĀHANAS

Besides furnishing us with a list of the Sātavāhana kings with their regnal years, the *Purāṇas* make some broad statements that have caused serious differences of opinion among the scholars, especially in regard to the starting point of the dynasty:

1. Relying on the unanimous statement of the Purāṇas that Simuka (Śiśuka, Sindhuka etc.), who heads the list of the Āndhra-Sātavāhana kings, came to power after overthrowing Suśarman, the last ruler of the Kāṇva dynasty, some scholars hold that the Sātavāhanas began their rule in the first century B.C.[1]

2. Another group of scholars takes into account the Purāṇic statement that the dynasty ruled for more than four centuries and a half, and further considering the fact that the end of the dynasty cannot be placed later than the first quarter of the third century A.D., as proved by the epigraphs, it is held that the Sātavāhanas came to power under Simuka in the third decade of the third century B.C., evidently after Aśoka's death, when the Mauryan empire showed signs of disintegration. These scholars maintain that the last Kāṇva king Suśarman was overthrown not by Simuka but by one of his successors.[2]

1. Following this tradition, Simuka is placed in the second half of the first century B. C. by H.C. Raychaudhuri, D.C. Sircar and others. R.G. Bhandarkar places the king about 75 B.C., for he propounded the theory that the Kāṇvas ruled contemporaneously with the later Śuṅgas and this Śuṅga-Kāṇva rule came to an end about 75 B.C. This theory, however, is not favoured by later scholars.
2. V.A. Smith, K.P. Jayaswal, K. Gopalachari, M. Rama Rao follow this view. G. Rao pushes Simuka as early as 271-248 B.C. Rao makes the following interesting observation, 'Simuka is called a Rājā by the *Purāṇas* and he is styled Rāya Simuka in the Nanaghat inscription. This title itself need not mislead us into thinking that he was in any sense of the term the supreme sovereign of an independent state. The inscription was a later one, subsequent to the attainment of *Sārvabhaumatva* by a descendant of Simuka. The authors of the *Purāṇas* were

In the *Proceedings of the Indian History Congress*, 1952, pp. 40ff., A.S. Altekar discussed both the above theories, and ultimately supported the second one with the following interesting arguments:

(a) The Mauryan empire collapsed about 187 B.C.; if we assume that the Sātavāhanas came to power about 30 B.C., then there would be a big 'vacuum (in the history of the Deccan) of more than a century which cannot be explained.'

(b) Simuka cannot have overthrown the last Kāṇva king; one of his successors must have done so, for he could not have become so powerful suddenly as to overthrow the Kāṇva imperial ruler at Pāṭaliputra.

(c) Though from the coins and inscriptions, we get only a few names of the Sātavāhana kings, archaeological evidences are likely to be discovered in future to show that there were nearly 30 kings in the dynasty, as asserted by the *Purāṇas*; and thus the Purāṇic tradition that the Sātavāhanas ruled for more than 450 years would be confirmed.

Though the above arguments are no doubt very forceful, it is at the same time difficult to dismiss the unanimous statement of the *Purāṇas* that Simuka overthrew the last Kāṇva king (c. 33 B.C.) and it is the *only unanimous* broad statement regarding the dynasty. On the other hand, there is hardly any unanimity regarding the period of the Sātavāhana rule; it ranges from 272½ years to more than 450 years. This naturally leads us to the problems: Shall we accept the unanimous statement of the *Purāṇas* or shall we reject it and prefer one about which there is no such unanimity ? Shall we write history on the evidences available or on the supposition that fresh evidences will come forth from the womb of the future ? A.S. Altekar further presupposes that the Kāṇvas ruled as an imperial

writing the past history of a contemporary royal family, an old old family of unbroken succession, which could proudly trace its beginnings to the early half of the third century B.C. If through the whole line the succeeding chieftains were all kings, the authors would surely 'not refer to their great ancestor as being anything less than a king.' (*EHD*, ed. G. Yazdani, 113)

power at Pāṭaliputra and that Simuka captured the imperial city. Before him K.P. Jayaswal also worked on a similar hypothesis.[1] It is assumed that the dynastic account of the *Purāṇas* has been written from the point of view of Magadha. Available evidences show, on the other hand, that after the fall of the Mauryas, Puṣyamitra lived at Pāṭaliputra and maintained the imperial tradition, but his successors were reduced to the position of a petty local dynasty at Vidiśā.[2] The *Purāṇas* give simply the account of the dynasty without any reference to the kingdom and capital, and so we can easily perceive that after Puṣyamitra the point of view of the Purāṇic writers naturally shifted from Magadha to the Vidiśā region in the Madhya Pradesh. The Kāṇvas also ruled in that region. The rest of North India became divided into a number of petty states as proved by the evidence of coins.[3] When the Sātavāhana Simuka overthrew the last Kāṇva ruler, naturally his dynasty also came within the viewpoint of the Purāṇic writers. Thus there is no reason to think that Simuka overthrew a very powerful dynasty at Pāṭaliputra.

Such problems as envisaged by Altekar and others are bound to arise as in writing the history of the Sātavāhana dynasty emphasis has been laid on the *Vāyu* and *Matsya* accounts only. In view of the fact, however, that the Purāṇas have hopelessly confused the account of the dynasty, we should make a comparative study of all the available Purāṇic evidences so that we may get the proper light, and should not be biased by one account against the other. Now, while all the Purāṇic accounts start with Simuka, as already stated, the Brahmāṇḍa Purāṇa makes the following interesting statement in concluding the account of the Kāṇvas:

> *Kāṇvāyanās tu catvāraś catvāriṃśacca pañca ca*
> *Samā bhokṣyanti pṛthivīṃ punar Andhrān gamiṣyati.*[4]

1. *JBORS*, xiii. 221-46, cf. *EHI*, 216-7
2. *EHNI*, 23-4
3. Cunningham, *Coins of Ancient India*, 79-80; Allan, *Catalogue of Ancient Indian Coins in the British Museum*, Intro.
4. *DKA*, 35, fn. 42. It is admitted that there is some confusion in the exact connotation of the term *punaḥ*, for it may mean *once more* as well as *afterwards*. In fact, in the Aihole inscription of Pulakeśin II it is used in the latter sense. (*'punar=api ca jighṛkṣos=sainyam=ākkrānta-*

'The four Kāṇvas will rule the earth for forty-five years; *then* (it) will *again* go to the Āndhras.

The verse quoted above shows that before the rise of Simuka, the Sātavāhanas had been in power, and a new rise of the dynasty (*punar*) happened after the fall of the Kāṇvas, when Suśarman, the last Kāṇva king, was overthrown by his servant Simuka. The independent Sātavāhanas might have been brought under subjection by the Kāṇvas who are described as *praṇata-sāmantāḥ*, and this evidently eclipsed their glory for the time being.

In the background of the above note, let us now study the other accounts in the Purāṇas.

(a) The *Matsya Purāṇa* makes the broad statement that there were nineteen kings in the dynasty, while three manuscripts actually name thirty kings. The *Vāyu*, on the other hand, speaks of thirty kings, but the different manuscripts actually name seventeen, eighteen and nineteen kings.

(b) The duration of the dynasty is said to have been 460 years according to the *Matsya*, 456 years according to the *Brahmāṇḍa*, *Viṣṇu*, and *Bhāgavata*, 411 years according to the *Vāyu*, (though only 300 years according to another manuscript of the same Purāṇa).

(c) The actual reign-period assigned to the kings according to the *Matsya* make a total of 448½ years; it is only 272½ years according to the Vāyu.

An analysis of the above statements would clearly show that there were two different traditions about the dynasty :

(1) that the number of the different Sātavāhana kings had been 17/19 or 30 ; and

(2) that the dynasty ruled for 272½/300 years or 411/448½/460 years.

sālam rucira-bahu-patākaṁ Revatī-dvīpām=āśu'—Ep. Ind vi, 5). So every case is to be decided with reference to the context of the account. As the *Matsya* and the other Purāṇas excepting the *Vāyu*, (leaving the M mss.) maintain that the Sātavāhanas ruled for more than four hundred years, and as again all the Purāṇas unanimously make Simuka overthrow the last Kanva king, it is quite clear that the term *punaḥ* in the *Brahmāṇḍa* text quoted above must be taken in the sense of *once more* and not *afterwards*.

As already indicated we have got three fixed points in the history of the dynasty :

(a) it came to power sometime before Simuka;

(b) Simuka re-asserted the independence of the dynasty about 30 B.C. ;

(c) the dynasty came to an end about 220-5 A.D.

As all the Puranic lists begin with Simuka, we can accommodate 17/19 kings only between C. 30 B.C. and C. 220/5 A.D., covering a period of 270/5 years. On the other hand, about 30 kings can be accommodated only on the supposition that the dynasty ruled for 411/448½/460 years. The starting point of this period cannot be C. 30 B.C., for, in that case, the dynasty would continue upto the fifth century A.D., which goes contrary to the archaeological evidences. This tradition evidently has, as its background, the fact that the Sātavāhanas started their rule sometime in the second half of the third century B.C., but as this list also puts Simuka at the beginning, we can clearly perceive how the compiler of the record has jumbled up two different phases of the dynasty, the Sātavāhanas ruling before and after the Kāṇvas.

This leads us to enquire what may possibly be the source of confusion. To understand it we have to bear in mind the fact as noted before, that after Puṣyamitra, the Purāṇic accounts have been compiled from the Vidiśā point of view :

(a) Thus when the *Vāyu Purāṇa* names only 19 or 17 rulers of the dynasty, but observes simultaneously that there were nearly 30 kings without mentioning the names of others, we have to understand clearly that it is dealing with the successors of Simuka, but indicating at the same time that there were a number of kings before him as well. The predecessors of Simuka have not been mentioned, evidently because they do not come within the Vidiśā point of view

(b) The *Matsya Purāṇa*, on the other hand, makes the broad statement that there were 19 kings evidently from the same point of view (i.e. Simuka and his successors), but simultaneously names about 30 kings of the dynasty to make the list complete. The writer was evidently in confusion; he has put Simuka at the top of the list (who heads the list of the second group of kings) and has thus jumbled up earlier and later kings together.

R. G. Bhandarkar who first dealt with the Purāṇic accounts

critically observed that 'the period of three hundred years (300 years is a general statement, the total of the different kings is 272½ years) and the seventeen (18 or 19) names given in the *Vāyu Purāṇa* refer probably to the main branch. The *Matsya* seems to me to put together the princes of all the branches (the main line and the branches that ruled after the fall of the main line) and thus makes them out to be thirty......Thus then both the *Vāyu* and the *Matsya* Purāṇa each gives a correct account, but of different things'. This interpretation, though accepted by many scholars, seems now to be a little out of the mark, in view of the *Brahmāṇḍa* account quoted above. The *Vāyu* states that it was giving the *pradhānyataḥ* account of the dynasty,[1] which has been interpreted as the Purāṇa giving the leading names of the family. But in that case one fails to understand why the Purāṇa has excluded the names of Pulumāyi and his immediate successors, for Pulumāyi was undoubtedly an important Sātavāhana ruler. Relying too much on the authenticity of the *Vāyu* list, R.G. Bhandarkar observed that Pulumāyi, Śiva Śrī and Śivaskanda who intervened between Gautamīputra and Yajña Śrī never sat on the throne and that they died as princes, though elsewhere the same scholar states that Pulumāyi 'reigned in his own right for four years'. This is evidently a defect in the *Vāyu* list, but this shows at any rate that it was not giving the leading names of the dynasty only. Epigraphic and literary evidences clearly prove that Simuka and his successors who ruled after the restoration of the Sātavāhana power played an important part in the political life of India, in contrast to the earlier members of the dynasty of whom we find no records showing that they played no important role. Had any of the earlier members played a striking part, that would have been mirrored, directly or indirectly, in the literature or epigraphs of the country. So by the expression '*pradhānyataḥ pravakṣyāmi*', the *Vāyu* refers not to the leading kings, but to the leading branch of the dynasty. It may be mentioned here that the *Brahmāṇḍa* list is in close agreement with the *Vāyu*, with minor differences here and there.

With the above defects in the *Vāyu* list and the jumbling up of names in the *Matsya*, it is apparent that we have to proceed

1. *JBORS*, xvi, 264 (*pradhānyataḥ*) ; Rao, *EHD* ed: G. Yazdani, 86.

very cautiously in using the Purāṇic material for writing a sober history of the dynasty. Epigraphic and numismatic evidences show that from Gautamīputra onwards, the *Matsya* list has been preserved in a rather satisfactory manner, and hence it is apparent that the confusion of the names of the earlier and the later members of the dynasty occurs in the earlier portion.

In any case, we may arrive tentatively at the following conclusions :

(a) the Sātavāhana dynasty came to power in the third century B.C.

(b) it subsequently lost its independent status but Simuka regained the independence of the dynasty;

(c) there were in all about thirty kings in the family;

(d) Simuka and his successors numbered about nineteen.

Caste of the Sātavāhanas

In determining the caste of the Sātavāhanas, we have to remember the fact that they were living in an age when both the *varṇa* and the *jāti* systems prevailed. The first denotes literally colour, whence character, nature and quality, while the second '*the form of existence fixed by birth*'.[1] D. R. Bhandarkar has shown how in ancient period various tribes of foreign extraction that entered into India were admitted into the *varṇa* fold which divided people into four grades, *brāhmaṇas*, *kṣatriyas*, *vaiśyas* and *śūdras*.[2] The orthodox *Dharmaśāstra* writers, who wrote from the Āryāvarta or the Madhyadeśa[3] point of view, strongly advocated the *jāti* theory as the basis of the four-fold division and postulated further the theory of *mixed castes* to account for the presence of various tribal elements in society, a hard fact which their orthodoxy evencould not deny.[4]

The operation of both the systems are found in case of the Sātavāhanas. When the Purāṇas state that they are of Āndhra-

1. S. Chattopadhyaya, *Social Life in Ancient India*, 7 ff
2. *Ind. Ant*, 1911, 1 ff
3. *Baudhāyana Dharma Sūtra*, I. i. 2.9; *Vasiṣṭha Dharma Sūtra*, i.8; *Mahābhāṣya*, ii. 4.10. Later on the whole of North India, however, came to be regarded as Āryāvarta or the Aryandom. *Manusaṃhitā*, ii. 22.
4. *Manusaṃhitā*, v: *Mbh.* xiii 46, 48

jāti, the stock to which they belonged is evidently meant. The Āndhras or the present Telegu speaking people are described as *dasyus* in the *Aitareya Brāhmaṇa*,[1] while Manu regards them as of mixed origin born of a Vaidehaka man and Niṣāda woman,[2] and living by 'the slaughter of wild animals'.[3] So from the strict *jāti* point of view they were not yet of a very high order.

The *varṇa* theory was nevertheless working simultaneously within the fold. Thus in the Nasik inscription of Gotamī Balasiri, her son is described as *ekabamhaṇa and khatiyadapamānamadana* like the great Brāhmaṇa hero Paraśurāma.[4] E. Senart translates the first expression as meaning 'the unique Brāhmaṇa',[5] while D.R. Bhandarkar takes it to mean 'the only protector of brāhmaṇas'.[6] E. Senart's translation seems to be the correct one, showing that the Sātavāhanas claimed to belong to the brāhmaṇa *varṇa*, but to Āndhra *jāti*, as asserted by the Purāṇas. In the same inscription, however, Gotamī calls herself a *rājarṣibadhu*. K. Gopalachari points out that the title of *rājarṣi* could only be taken by a kṣatriya, and preferring D.R. Bhandarkar's interpretation, which cannot be accepted, considers the Sātavāhanas to be of kṣatriya caste.[7] Such expressions of diverse connotation in the same record shows only that the *varṇa* had not yet crystallised into the strict *jāti* system in the Sātavāhana society. In other words, the Sātavāhanas had not come fully as yet under the social patterns of the orthodox (Midlanders) and were still maintaining a liberal frame of society, in which persons were judged according to their quality of head and heart and not by the accident of birth. Their description as *vṛṣala* in the *Bhāgavata Purāṇa* (*supra*) proves that even as late as the ninth century the orthodox society was not prepared to accord them a higher status in the *jāti* scale.

1. *Ait Br.* vii. 92.18
2. *Manusaṁhitā*, x. 36
3. *ib.*, x. 48
4. *Select Ins.*, 197f
5. *Ep. Ind.* viii. 60ff
6. *Ib.*, xxii, 32ff
7. *CHIN*, 300

Chapter III

THE EARLY SĀTAVĀHANAS

There is still some difference of opinion regarding the methodology to be followed in studying the history of the Sātavāhana rulers, especially before Gautamīputra. We have on the one hand the list of the Āndhra-Sātavāhana kings preserved in the Purāṇas, and on the other the archaeological evidences, the coins and epigraphs, besides some important literary references bearing on them. The evidence of the second group does not always tally with the Purāṇic lists, and thus writing as early as 1919, G. J-Dubriuel realised the unsoundness of the Purāṇic account and used them only in the background of other reliable sources.[1] That methodology should be followed even now. But unfortunately the cause of the *Matsya* account is still championed, and attempt is made to utilise archaeological evidences only to justify the *Matsya* list. The latest attempt in this direction has been made by K. Gopalachari.[2] He realised that if the *Matsya* account is to be maintained, Simuka must be kept at the head of the Sātavāhana list. But coins of king Sātavāhana have been discovered proving that he, and not Simuka, was the progenitor of the Sātavāhana *kula* (*infra*). Hence to maintain his thesis he identifies Sātavāhana with Lambodara,[3] the seventh king in the *Matsya* list, on what grounds one does not know. M. Rama Rao found a similar difficulty and observed that 'the Purāṇas did not include the name of this Sātavāhana because he was the small ruler of a petty kingdom and not a ruler with imperial dignity'.[4] Here we should only remember that during the Kṣaharāta interregnum lasting for nearly fifty years many kings of the dynasty were not rulers of imperial dignity, but some of their names have crept in the Purāṇas. On the other hand, names

1. *AHD*, 13-15, 37ff
2. *CHIN*, 293ff
3. *ib.*, 304
4. M. Rama Rao, *Sātavāhana Coins*, 12

of several Sātavāhana kings known from coins are missing from the list.

Though scholars like K. Gopalachari favour the *Matsya* list, we may note an important observation by him in this connection. Thus he states that 'from Āpilaka to Hāla (eighth and seventeenth respectively in the Purāṇic lists) there stretches a long period of darkness relieved only by a single point of light (e.g. Kuntala Śātakarṇi). But it is probable that fresh evidence, like the Āpilaka coin may not only confirm the order in the Purāṇic lists, but also open a vista into the period.'[1] Such an observation betrays at least *two* lacunae : *first*, what about the names of the kings known from coins but not found in the list; and *secondly*, the methodology of history is dependent on what is available, not on an imaginary one to be found in future. The observation only shows the helplessness of a scholar in dealing with the *Matsya* account. This becomes further apparent when after modifying the Purāṇic list of Āndhra kings 'in the light of inscriptions and coins', he finds that the number of kings becomes thirty-two instead of thirty as given in the *Matsya Purāṇa*, and then observes that the names of two kings nos. 5 and 10, Skandastambhi and Svāti 'have to be deleted from this list,'[2] but why and on what ground we are not told again.

As already stated, the *Matsya* list from Gautamīputra onwards agrees very satisfactorily with the archaeological evidences. So for studying the history of the early kings we shall depend primarily on archaeological evidences and utilise the Purāṇic sources only in so far as it agrees with them. We should refrain from starting with any preconceived idea about the authenticity of the sacred texts. Unfortunately, we get very little information about the period immediately after the fall of the Mauryas. Our study begins with Sātavāhana who flourished at the beginning of the first century B.C.

Sātavāhana

It was presumed that the Sātavāhana *kula* was probably named

1. *CHIN*, 304
2. *ib.*, 326-27

after the progenitor of the dynasty, like the Gupta-*vaṃśa* named after *mahārāja*-Gupta. The supposition proved true when coins bearing the name Sātavāhana came to light. One such coin bearing the legend *Siri Sadavaha* was discovered at Kondapuram, while another with the legend *raño Siri Sadavaha* (*nasa*) came from the collection of Hurmuz Kaus of Hyderabad said to have been purchased from Warangal. Another such coin was purchased at Aurangabad and a fourth one came from Poona.[1]

From such meagre finds of coins, we shall probably be not justified to infer what was the region exactly under the rule of this ruler, for a single coin could have migrated easily from one place to another. The name Sātavahana is not mentioned in the Purāṇas.

These four coins make a very interesting study. V.V. Mirashi assigns Sātavāhana 'two or three generations' before Simuka and thinks that he was 'the founder of the Sātavāhana dynasty'.[2] Katare identifies Sātavāhana with Kumāra Sātavāhana mentioned in the Nanaghat cave relievo inscription.[3] M. Rama Rao maintains that 'Sātavāhana must be taken to have flourished before *Simuka* and *Kṛṣṇa*. He could not, however, have lived long before them'.[4]

Sātavāhana, as already stated, should properly be regarded as the progenitor of the Sātavāhana dynasty and his identification with Kumāra Sātavāhana cannot stand as the prince appears to have never ruled at all, evidently dying young. It is of course certain that the 'characters of the legends found on the coins of Sātavāhana, particularly *s* with its lower part bent below the body of the letter, *r* with a wide top and pointed bottom and *h* with a round bottom resemble the characters of the legends found on the coins of Śātakarṇi, on the one hand, and of the bigger Nanaghat inscription on the other'.[5] This shows that Sātavāhana was not far away from the time of Śātakarṇi (identified with Śātakarṇi I or Śātakarṇi II of the Purāṇic list). As the Nanaghat record is palaeographically later than the Bes-

1. M. Rama Rao, *Sātavāhana Coins*, 9ff
2. V.V. Mirashi, *Studies in Indology*, i, 119ff
3. *IHQ*, xxvii, 210ff
4. M. Rama Rao, *l.c.*, 12
5. M. Rama Rao, *l.c.*, 11-12

nagar inscription of Heliodoros of c. 100 B.C., Sātavāhana appears to have ruled after this date. Thus though the Āndhra rule started about c. 232 B.C., after the death of Aśoka,[1] the Āndhra-Sātavāhana dynasty appears to be a separate one from the dynasty that came to power at the time of the later Mauryas.

Sātavāhana possibly came to power in Upper Deccan during the period following the tragic end of the last Śuṅga king Devabhūti in c. 75 B.C.[2] when the Kāṇvas came to power in Vidiśā and ruled for forty-five years (c. 75-30 B.C.). The Kāṇvas are described as *praṇatasāmanta*,[3] which seems to indicate that Sātavāhana lost his independence later on. According to a very late Jaina account which can hardly be taken as historical Sātavāhana was at first a pious man and built Jaina temples and *cetiyas*. Later on he became wicked and was dethroned and killed.[4]

The meaning of the term Sātavāhana is obscure. J-Przyluski derives it from the Austric word *sādaṁ*, *sadāṁ* and *sādāṁ* meaning *horse* and *han* or *hapan* meaning son, later on Sanskritised into vāhana. Thus the word, according to the French scholar, meant originally '*son of horse*' and it is supposed that princes born of union between the queen and the sacrificial horse or during performance of the Aśvamedha sacrifice would generally be called 'sons of the horse'.[5] As we have no evidence at our disposal to show that the father of Sātavāhana ever performed an Aśvamedha sacrifice it is difficult to accept the theory. In the *Kathāsaritsāgara* the word is explained as meaning 'he who rode a yakṣa (named Sāta in the form of a lion)', a fanciful account similar to one given by the Jaina author Jinaprabhasūri.[6] K. Gopalachari points out that *Saptavāhana* is one of the thousand names of Viṣṇu who is closely associated with the Sun in the *Mahābhārata* and the term Sātavāhana being derived from it may denote a king of the Solar line which would make the prince a kṣatriya[7], a

1. *supra*
2. *PHAI*, 332
3. *DKA*, 35
4. *JBBRAS*, x, 133f
5. *JRAS*, 1929, 273
6. *Kathāsaritsāgara*, trans. i, 37; *JBBRAS*, x, 132
7. *CHIN*, 300

theory which cannot be accepted (*supra*). He rejects the explanation of the term as meaning 'seven arrows' or 'seven rays of the Sun' suggested by S.A. Joglekar.[1]

Simuka

If the Purāṇic accounts may be taken to allude to the status of the Āndhra-Sātavāhanas, the subordinate role of the dynasty continued till c. 30 B.C., when Simuka, 'a servant of the last Kāṇva king' killed his master and became independent. As already stated, all the Purāṇas place him at the head of the dynastic list of the Āndhras, evidently because an independent Āndhra line came within the purview of the Purāṇic writers who were now composing their accounts from the Vidiśā point of view.[2] In the Nanaghat cave relievo inscriptions Simuka is described as '*rāyā-Simuka-Sātavāhano sirimālo*.[3] D.C. Sircar has suggested that the *lacuna* in line *two* of the big Nanaghat record of Nāganikā contained probably the reading *Simuka Sātavāhanasa vaṁsa-vadhanasa*.[4] This restoration was evidently suggested in view of the Purāṇic accounts making Simuka the founder of the Sātavāhana-kula. But after the discovery of the Sātavāhana coins the picture has changed altogether. As all the Purāṇas maintain that Simuka ruled for 23 years we may tentatively put his period as extending from c. 30 B.C. to 7 B.C.

Simuka appears to have been a very shrewd politician. He realised that to overthrow the Kāṇvas was a difficult task and hence entered into an alliance with the mahārathī Tranakayira whose daughter was married to his son Śātakarṇi (*infra*). Tranakayira was a Nāga, possibly a vassal under the last Kāṇva ruler. Thus several *servants* combined together to overthrow the Kāṇva regime and the powerful among them ultimately won the crown.

Kṛṣṇa

According to the Purāṇas, Simuka was succeeded by his

1. *ABORI*, xxvii, 237ff
2. *EHNI*, 30
3. *Select Ins.*, 184
4. *ib.*, 187

brother Kṛṣṇa. We have in a cave at Nasik an inscription[1] of Kanha's reign which appears to be important for at least three reasons : *first*, it states that the cave was constructed by the 'officer in charge (mahāmātra) of the śramaṇas at Nasik', showing that king Kanha favoured Buddhism and maintained a separate administrative department to look after the Buddhist monks; *secondly*, the art critics assign, the 'Nasik Hall to the latter half of the first century B.C.' on stylistic grounds and the theory is supported by the *angular* forms of some letters in the epigraph. This furnishes us an important clue in determining the period when Kanha came to power. It goes against assigning Simuka and Kṛṣṇa of the Purāṇas to an early date at the close of the third century B.C.; *thirdly*, the mention of *mahāmātra* in the record shows that the early Sātavāhana administration was based on Maurya model.

The prevalence of Buddhism in western Deccan, as proved by the Nasik record, was another legacy of the Mauryas. According to the *Mahāvaṁsa*, Aśoka sent Mahādhammarakkhita to Mahārāṣṭra and Yavana Dharmarakkhita to Aparāntika for preaching Buddhism.[2] It is difficult to determine how far the account is authentic, but from his edicts it is clear that his missionaries worked in Aparānta which included a part of western Deccan strip while his edicts have been found in Maharashtra itself. The Buddhists of Nasik possibly belonged to the Bhadāyanīya school. The employment of a Yavana for preaching an Indian religion is indeed interesting.

Śātakarṇi

According to the Purāṇas,[3] Kṛṣṇa was succeeded by his son Śātakarṇi; Mallakarṇi according to the *Matsya* version. This, however, seems to go against the evidence of the Nanaghat cave relievo inscriptions[4] referring to :

(a) Rāyā Simuka-Sātavāhano sirimāto

(b) Devi-Nāyanikāya raño ca siri-Sātakanino

(c) Kumāro Bhā......ya

1. *Select Ins.*, 183
2. *ANM*, 216
3. *DKA*, 39
4. *Select Ins.*, 184f

(d) Mahāraṭhi Tranakayiro
(e) Kumāro Hakusiri
(f) Kumāro Sātavāhano

It will be seen that in the above epigraphic account which names the different members of the family of Śātakarṇi, including his father-in-law Maharathi Tranakayira, no reference is made to Kṛṣṇa, evidently because he was not in the direct line. It has been inferred that Śātakarṇi was the son of Simuka, who is, therefore, placed first in the line of the relievos. As Rapson observes: 'The lists given in such records are genealogical rather than dynastic. Members of the ruling family not in direct descent are often omitted.[1] V.S. Bakhle maintains that Kanha or Kṛṣṇa's name has been omitted from the relievos because he set aside the legal claims of Śātakarṇi and usurped the throne.[2]

An altogether different view is maintained by G.V. Rao. He argues that Kṛṣṇa finds no place in the relievos since Śātakarṇi mentioned there is Śātakarṇi II of the Purāṇic list while Kṛsṇa was the father of Śātakarṇi I. Simuka is mentioned because he was the founder of the dynasty.[3] For the sake of clearness we may quote the Purāṇic list below :

	Matsya P.		*Vāyu* P.	
1.	Simuka	23 yrs.	Sinduka	23 yrs.
2.	Kṛṣṇa	18 yrs.	Kṛṣṇa	10 or 18 yrs.
3.	Śrī-Mallakarṇi	10 yrs.	Śātakarṇi	56(10 ?) years
4.	Pūrṇotsaṅga			
5.	Skandastambhi			
6.	Śātakarṇi			

F.E. Pargiter corrected Śrī-Mallakarni of the *Matsya* list into Śrī-Śātakarṇi on the analogy of the *Brahmāṇḍa* and *Viṣṇu* versions and thus he came to be regarded as Śātakarṇi I, while the *sixth* king of the list as Śātakarṇi II.[4] F.E. Pargiter,

1. *CIC*, xix, fn. 4
2. *JBBRAS*, iii, 53
3. *EHD*, ed. Yazdani, 88f
4. *DKA*, 39

however, himself has pointed out that the *Matsya* version of the Sātavāhana is the earliest one and the other Purāṇas copied from it.[1] Now, regarding the third king the *Matsya* gives[2] the reading:

Śrī Mallakarṇir bhavitā tasya putrastu vai daśa

The reading in the *Vāyu* is as follows:

Śrī Śātakarṇir bhavitā tasya putrastu vai mahān[3]

Apparently *mahān* is a variant reading for *daśa* and the two lines show that the *Vāyu* and the *Matsya* are speaking of the same king. It is clear that Śātakarṇi or Śrī-Mallakarṇi ruled for ten years and further the reading Śātakarṇi is the correct one. The confusion arises from the later versions of the texts which underwent several revisions and finally got the forms in which we have received them. Evidently both the revisionists of the *Matsya* texts on the one hand, and the *Vāyu* on the other, fell in a faulty circle. The revisionists of the *Matsya* text corrupted Śātakarṇi into Mallakarṇi and they had to find out another Śātakarṇi among the earlier kings whom they placed sixth with a total reign of fifty-six years. The later revisionists of the *Vāyu* then followed *Matsya* and assigned the third king Śātakarṇi fifty-six years instead of original ten. Thus the existence of a second Śātakarṇi is very doubtful.

The above conjecture must be supported by extra evidences as a large number of scholars believe in the existence of two Śātakarṇis. K. Gopalachari maintains that while the Nanaghat inscription and the relievo inscriptions belong to the reign of Śātakarṇi I, the Sanchi inscription should be assigned to the time of Śātakarṇi II who should also be identified with Śātakarṇi mentioned in the Hathigumpha record.[4] G.V. Rao holds that Śātakarṇi II is mentioned in all the records referred to above.[5] While editing the Hathigumpha record D.C. Sircar observes:

1. *DKA.*, xx
2. *ib.*, 39
3. *ib.*, fn. 29
4. *CHIN*, 301-3
5. *EHD*, ed. G. Yazdani, 81-9

'This king seems to be Śātakarṇi who ruled shortly after the husband of Nāganikā according to the Purāṇas. Palaeographically the Hathigumpha record is slightly later than the Nanaghat record. It may be pointed out that the letters of the Sanchi inscription of Śātakarṇi resemble the script of the present record and may belong to Śātakarṇi II. Of course, if this slight development is overlooked, we may identify both these Śātakarṇis with Śātakarṇi I. But it should be remembered that the big Nanaghat record was possibly engraved after the death of that king'.[1]

It will be seen that on matters of palaeography, the opinion of D.C. Sircar tallies with that of K. Gopalachari, while G.V. Rao depends on the view of Buhler that 'the alphabet of the Nanaghat inscription agrees generally with that of the Hathigumpha epigraph'. As there is so much difference of opinion on matters of palaeography and as the difference between the Nanaghat and the Hathigumpha records is only of a few decades, let us turn to the internal evidences of the epigraphs for determining whether there were one or more Śātakarṇis.

In 1.4 of the Hathigumpha record Khāravela says that in the second year of his reign he sent an army against Śātakarṇi, while in 1.6 we read that in his fourth year the Kaliṅga king compelled the Raṭhikas and the Bhojakas to adore his feet.[2] The Bhojakas were the ruling chiefs of Berar while the Raṭhikas the chiefs of the Marathi-speaking districts of Khandesh. The simultaneous mention of Śātakarṇi and the chiefs points to a time

1. *Select Ins.*, 207, fn. 7
2. '*Raṭhika-Bhojaks* stand for the Mahāraṭhis and Mahābhojas of Sātavāhana inscription and the minor inscriptions of the same period at Kānheri, Kuḍā and Bedsā. The Raṭhikas are mentioned as *Risṭikas* in the Girnar, *Raṭhikas* in the Shahbazgarhi and *Raṭhakas* in the Mānsehrā version of the 5th edict of Aśoka. The Dhauli version supplies the analogous form in *Laṭhika*. In the 13th edict we find the *Bhojakas* mentioned with the *Pitinikas* in Shāhbāzgarhi, Mānsehrā and Kālsī versions. In the Kānheri cave inscription of the time of Viṇhukaḍa Chuṭukulānanda a Mahābhoja is also called a *Mahārāja* showing that Bhoja probably was a title. Mahābhoja or Mahābhojis are mentioned in five votive inscriptions in the Kuḍā cave. In later periods a Bhojaka is mentioned in the copper-plate inscription of the Pallava king Śivaskandavarman'. (*Ep Ind*, xx, 84)

when the Sātavāhana empire was a small one evidently confined to the western Maharashtra region. On the other hand, the title of the *Lord of Dakṣiṇāpatha* given to Śātakarṇi, in the Nanaghat record, shows that he was flourishing after the fifth year of Khāravela as a great king. Had Khāravela met Śātakarṇi II, then it would not have been necessary for him to conquer afresh the Raṭhikas and the Bhojakas for they had already lost their separate existence during the time of the first Śātakarṇi who must, therefore, be regarded as a contemporary of Khāravela.

There are other reasons for thinking that the contemporary of Khāravela was the third king of the Sātavāhana dynasty and not the sixth one. As already stated, we cannot reject the unanimous testimony of the Purāṇas that Simuka overthrew the last Kāṇva king Suśarman and we have seen that Simuka ruled from c. 30 B.C. to c. 7 B.C. The sixth king of the dynasty, according to the *Matsya* chronology, would rule from 64 A.D. to 120 A.D., when, in fact, the Kṣaharātas were ruling over the Maharashtra region. Khāravela again can hardly be assigned to such a late date. As D.C. Sircar has himself pointed out, 'the angular forms and straight bases of letters like *b*, *m*, *p*, *h* and *y*, which are usually found in the Hathigumpha record, suggest a date not much earlier than the beginning of the 1st century A.D. (cf. *ḍ*)'.[1] This is exactly the time when the third king of the Sātavāhana dynasty had been ruling.

The grand stūpa at Sanchi contains an inscription informing us 'that an image is due to the sculptor of the great king Śātakarṇi'. It has been inferred that the empire of the third Sātavāhana monarch thus extended in the north upto East Malwa. The record in fact is incised on the southern gateway of the stūpa itself. Sanchi was a place of pilgrimage where people from different parts flocked for dedication. So on its evidence *only* it will not be proper to come to any definite conclusion. E.J. Rapson, however, maintains that the conquest of West Malwa is probably suggested by round coins bearing the legend *Sri Sāta*.[2] If this view be accepted then in the background of the Sanchi record we may hold that Śātakarṇi really conquered the Malwa region.

1. *Select Ins.*, 206, fn. 1
2. *CIC*, xciii

The Nanaghat inscription speaks of the second 'horse sacrifice', besides other sacrifices, performed by Śātakarṇi. The mention of the second sacrifice shows that 'two Aśvamedhas were performed, but the account of the first is lost'. Aśvamedha sacrifices were generally performed by kings after some victory in battle, though at a later period it lost its original significance and even petty chiefs performed more than one such sacrifices without possibly seeing the battlefield. In case of Śātakarṇi I, however, there is no reason to believe that he performed the sacrifice without any cogent reason for the degradation of the Aśvamedha had not yet started.

G. Buhler thinks that the Aśvamedha sacrifices referred to in the record were performed by the queen Nāganikā when she had been acting as the regent of her minor sons on behalf of her late husband, though according to the śāstras women are not allowed to offer *Śrauta* sacrifices. D.R. Bhandarkar has criticised the theory and holds that, 'it is inconceivable that Nāganikā, even as queen-regent, celebrated it of her own accord and to indicate her paramount sovereignty. An Aśvamedha sacrifice is performed by a king who lays claims to universal monarchy by conquering all neighbouring princes, and as Nāganikā's husband Śātakarṇi has been styled *apratihatachakra*, it is proper and natural to suppose that it was he who celebrated the sacrifice twice. What appears to be the case is that Śātakarṇi it must be, who carried out the sacrifices referred to in the epigraph, and as all sacrifices are performed by yajamānas along with their consorts, Nāganikā has been associated with him'.[1] Indeed, a critical study of the epigraph conveys the idea that Nāganikā was only describing the sacrifices performed by her illustrious husband who was *vira*, *śūra*, *dakṣiṇā* (*patha*) *pa*(*ti*) and *apratihatacakra*.

The Hathigumpha record gives possibly a clue to at least one such sacrifice. The inscription speaks of many victories of the Kaliṅga king in different directions. While some of the statements may undoubtedly be record of true facts, we may scent some amount of exaggeration in others. We should note that there is no mention of any actual fight between Śātakarṇi

1. *Ind. Ant.* 1918, 72, fn. 11

and the Kaliṅga king. In the background of the verbose nature of the Hathigumpha record it will possibly be not improper to infer that Khāravela could not fare well in the struggle. The Kaliṅga king's advance was evidently resisted by the Sātavāhana monarch who might have then performed an Aśvamedha sacrifice to celebrate the incident, a victory on his part. The statement *acitayita Satakaṃniṃ* which is generally interpreted to mean 'without caring for Śātakarṇi' seems to allude indirectly to the fact that the Kaliṅga king had not thought properly the might of his adversary.

The Nanaghat inscription of the queen gives us an important insight into the condition of religion prevailing in the Maharashtra region at the period. The performance of the *aśvamedhas* shows the presence of Vedism which is further proved by reference to Rājasūya and other sacrifices in which, it is stated, large *dakṣiṇās* were paid to the *purohitas*. The epigraph also refers to Dharma, Indra, Saṃkarṣaṇa and Vāsudeva, Candra and Sūrya and the *lokapālas* Yama-Varuṇa-Kuvera and Vāsava.

The reference to four *lokapālas* is interesting showing that the conception of ten *lokapālas* described in later Brāhmaṇical literature had not yet taken root in popular imagination. As we find its first use in an inscription from the Maharashtra region, it is not unlikely that this particular form of worship developed among the Aryans of the Outer Band, though it is difficult to determine to what extent the Dravidian and the Austric ideas played at the bottom. Ordinary people are concerned with the four main directions (north, south, east and west) and thus the worship of the four *lokapālas*, each guardian of a particular quarter, was but a natural one.

Salutations to the luminaries, though several planets are referred to in earlier literature, show also how luminary worship was gradually gaining momentum in the south. A passage of the *Aitareya Brāhmaṇa* makes the interesting statement *ādityād vai candramā jāyate*[1] which not only presupposes many astral theories that are budding forth at the present time but also shows how

1. W. Kirfel, Die *Kosmographie der Inder*, 32

since c. 800 B.C. the luminaries were influencing the minds of the common man. In this record we find the earliest epigraphic evidence of their worship.

Mention of Saṃkarṣaṇa and Vāsudeva together contains the earliest germ of the *vyūha* doctrine which is met with for the first time in the *Nārāyaṇīya* section of the *Mahābhārata* in which Vāsudeva, Saṃkarṣaṇa, Pradyumna and Aniruddha are worshipped together.[1] With the help of the epigraphic evidences we can trace the gradual evolution of the belief. Thus the Besnagar inscription of Heliodoros refers to Vāsudeva alone. The Ghosundi (Rajasthan) stone inscription of *mahārāja* Sarvatāta and the present Nanaghat record mention Vāsudeva with Saṃkarṣaṇa, while the Mora (Mathura) inscription of the time of Sodāsa refers to the *pañcavīras* which has been taken to mean Vāsudeva, Saṃkarṣaṇa, Pradyumna, Aniruddha and Śāmba. Later on Śāmba became dropped from the Vaiṣṇava pantheon and found his way in Solar mythology.

Thus the Nanaghat inscription is not only an important document of political history but throws interesting sidelight on the development of Brāhmaṇical cults as well.

Śātakarṇi I, the son of Simuka and the third king of the restored Sātavāhana line, was thus a valiant warrior who saved his kingdom from outside danger and extended its boundaries. He is the issuer of *Siri-sāta* coins and also of coins bearing the legend *Satakanasa* or (*Siri*) *Satakanasa* or *Rajño Siri Satakani*. It is very doubtful whether we can ascribe to him the coins with the legend (*Sa*)*takani Maharath*(*i*) *Sadaka.*[2]

Vedi-Siri

It is not easy to determine who succeeded Śātakarṇi. The Nanaghat relievo inscriptions refer to Kumāra Bhā......ya, Kumāra Hakusiri and Kumāra Sātavāhana, while the big Nanaghat record refers to princes Vedi-siri and Sati-siri. The non-

1. *Mbh.* xii. 336 ff; for the Pāñcarātras, F.O. Schrader, *Introduction to the Pāñcarātra and the Ahirbudhnya Saṁhitā*, Madras, 1916
2. We may agree with M. Rama Rao that 'these coins indicate that there was a line of *Maharaṭhis* who issued coins of the lion type and who were subordinates of Śātakarṇi I.' (*l. c.*, 16)

mention of the first three princes in the Nanaghat inscription seems to show that they were evidently dead when the record was incised long after the death of king Śātakarṇi. One Mahā-Hakusiri is mentioned in a Nasik cave inscription incised by his granddaughter Bhaṭapālikā.[1] But this Mahā-Hakusiri can hardly be identical with Kumāra Hakusiri mentioned above.

As pointed out by D.R. Bhandarkar, Śātakarṇi was possibly succeeded by his son Vedi-siri. V.V. Mirashi also accepts this view and points out that in the Nanaghat record of Nāganikā, he, and not Śātakarṇi, is given the epithet raño and described as *apratihatacakra* and *Dakhiṇāpathapati*.[2] If this view be accepted (though it has not been accepted in these pages) then there is no reason to think that queen Nāganikā had been acting as a regent, while the Nanaghat record is nothing but a funeral oration of a disconsolate wife.

Vedi-siri, like king Sātavāhana, the progenitor of the Sātavāhana dynasty, is not mentioned in the Purāṇas showing that the texts have got many loopholes.

Āpilaka

A coin found in the Madhya Pradesh region bears the legend *Raño Siva Siris Āpilakasa*. It has been held that palaeographically it must be assigned to a late date;[3] but there is really no such difficulty on this score. The *Vāyu* puts him after Śātakarṇi I while in the *Matsya* he is the eighth in the list.

A note of caution should be uttered here. The find of a few coins of a particular king in a certain area should not be taken as indicating that the region was under his sway, for it is well-known that coins often travel from one place to another. It is really

1. *Ep. Ind.* viii, 91
2. *Ind Ant*, 1918, 72; V. V. Mirashi, *Studies in Indology*, i, 119ff
3. K.N. Dikshit maintains that on numismatic grounds the place of this ruler is more with the later kings of this dynasty than with the earlier ones as indicated in the Purāṇas. K. Gopalachari points out that the blank reverse of the coins certainly attests its early age. The early forms of *s* and *r* which are only slightly developed forms of those of the Sri-Sāta coins and the primitive *i* sign shows that the coin is an early one.

curious, therefore, that the discovery of a single coin of king Sātavāhana in Kondapuram, near Hyderabad, has led an eminent scholar to infer that the 'Sātavāhana empire started from Telengana of modern Andhra Pradesh.'[1] Similarly, it has been held that a copper coin of king Āpilaka, discovered in the Madhya Pradesh, 'attests the extension of Sātavāhana power in the north-east in or before his reign'.[2]

1. *Sātavāhana Coins*, 23
2. *CHIN*, 304

APPENDIX I

ON THE DATE OF KHĀRAVELA

Some scholars are inclined to think that Khāravela flourished at the first quarter of the second century B.C., on the following grounds:

(a) that the Hathigumpha inscription is dated in the 165th year of the Maurya era corresponding to the thirteenth year of Khāravela (*l*.16) (Dubrevil);

(b) that Bahasatimita who was compelled to adore the feet of the Kaliṅga king (*l*.12) is no other than Puṣyamitra (Jayaswal);

(c) that in *l*. 6 of the Hathigumpha record, Khāravela claims that he caused a canal to be dug out again that was originally constructed by king Nanda who must be identified with Nandivardhana (Jayaswal);

(d) that in *l*. 8 of the record, we have a reference to the Yavana-rāja Dimita who fled away to Mathurā on the approach of Khāravela, and this Dimita can only be identified with Demetrius I who was the contemporary of Puṣyamitra Śuṅga (Sten Konow).

None of the above arguments appears to be valid; (a) what has been read in the *l*. 16 of the Hathigumpha record as *Muriya-kāla* is really *mukhiya-kāla* or *mukhya-kāla*, and further there is no evidence of any Maurya era starting from the accession of Candragupta Maurya in c. 324 B.C. Had such been the case, Aśoka would have dated his records in that era instead of in his regnal years; (b) the identification of Bahasatimita with Puṣyamitra is far from certain. K. P. Jayaswal's argument that as Bṛhaspati is the lord, nakṣatrādhipa, of the nakṣatra Puṣya or Tissa in the house of Cancer in which the planet becomes ascendant (*tuṅga*), Bahasatimita should be identified with Puṣyamitra who occupied an ascendant position in North India, has got no historical basis. As H.C. Raychaudhuri points out, the *Divyāvadāna* makes a distinction between a king named Bṛhaspati and

Puṣyamitra.[1] R.P. Chanda aptly remarks: 'Even if we admit that Bṛhaspati was also identified by the ancient Hindus with Puṣya, that does not justify the identification of Bṛhaspatimitra with Puṣyamitra any more than the denotation of the same god by the terms Skanda and Kumāra justifies the identification of Skanda Gupta with Kumāra Gupta.'[2] Bahasatimita was possibly a king of the Kauśāmbī region, and his jurisdiction may have extended over Magadha as well;[3] (c) similarly, there is some difficulty in accepting the identification of Nandarāja mentioned in the Hathigumpha record with Nandavardhana or Nandivardhana. Nandivardhana was a king of the dynasty of Śiśunāga, and there is no evidence that the Śiśunāgas had to do anything with Kaliṅga. As H.C. Raychaudhuri points out: "It is not Nandivardhana but Mahāpadma Nanda who is said to have brought 'all under his sole sway' and 'uprooted all Kṣatriyas' or the old ruling families. So we should identify 'Naṃdarāja' of the Hathigumpha inscription, who held possession of Kaliṅga either with the all-conquering Mahāpadma Nanda or one of his sons."[4] L.D. Barnett thinks that Nandarāja may have been a local king of Kaliṅga, but the view goes against the internal evidence of the Hathigumpha inscription. As Nandarāja is said to have ruled some 300 years before Khāravela, the latter evidently flourished at the second half of the first century B.C., or somewhat later; (d) as regards the identification of the Yavanarāja Dimita with Demetrius I, it may be noted what R.P. Chanda has stated in *IHQ*, v.p. 598: 'The chronological impossibilities in these identifications become still more apparent when attempt is made to reconstruct the history of Magadha from 175 to 170 B.C. on their basis. If Demetrius, son of Euthydemus, retired from India to face Eucratides when Khāravela laid siege to Rājagṛha, the latter event must have happened in the year 175 (Jayaswal) or 174 (Sten Konow) B.C. As this year corresponds to the eighth year of Khāravela's reign, he must have ascended the throne of Kaliṅga in 183 or 182 B.C. With Khāravela's siege of Rājagṛha, the revolt of Eucratides in Bactria and the retreat of Demetrius, Messrs. Sten Konow

1. *PHAI*, 374
2. *IHQ*, v. 597
3. *supra*
4. *PHAI*, 377

and Jayaswal link two other events, the siege of Sāketa and Madhyamikā by Demetrius and a horse sacrifice (the first horse sacrifice according to Mr. Jayaswal) of Puṣyamitra. As we have already seen, Patañjali's statements in the *Mahābhāṣya* clearly indicate that the siege of Sāketa and Madhyamikā by the Yavana (i.e., the Yavana king) and the horse sacrifice of Puṣyamitra were not, strictly speaking, contemporaneous events'. In fact, the siege of Demetrius took place before Puṣyamitra ascended the throne of Magadha after murdering Bṛhadratha, and this goes strongly against the proposed identification.

Thus it appears that in determining the date of Khāravela we have to depend on the palaeographical evidence of the Hathigumpha record, which as already stated,[1] points to a date in the second half of the first century B.C., and the meaning of the expression '*Pañcame ca dāni vase Naṃda—rāja-ti-vasa-sata-o (gh) ātitaṃ Tanasuliya-vāta panādim nagaram pavesayati*' showing that Khāravela flourished some *ti-vasa-sata* years after Naṃda-rāja. Now, the expression *ti-vasa-sata* may mean either 103 or 300. As it is stated that in fifth year of his reign Khāravela caused the canal opened out by king Nanda *ti-vasa-sata* years back to be brought into the capital, we have to place the accession of Khāravela either 98 or 295 years after the time of the Nanda-rāja. If taken in the former sense, Khāravela becomes king in 324 – 98 = 226 B.C. This date can in no case be later, though there is every possibility that it may be somewhat earlier. The Hathigumpha record further states that he was elevated to the position of *yuvarāja* nine years before his accession, i.e., in c. 235 B.C. It appears also from the above discussion that in c. 235 B.C. Khāravela's father was on the throne of Kaliṅga and he also had his predecessor or predecessors who thus become a contemporary of Aśoka along with Khāravela's father as well. But from the inscriptions of Aśoka we learn that in his time Kaliṅga was governed by a Maurya Kumāra under the suzerainty of Aśoka. This shows that the expression *ti-vasa-sata* cannot be taken in the sense of 103, though on the analogy of the earlier records it may be assumed that it has been used not with mathematical accuracy.

1. *supra*

The above discussions clearly show that we can take the expression roughly in the sense of 300, which would place Khāravela in the second half of the first century B.C. or the first half of the first century A.D. This interpretation, as we have already seen, is supported by the literary and the archaeological data at our disposal.

Chapter IV

KṢAHARĀTAS AND SĀTAVĀHANAS

From Simuka who became independent in c. 30 B.C. to Āpīlaka there now appears to have ruled five kings. The Purāṇic reign periods assigned to four of them (Simuka, 23; Kṛṣṇa, 18; Śātakarṇi, 10; Vedisiri, ?; Āpīlaka, 12) give us a total of 63 years. We may assign 15 years to Vedisiri and thus the early Sātavāhanas would appear to rule for 78 years, i.e., up to c. 48 A.D. or c. 50 A.D. in round numbers.

In the middle of the first century A.D. the Scythian—*Kṣaharātas* made their first encroachment over South India and gradually a considerable portion of the country passed under their heels. The Sātavāhana dynasty was pushed to the background and the Sātavāhana princes maintained a precarious existence evidently as petty local rulers outside the territory of the *Kṣaharāta* kings and some of them might have acknowledged temporarily the suzerainty of the foreign masters. This is proved to a certain extent by the fact that no king mentioned in the Purāṇas as ruling between Āpīlaka and Gautamīputra who ultimately restored the lost glory of the dynasty is known from either inscriptions or coins (see, *infra Numismatic Notes*). Evidently the kings were too insignificant to issue any of them, though at least one of them, Hāla, is mentioned in a literary work (*supra*).

For a proper understanding of the *Kṣaharāta* exploits in South India we have to turn for a moment to the events happening on the northern side of the Vindhyan range. A branch of the Scythians, who originally lived in Central Asia, ultimately migrated to India and caused the downfall of the Greek rule in the Punjab and the North-Western-Frontier Province in Pakistan. Available archaeological records show that a Scythian dynasty using the title of *king of kings* ruled in Taxila while there were several Scythian satrapal dynasties ruling over Kāpiśa, Puṣkalāvatī, Abhisāraprastha, Mathura and other places. During the reign of Azes II, the fourth Śaka or Scythian king of Taxila, we find that the currency 'suffered a sudden and surprising eclipse. The design deteriorated and the workmanship came to a very low ebb'. It has been surmised that such a state of affairs happened due to 'some local catastrophe such as an earthquake or plague, which had wiped out the mint and its skilled engravers.'[1]

Evidently taking advantage of this calamitous situation, the Parthians of Eastern Iran made an inroad into India, wiped out the Śaka rule in W. Punjab and occupied Taxila. This event occurring in the remote Western Punjab bore an indirect effect. The Śakas now became scattered and a branch of them moved towards the south putting pressure on the dominion of the Sātavāhanas.

Let us now try to determine the approximate time when the process started. When Apollonius of Tyana visited Taxila c. 43-44 A.D., the throne of the country was occupied by one Phraotes, evidently a Parthian as his name indicates. Following Herzfeld, Tarn thinks that Phraotes was Gondopharnes, for the term Phraotes may be a Graecised corruption of the word *apratihata* which is a title of Gondopharnes on his coins.[2] Marshall points out, however, that 'the title *apratihatacakra* had been used by the satrap Rañjubula in the Eastern Punjab......It may be noted that Philostratos represents Phraotes as being only 27 years of age at the time of Apollonius' visit, which could mean that he (if he could be identified with Gondopharnes) was about 12 years of age when he came to the throne in 19 A.D. On all his coins, however, Gondopharnes appears as a bearded middle aged man.[3] The famous Takht-i-Bahi inscription of the (Vikrama) year 103 shows that Gondopharnes was king in 45 A.D., and that his reign began in 19 A.D., because the record is dated in his 26th regnal year as well. The Orthanges coins prove that he came to power in Eastern Iran,[4] and so 19 A.D. is evidently the date when he began his rule there and evidently it was at a later period that he occupied Taxila. From the Takht-i-Bahi epigraph it does not necessarily follow that Gondopharnes

1. J. Marshall, *Taxila*, i, 54
2. *GBI*, 341
3. J. Marshall, *Taxila*, i, 64, fn.3
4. *CHI*, 578

was in possession of Taxila in 45 A.D. By that time the Gandhāra country must have been under him—Takht-i-Bahi is in Gandhāra country—and it is more probable that he occupied Taxila a few years later. Phraotes ruled over Taxila in 43-44 A.D. and he did not disturb the Scythian equilibrium very much. Azes II still had been in power, evidently somewhere outside Taxila, and his rule came to an end under the pressure of Gondopharnes as the coins show that one Aspavarman who had been a *strategos* under Azes II served later on under Gondopharnes as well. The empire of Gondopharnes comprised Seistan, Sind, the Southern and Western Punjab, the North Western Frontier Province and Southern Afghanistan.[1] He might have also conquered and annexed to his empire a part of the Parthian dominion to the west of Seistan.

It would thus appear that though the conquest of Phraotes dislodged the 'Śakas from Taxila, the real disturbance to the Śakas in general was caused by the conquest of Gondopharnes, and this pressure compelled some of the Śaka Chiefs to move towards the south'. If this view be accepted then we may place the beginning of the Scythian pressure on the Sātavāhana empire sometime about c. 48 A.D. i.e. just after the reign of Āpīlaka.

Inscriptions and coins reveal the existence of two Scythian dynasties—the *Kṣaharātas*, and the family of Caṣṭana—that put pressure on the Sātavāhanas. Of these two dynasties, the earlier and the short-lived one was that of the *Kṣaharātas* consisting of two members only, Bhūmaka and Nahapāna. Bhūmaka's coins have been found in Gujarat, Kathiawad and the Malwa region. We are absolutely in the dark regarding the relationship of Nahapāna with Bhūmaka. Rapson thinks that the forms of the Brāhmī and Kharoṣṭhī letters on their coins make a long interval between them almost impossible.[2] As Bhūmaka

1. *EHNI*, 81
2. E.J. Rapson, *CIC*, cviii; Dr. D.C. Sircar thinks that 'the use of both the Kharoṣṭhī and Brāhmī scripts in Bhūmaka's coin-legends probably points to the fact that the Kshatrapa territories not only comprised such districts as Malwa, Gujarat and Kathiawad where Brāhmī was prevalent, but also some regions about Western Rajputana and Sind where Kharoṣṭhī appears to have been in use.' (*AIU*, 179) But the inclusion of Sind within Bhūmaka's kingdom goes against the evidence of the *Periplus* which makes Nahapāna rule at a time when the Parthians were fighting in Indo-Scythia=Sind.

appears to have been one of the earliest victims of the Parthian pressure, he might have begun his rule about 50 A.D. and thus it is not possible to place the beginning of Nahapāna's reign later than c. 70 A.D.

The distribution of Bhūmaka's coins show that he could not attack the citadel of the Sātavāhana power in the south though he might have snatched away a portion of the Madhya Pradesh from some successor of Āpīlaka (?). Nahapāna was more successful in his bid and in studying the history of his reign we have to bear in mind the following facts:

(a) The geographical references in the inscriptions of Uṣabhadāta, son-in-law of Nahapāna, show that the latter's rule extended as far north as Ajmer in Rajasthan as well as over Kathiawad, South Gujarat, Western Malwa, North Konkon from Broach to Sopara and Nasik and Poona districts.[1]

(b) The Jogalthembi hoard has brought to light numerous coins of Nahapāna, two-thirds of which have been re-struck by Gautamīputra Śrī-Śātakarṇi, a fact which shows that the two kings were contemporaries and that the *Kṣaharāta* ruler was conquered by the Sātavāhana king.[2]

It is thus apparent that the successors of Āpīlaka (?) lost Western Maharashtra region to the *Kṣaharātas* and maintained a precarious existence till the time of Gautamīputra who uprooted the alien rule and restored the glory of the dynasty. From a Nasik inscription[3] it appears that Nahapāna was over-

1. *Ind Ant*, 1918, 75
2. H.R. Scott, who made a critical study of the coins, came to the conclusion that the coins re-struck by Gautamīputra did not all belong to the Kṣaharāta king. We are noting his views here as since not only J.G.-Dubreinl accepted it as early as 1919, but some recent scholars have tried to revive his theory. Scott points out that the faces on the coins vary 'greatly in age and not in age only, but in every feature' and so he concludes 'We may have here the coins not of a single king, but of a series of kings, sons and grandsons perhaps of Nahapāna, who retained on their coins the name of their great ancestor as title of honour.' It will be seen that Nahapāna ruled for more than 46 years and so the face on his coins must have taken various shapes with the variation of age. We are unable to accept Scott's views though G.V. Rao has recently advocated in his favour. (*EHD*, ed. G. Yazdani, 95f)
3. *Ins.*, 191

thrown by Gautamīputra in his 18th regnal year. This gives us the equation:

The last year of Nahapāna = the 18th regnal year of Gautamīputra.

This leads us to a discussion of the date of Nahapāna, which would help us in determining the time of restoration of the Sātavāhana power. Nahapāna has been mentioned in eight cave inscriptions. Of these six have been cut in cave no. 10 of Pandu Lena, near Nasik, one in the Caitya Cave at Karle and one in a cave at Junnar. The Pandu Lena (Nasik) records give the dates 41, 42 and 45. The Junnar epigraph specifies the year 46.

There has been great controversy regarding the era to which these dates are to be referred:

(a) Cunningham, G. J-Dubreuil, R.D. Banerjee and some other scholars are in favour of assigning these dates to the Vikrama era of 58 B.C.

(b) Following A.M. Boyer, E.J. Rapson refers these dates to the Śaka era of 78 A.D. and this view has been accepted by a large number of scholars.

(c) A third view has recently gained ground according to which these dates refer to the regnal years of Nahapāna.

We cannot clearly accept the first view, for Nahapāna is referred to as a contemporary prince in the *Periplus of the Erythraean Sea*. Some scholars preferring the variant reading Mambarus or Nambarus maintain that the prince of the *Periplus* cannot be Nahapāna.[1] It has been pointed out, however, that 'the king of the *Periplus M.E.* Ch. 41, is Nahapāna' and this 'no longer admits of doubt. The text, as based on the latest examination of the manuscript, suggests the view that the name was originally Nambarus and eliminates the Mambarus of earlier texts.'[2] It has been pointed out that the *Periplus* mentions Malichos (Maliku), the king of the Nabateans, who died in 75 A.D., and Zoscales (Za Hakale), king of the Auxumites, who reigned from 76 A.D. to 89 A.D.[3] The work on the other

1. This theory has been accepted by D.C. Sircar in *AIU*, 178-79.
2. *JRAS*, 1946, 170
3. *ib.*, 1917, 827-30

hand, confines the Kuṣāṇas in Bactria[1] and this appears to point to a date before 64 A.D., for the Panjtar inscription of that year proves the presence of the Kuṣāṇas on the Indian soil. In face of all these evidences, we can only conclude that the different section of the monograph were composed at different times between 60 and 80 A.D. Thus Nahapāna appears to have been ruling sometime between these two dates.[2]

So we have to select between the second and third theories. How adamant the advocates of the theories are in their views will be apparent from the pages of the *Comprehensive History of India*, ii, ed. K.A.N. Sastri, where J.N. Banerjea refers the dates in the records of Nahapāna to the Śaka era of 78 A.D. and K. Gopalachari considers that they refer to the regnal years of the prince. Noting this contradiction in the same volume, the editor added the following note:

> 'By following the Purāṇic data closely, Dr. Gopalachari arrives at A.D. 72-95 as the period of Gautamīputra's reign and considers that the dates in Nahapāna's inscriptions represent his regnal years. Dr. J.N. Banerjea, on the other hand, following Rapson, refers the dates to the Śaka era, holds that Nahapāna began to rule first as a satrap of Kaniṣka and became independent later and discusses at some length the position taken up by Gopalachari. It would seem, however, that the eulogium on Gautamīputra's conquests recorded in the Nasik inscription of the nineteenth year of his son and successor Pulumāyi II about twenty-five years after they were effected, goes to show that the results of Gautamīputra's success were not so short-lived as they must be held to have been if Nahapāna's dates are referred to the Śaka era'.[3]

E.J. Rapson's theory cannot be accepted on other grounds as well. Since the year 46 is the last known date of Nahapāna, according to this theory then Nahapāna's reign would come to an end in 124 A.D. and as this would correspond to 18th year of Gautamīputra's reign, his accession should be placed in 106 A.D.

1. *The Periplus*, ed. Schoff, 185
2. For a discussion of the date of the *Periplus*, B.N. Mukherjee, *The Kushāṇas and the Deccan*, 123-27
3. *CHIN*, xviii

From the epigraphic evidences it is absolutely clear that Gautamīputra ruled at least for 24 years, while a Karle epigraph shows that his son Pulumāyi also ruled at least for the same number of years. This would show that, according to E.J. Rapson's view, Pulumāyi ruled from 130 A.D. to 154 A.D. This goes against the mention of Śātakarṇi as the lord of Dakṣiṇāpatha in the Junagadh inscription of Rudradāman of 150 A.D., for Pulumāyi never takes the title of Śātakarṇi in inscriptions or coins. Those who follow Rapson suggest that Śātakarṇi of the Junagadh record is to be identified with Vāśiṣṭhīputra Śrī-Śātakarṇi of a Kanheri Cave inscription or with Vāśiṣṭhīputra Chatrapana Śātakarṇi of a Nanaghat record. The Junagadh record shows that Śātakarṇi was the *Lord* of Dakṣiṇāpatha about 150 A.D. and in that case we have to infer, if we follow Rapson, that either Pulumāyi and Vāśiṣṭhiputra Śrī Śātakarṇi or Vāśiṣṭhīputra-Śrī (Chatrapana) Śātakarṇi had been ruling conjointly or that there was a partition of the empire, the latter prince being more powerful than Pulumāyi. But we have absolutely no evidences for either supposition. This shows that Rapson's theory is untenable.[1] (For further discussions, *infra*).

J.N. Banerjea and some other scholars maintain that Nahapāna was a viceroy of the Kuṣāṇas;[2] in other words, the Sātavāhanas after Āpīlaka were pushed to the background not under the pressure of the Kṣaharātas, but under the pressure of the Kuṣāṇas. The Kuṣāṇa domination over the Maharashtra region is not supported directly by any archaeological evidence. Such a view rests on the following untenable theories :

1. E.J. Rapson made the above observations before the Andau Stone inscription of the (Śaka) years 52 came to light and so the question of Nahapāna's date must be discussed afresh. To understand the problem, as Prof. Nilakantha Sastri has observed, we have to discuss the following questions:—
(a) In what relation does Nahapāna stand to Caṣṭana and his line?
(b) What is the relation between these two lines of foreign rulers and the Sātavāhanas?
(c) Among the Sātavāhanas themselves what is the relation in which the reign of Gautamīputra Śātakarṇi stands to that of Pulumāyi?
Prof. Sastri has discussed all these problems in *JRAS*, 1926, 644.
2. *CHIN*, 274f

(a) S. Levi thinks that the sway of Kaniṣka extended over the North-Western part of the Deccan. He equates Sandanes, who had the port of Calliena or Kalyan under his control, mentioned in the *Periplus of the Erythraean Sea*, with Candra or Candana, Chinese Chen-tan, a royal title given to Kaniṣka. Further, he thinks that Tong-li of the Chinese historian should be identified with Dravida and thus concludes that the Yueh-chi were the rulers of different principalities in the Deccan.[1] The theory is not a conclusive one and does not tally with the known epigraphic evidences of the dynasty.[2]

(b) E.J. Rapson makes Nahapāna a subordinate ruler under the Kuṣāṇas because one of his Nasik inscriptions contains 'the important information that the rate of exchange between the Kārṣāpaṇa and the gold coin of the period, the Suvarṇa, was as 1 to 35. The reference here must surely be (according to E.J. Rapson) to the contemporary gold currency of the Kuṣāṇas, the standard of which was apparently that of the Roman Aureus.'[3] The mere mention of suvarṇa or gold coins cannot at once refer to the currency of the Kuṣāṇas, for suvarṇa as a coin was prevalent in India as early as the Vedic times.

(c) D.R. Bhandarkar has adduced still another ground to connect the *Kṣaharātas* with the Kuṣāṇas. The Nasik cave inscription, No. 12, of Nahapāna's son-in-law Uṣavadāta contains the line '......data cānena akṣaya-nivi-Kāhāpanasahasrāṇi trīni 3000 saṃghasa cātudisasa ye imasmin lene vasāṁtāna (ṃ) bhavisaṃti civarika Kuśāṇa mule ca'. D.R. Bhandarkar observes that the name Kusāṇa 'appears to have been given to the silver coinage of Nahapāna, because he issued it for his overlord, who must have been known as kuśaṇa i.e., Kuṣāṇa.'

1. *JA*, 1936, 61-21
2. For a discussion of Levi's theory B.N. Mukherjee, *The Kushāṇas and the Deccan*, ch. ii.
3. *CIC*, clxxxv

He further connects this Kuṣāṇa with the Kuṣāṇa sovereign referred to in the Taxila Scroll inscription of the year 136, and thinks that he can be no other than Kujula Kadphises or Kadphises I.[1] The sense of the passage does not admit of Bhandarkar's interpretation. Kuśāṇamula here evidently refers to expenses of outside life as pointed out by E. Senart. Further there are objections to the equation kuśaṇa to Guṣaṇa or Kuṣāṇa.

It is thus apparent that there is no valid ground for thinking that the Kuṣāṇas ever extended their sway over the Maharashtra country or that the records of Nahapāna are dated in the Śaka era of 78 A.D. As we have already indicated the date of Nahapāna is intimately connected with the date of Gautamīputra and his successors. V.A. Smith has pointed out that the silver coins of the Sātavāhana king Yajñaśrī Śātakarṃi imitate the coinage of the Śaka rulers of Ujjayinī, a fact which possibly proves his victory over the latter. We know that on several occasions the later Śaka satraps of Ujjayinī had to acknowledge the authority of some other power and on such occasions there was no issue of the *mahākṣatrapa* coins. Now, before the Sātavāhana dynasty came to an end in the first quarter of the third century A.D., these were two occasions when the exalted office remained in abeyance—179-181 A.D. and again 188-190 A.D. During one of these periods Yajñaśrī Śātakarṃi apparently subdued the Śakas of Ujjayinī, as proved by his coins referred to above. The Gunda inscription of 181 A.D. shows the Ābhīra general Rudrabhūti referring to Rudrasiṃha as the satrap ignoring the existence of any *mahākṣatrapa* altogether.[2] It is not unlikely that Rudrabhūti was an overpowerful general who usurped the *mahākṣatrapa* power, but like Puṣyamitra did not adopt any higher title. Thus by process of elimination we may infer that Yajñaśrī Śātakarṃi extended his sway over the satrapal dominion during the period 188-90 A.D. and after this victory of the Sātavāhana king the then Śaka ruler Rudrasiṃha I became a mere *kṣatrapa* of the subordinate rank. It was evidently after the death of the Sātavāhana emperor that the Śakas recovered

1. *Ind Ant*, 1918, 76
2. *Ep Ind*, xvi, 233

their independence and the office of the mahākṣatrapa revived again. This gives us a fixed point in the Sātavāhana chronology :

The year 190 A.D.=the last year of Yajñaśrī Śātakarṇi's reign.[1]

If with this fixed point we go back and build up the chronology of Gautamīputra and his successors, we get admirable results that tally with all other evidences. Here we may first bring in the evidences of the *Vāyu* and the *Matsya* Purāṇas :

Vāyu P.		*Matsya P.*	
Gautamīputra	21 yrs.	Gautamīputra	21 yrs.
		Pulomāt	28 "
		Śivaśrī	7 "
		Śivaskanda	7 "
Yajñaśrī	29 "	Yajñaśrī	29 "
Vijaya	6 "	Vijaya	6 "
Daṇḍaśrī	3 "	Candaśrī	10 "
Pulomāvī	7 "	Pulomāvi	7 "

An examination of the above accounts in the background of the available epigraphs reveals that the *Matsya* version is more faithful for the later Sātavāhana kings, though for the earlier kings the *Vāyu* account, as we have already indicated, appears to be a more correct one:

(a) Inscriptions show that Gautamīputra was succeeded not by Yajñaśrī, as the *Vāyu* asserts, but by Vāsiṣṭhīputra Pulumāyi=Pulomāt of the *Matsya* list.

(b) Śivaśrī is evidently identical with Vāsiṣṭhīputra Śivaśrī Śātakarṇi of the coins and Vāsiṣṭhīputra Śrī Śātakarṇi of the Kanheri epigraph that represents him as the husband of the daughter of the mahākṣatrapa Ru(dra)= Rudradāman.

1. We shall see later on that Yajñaśrī Śātakarṇi conquered the Śakas of Ujjayinī, and it was evidently after his death that the office of mahākṣatrapa was revived again in the Śaka kingdom. The Sātavāhana conquest must be ascribed to the period A.D. 188-90, for on other occasions when we find no mahākṣatrapa, a sign of the Śaka kingdom passing under some foreign rule, the Śakas were under the suzerainty of the Ābhīras and the Sassanids.

(c) Śivaskanda is evidently identical with king Sivamaka Sata of an Amaravati record, as D.C. Sircar has suggested.

(d) Vijaya is known from coins of the Akola hoard.

(e) Candraśrī has been identified by E.J. Rapson with Śrī Canda II of the coins.

(f) The last king Pulomāvi is evidently mentioned in the Myakadoni epigraph. While editing the record in *Ep. Ind.* xiv, pp. 151 ff, V.S. Sukthankar opined that the Pulumāyi of the record should be identified with Vāsiṣṭhīputra Śrī Pulumāyi, son of Gautamīputra. 'The absence of the metronymic and the honorific prefix *sāmi* which are always borne by the son of Gautamīputra siri-Sātakarṇi, and the alphabet of the Myakadoni inscription, which approaches that of the Nāgārjunikonda and the Jagayyapeta inscriptions, make it highly probable that the Pulumāyi of this inscription is the last of the Sātavāhanas in the Purāṇic lists'.[1]

The above discussions clearly demonstrate that for Gautamīputra and his successors the *Matsya* account is a more faithful one, though in the reign-period assigned to these kings we find some discrepancies with the data supplied by the archaeological sources. In this connection we may note the following facts :

Epigraphic records show that both Gautamīputra and Pulumāyi ruled at least for 24 years.

The Junagadh record shows that one Śātakarṇi, the lord of Dakṣiṇāpatha, had been ruling about 150 A.D. This Śātakarṇi is evidently identical with Vāsiṣṭhīputra śrī Śātakarṇi of the Kanheri record, same as Śivaśrī Śātakarṇi of the Purāṇas and Vāśiṣṭhīputra Śivaśrī Śātakarṇi of the coins, as already stated.

Yajñaśrī Śātakarṇi's inscriptions prove that he ruled at least for 27 years and thus the Purāṇic account that he ruled for 29 years may be correct.

On the basis of the above discussions, and taking 190 A.D. as the last year of Yajñaśrī Śātakarṇi, the chronology of the later Sātavāhanas would stand thus :

1. *EHAC*, 72

Gautamīputra Śātakarṇi	.. c.	99 A.D.—123 A.D.
Vāsiṣṭhīputra Pulumāyi	.. c.	123 A.D.—147 A.D.
Śivaśrī Śātakarṇi	.. c.	147 A.D.—154 A.D.
Śivaskanda Śātakarṇi	.. c.	154 A.D.—161 A.D.
Yajñaśrī Śātakarṇi	.. c.	161 A.D.—190 A.D.

In his *Early History of the Andhra Country*, pp. 55f, K. Gopalachari assumes that Gautamīputra Śātakarṇi became king in 82 A.D. and ruled up to 106 A.D., while in the *Comprehensive History of India*, ii, p. 312, the same scholar holds that Gautamīputra's reign period was c. A.D. 72-95. It is difficult to accept any of his theories since Gautamīputra's empire, as we shall see later on, included Ākar-āvanti (East and West Malwa), while we have got an inscription of Vāsiṣka from Sanchi dated in the year 106 A.D. showing that the Kuṣāṇas still controlled the Eastern Malwa region. It was evidently conquered by Kaniṣka I who came to the throne in 78 A.D. and not a new conquest by Vāsiṣka himself. This shows that Gautamīputra must have been living after 106 A.D. and it was evidently after his death that the Sātavāhana monarch conquered the Avanti region.

Recently, Prof. G.V. Rao has suggested the following dates for Gautamīputra and his successors :[1]

Gautamīputra Śātakarṇi	..	A.D. 62-86
Vāsiṣṭhīputra Pulumāyi	..	A.D. 86-114
Śivaśrī Śātakarṇi	..	A.D. 114-121
Śivaskanda	..	A.D. 121-128
Yajñaśrī Śātakarṇi	..	A.D. 128-157[2]

1. *EHD*, ed. G. Yazdani, 107
2. According to Krishnasastri (*Ep Ind*, xviii, 318) the second year of Cada Sāti or Caṇḍaśrī (Śātakarṇi) is equivalent to A.D. 210. Now, Yajñaśrī Śātakarṇi was succeeded by Vijaya, whose successor was Cada Sāti. According to the *Matsya Purāṇa*, Vijaya ruled for 6 years. Thus if we take Krishnasastri's view and begin calculating backwards, we find that Vāsiṣṭhīputra Pulumāyi's reign falls between c. 135 A.D. and 160 A.D. But, as we have pointed out before, the Junagadh record of 150 A.D. speaks of king Śātakarṇi as being twice defeated by the Great Satrap Rudradāman, and this Śātakarṇi can hardly be identified with Vāsiṣṭhīputra Pulumāyi.

V.V. Mirashi gives us the following account of Sātavāhana geneology and chronology:

'It is well known that there was an interruption in the Sātavāhana rule

(*continued*)

over Gujarat and Maharashtra. The Śaka Satrap Bhūmaka established himself in Gujarat and Nahapāna in Maharashtra. The Sātavāhanas who were ousted from this part of the country, seem to have retired to Vidarbha. They attempted to reconquer their lost territory during the reign of Gautamīputra Śātakarṇi. This Sātavāhana king is said to have exterminated the Kshaharāta family to which Nahapāna belonged. The decisive battle seems to have been fought in the eighteenth year of Gautamīputra's reign; for, soon after the victory he donated a field to the Buddhist monks living in the caves near Nasik. The Kshaharata Satrap defeated by Gautamīputra is not named, but he was probably Nahapāna himself; for we know of no successor of the latter. Besides, Gautamīputra is known to have called back and restruck Kshatrapa coins in order to proclaim the establishment of his rule. The Jogalthembi hoard, discovered in 1906, contained hundreds of coins of this type. But among them there was not a single coin of any successor of Nahapāna, which shows that Gautamīputra came immediately after Nahapāna.

Now, the last known date of Nahapāna is 46, which it seems best to refer to the Śaka era. It is thus equivalent to *circa* 124 A.C. Supposing that Nahapāna suffered a defeat in this year, 124 A.C. becomes the 18th year of Gautamīputra's reign. Gautamīputra may, therefore, have come to the throne in *circa* 107 A.C. The Purāṇas name the successors of Gautamīputra and give their reign-periods as follows:—

Gautamīputra	...	21 years	*circa*	107-127 A.C.
Puḷumāvi II	...	28 ,,	,,	128-155 ,,
Śātakarṇi	...	29 ,,	,,	156-184 ,,
Śivaśrī Puḷumāvi III	...	7 ,,	,,	185-191 ,,
Śivaskanda	...	3 ,,	,,	192-194 ,,
Yajñaśrī	...	29 ,,	,,	195-223 ,,
Vijaya	...	6 ,,	,,	224-229 ,,
Chaṇḍaśrī Śāntikarṇa	...	10 ,,	,,	230-239 ,,
Puḷumāvi IV	...	7 ,,	,,	240-246 ,,

The find of potin coins at Tarhālā in the Akola District of Berar plainly indicates that all these kings continued to hold Maharashtra to the end of the Sātavāhana age. The reign-periods mentioned in the Purāṇas are not, however, absolutely trustworthy. In the first place, there are many variants, and even if we take the readings supported by the best MSS., their statements are in some cases contradicted by contemporary inscriptions. The Purāṇas, for instance, assign a reign-period of only 21 years to Gautamīputra, but from a Nasik cave inscription he is known to have reigned for at least 24 years. There may, therefore, be similar discrepancies in other reign periods also. Besides, it is not certain that the battle between Gautamīputra and Nahapāna was fought in the Śaka year 46 and not later. Notwithstanding these circumstances which render the accuracy of the dates doubtful, we may say that the Sātavāhanas continued to rule in Maharashtra till the middle of the 3rd century A.C.' (*Corpus*, iv, xxiiif)

We are unable to accept the above account for more than one reason. Ptolemy states in his *Geography*, composed in c. 140 A.D.,[1] that Siri Polemaios had been ruling in Baithana or Pratiṣṭhāna. Siri Polemaios is undoubtedly Śrī Pulumāyi and if he had been ruling in 86-114 A.D. then it is really curious that Ptolemy speaks of a king who ruled more than 25 years before his time, and ignores the contemporary king altogether. He speaks of Tiastenes or Caṣṭana of Ozene and this Caṣṭana is mentioned as a ruling prince in the Andau record of 130 A.D., and so Pulumāyi must have been his contemporary. Yajñaśrī Śātakarṇi was an important king and the non-mention of his name in Ptolemy's *Geography* appears to be significant, for Ptolemy's account of South India has been considered by competent critics to be more or less a contemporary one. Again, the close resemblance between the characters of Nahapāna's records and those of the Andau inscription of the time of Caṣṭana and Rudradāman of 130 A.D. shows that Nahapāna's dates cannot be so early as has been supposed by the scholar, for this would make his last year correspond to 80 A.D. [18 years of Gautamīputra, 62+18=80 A.D.=the last year of Nahapāna's reign.]

According to the scheme of chronology suggested by us, Nahapāna was uprooted by Gautamīputra Śātakarṇi in c. 117 A.D. This shows that the years mentioned in his records cannot be ascribed to the Śaka era of 78 A.D. Nahapāna ruled after Bhūmaka and thus it is not unlikely that the records of Nahapāna are dated in his regnal years. This appears to be supported by traditions preserved in the Jaina Paṭṭāvalis and Jinasena's *Harivaṃśa* which assign a period of 40 and 42 years respectively to Naravāhana or Nahapāna—a fact showing that Nahapāna ruled for more than 40 years.[2] The large number of coins issued by Nahapāna also attest a long reign.

1. 'So the *Geography* was composed between c. February of A.D. 141 and the death of Ptolemy some time in the period ranging from some time of c. A.D. 161 to c. March of A.D. 185......The more exact date for each of such sources has to be ascertained with the help of internal evidence.' (B.N. Mukherjee, *The Kushāṇas and the Deccan*, 129) Though Ptolemy might have composed his account about 140-1 A.D. the materials on which he depended were evidently of a little earlier date.

2. S. Chattopadhyaya, *The Śakas in India*, 57

Allan is inclined to place Nahapāna much earlier. His arguments are as follows :

'A *Kṣaharāta* satrap called Ghaṭāka is mentioned in an inscription from Mathura, while Nahapāna used the Indian title rājā on the *reverse* of his coins, and *rājā* and *kṣatrapa* in a very corrupt Greek legend on the *obverse* which suggests a date contemporary with Rañjubula or Rajula. His coins cannot be assigned to so late a date in the second century A.D. for this would make the interval between Nahapāna and the Mathura dynasty too great.'[1]

We cannot, however, agree with this view. The *Kṣaharāta* satrap Ghaṭāka need not be connected with the line of Nahapāna, and further, as Allan himself states, the coins of Nahapāna and Rañjubula may have been derived from the same prototype. Under the circumstances, there is no harm if the interval between Nahapāna and the Mathura dynasty becomes *too great*.

Much of the area ruled over by Nahapāna appears to have been conquered by his predecessor, for the only military achievement of his reign was the conquest of the Mālayas by Ṛṣabhadatta or Uṣabhadāta, the son-in-law of Nahapāna. This seems to show that between Bhūmaka and Nahapāna there was another king whose reign might have been short but who had extensive conquest in South India to his credit. In Nasik Cave inscription, no. 10, Ṛṣabhadatta states: "And by the order of the lord, I went to relieve the chief of the Uttamabhadras, who was besieged for the rainy season by the Mālayas; and the Mālayas fled as it were at the sound (of my approach) and were made prisoners by the Uttamabhadras. Thence I went to the Puṣkara lake and was consecrated, and made a donation of three thousand cows and a village."[2] Who these Uttamabhadras were we do not know. The Mālayas have been supposed to be either 'the inhabitants of the Mālaya hills in Southern India' or 'the Mālavas'. The latter identification is more probable.

The location of the capital of Nahapāna is a matter of great

1. *Cambridge Shorter History of India*
2. *Ep Ind*, viii 78; *Arch. Surv. West. Ind.*, vol. iv 99, no. 5

controversy among the historians. The *Periplus* states: 'Beyond the gulf of Baraca is that of Barygaza and the coast of the country of Ariaca, which is the beginning of the kingdom of Nambanus and of all India. That part of it lying inland and adjoining Scythia is called Abiria, but the coast is called Syrastrene ... The metropolis of this country is Minnagara, from which much cotton cloth is brought down to Barygaza. In these places, there remain even to the present time signs of the expedition of Alexander, such as ancient shrines, walls of forts and great well.'[1] In any case, it must have been an inland town, for, we are informed by the *Periplus* that, much cotton cloth was brought from here to the port of Barygaza. Its position is indicated by the fact that 'ordinary' cloth, i.e., of coarser sort, came to Barygaza 'through Ozene (Ujjayinī) and Minnagara'. Minnagara, therefore, lay on the route from Barygaza to Ozene. The name of the capital was probably 'Nagara' and the epithet *Min* signified its association with the Śakas.[2]

The name Nahapāna is completely un-Indian. *Naha* in Iranian and Armenian means people, while *pana* in Iranian means protege; cf. Artaban, Darapanah[3] etc. His son-in-law Ṛṣabhadatta takes an Indian name. Either he was an Indian or an Indianised Scythian. Inscriptions bear out the fact that he was equally tolerant towards the Buddhist and the Brahmanical creeds. We find him making *tīrtha-yātrās* to the Brāhmaṇical sacred places, on the one hand, and making donations to the Buddhist monks, on the other. His epigraphs may be taken indeed as throwing interesting side-lights on the religious belief of the Śakas of his age. We may note here the contents of a few of them ....

1. *Nasik inscription no.* 10, records his gifts mostly to the gods and the Brāhmaṇas, made by him on the river Barṇāsā, at the *tīrtha* of Prabhāsa at Bharukaccha,

1. *l.c.*, 39
2. For different locations of the capital, see Fleet *JRAS*, 1912, 788, where Minnagara is identified with Dohad in Panch-Mahals; *Ind Ant*, 1926, 143, where it is identified with Junnar; Bhandarkar thinks that it was Mandasor, cf. *Bomb. Gaz.* I.i. 15n. For Broach as the capital of Nahapāna, see *Āvaśyaka Sūtra*, *JBORS*, 1930, 290; also *IHQ*, 1929, 356.
3. *JRAS*, 1906, 211

Daśapura, Govardhana, Sūrpāraka, at the rivers Ibā, Paradā, Damana, Tāpī, Karabenā, Dahanukā, and at the village of Nānaṃgola to the congregation of *Carakas* at Piṃḍītākāvaḍa, Govardhana, Suvarnamukha, and the Rāmatīrtha in Śūrpāraka. It records further his *abhiṣeka* and donations at *Puṣkara* and his donations of a field to the congregation of monks of the four-quarters.

ii. *Nasik inscription no.* 12, records the dedication of a cave and an endowment of money to the community (saṃgha) of the four-quarters, besides a dedication of money to gods and Brāhmaṇas.

iii. *Nasik inscription no.* 14, records his gifts to gods and Brāhmaṇas at Chechinina, Dāhanukānagara, Kekāpura ....and the bestowing of money and *tīrtha* on the Barṇāsā river.

iv. *Kanheri inscription*, Lūders no. 1099, records his gift of the village of Karajika to the monks residing in the caves at Vāluraka for the support of the congregation (saṃgha) of the four-quarters and his donations to the Brāhmaṇas on the river Barṇāsā and at Prabhāsa.

Some of Ṛṣabhadatta's gifts might have been in favour of the Śaka-(Maga) Brāhmaṇas, who were present in South India, as evidenced by the *Geography* of Ptolemy,[1] but many of his gifts and actions were directed in favour of the Indian Brāhmaṇas, and his actions prove beyond doubt that he had great respect for the Brāhmaṇical religion. In this connection, the statement of the Nasik inscription no. 10 *Prabhāse puṇya-tīrthe Brāhmaṇebhyo'ṣṭabhāryāpradānena*, an epithet applied to Ṛṣabhadatta, may be compared with the *Mbh.* iii. 82.20 ff. Where Prabhāsa is called the best of the *tīrthas*, and the *Kūrma-Purāṇa* ii. 39.79, *Viṣṇusaṃhitā*, 19, and *Padma Purāṇa* (Brahmakhaṇḍa) ch. 24, where gifts of money, maidens, etc. to the Brāhmaṇas at sacred places are highly recommended. The Purāṇas, in fact, devote large spaces for the purpose of describing the importance of the various *tīrthas* or sacred places in different parts of India. The custom of going to

1. Ptolemy, ed. Renou, 33

pilgrimage, as Ṛṣabhadatta did, went throughout the ancient period and even Muslim writers have noted how thousands of pilgrims used to visit the Sun temple at Multan and the Śiva temple at Prabhāsa.

Ṛṣabhadatta favoured Buddhism also which, however, failed to deepen its root in the Maharashtra region. Nasik, as we have already seen,[1] was a stronghold of the Buddhists during the time of the early Sātavāhanas. In the age of the Śakas, however, Kanheri seems to have been the other Buddhist establishment of this region as evidenced by the epigraphic records discovered there. At the establishment of Nāgārjunikoṇḍa, we hear of the Śaka Moḍa and his sister Budhī who were followers of that creed,[2] but at Kanheri, which was included within the empire of the kṣatrapas, we hear of no Śaka worshippers. In the Deccan, Buddhism seems to have made no great progress and Fa-hian did not visit the country because he was told that the people there followed heretical views and did not follow the *śramaṇas* and the law of the Great Buddha. Similar was probably the case also in Western India in our period, though there may have been a few *saṃghārāmas* here and there, which flourished under the patronage of the later Sātavāhana monarchs.

We are fortunate in having in the *Periplus of the Erythraean Sea* an account of the trade and commerce of South India when Nahapāna had been ruling. The name of the author of the *Periplus* is unknown though he appears to have been an Egyptian Greek and a merchant who possibly visited India on more than one occasions. There were several factors that encouraged trade between South India and the Western world during this period. The rivalry between Rome and Parthia blocked the land route, while the discovery of the nature of monsoon winds about 45 A.D. on a scientific basis

1. *supra*
2. *Ep Ind*, xx, 37. 'The donor was Budhī (i.e., Buddhi), the sister of Moḍa, the Śaka. If this interpretation is correct, the mention of a Śaka or Scythian is a point of special interest. In this connection it should be noted that among the sculptures excavated by Mr. Longhurst at Nāgārjunikoṇḍa there are two showing a warrior in Scythian dress.'

gave a great impetus to the maritime trade.[1] (cf. supra, Kennedy's views) It was found that with the help of these winds a ship starting from the mouth of the Red Sea would reach the ports of South India in forty days or even less. The foundation of the Roman empire further gave peace which facilitated the adventure of the traders. On the high sea they could now feel secure against the operations of the pirates.[2] There was further great demand for Indian pepper, fine muslin and other luxury goods in the Western world and the large number of Roman coins discovered in South India bear witness to this voluminous trade. On the basis of these coins R. Sewell has arrived at the following facts regarding the nature of Indo-Western trade:

1. During the Consulate there was practically very little trade between Rome and India.
2. After Augustus came to the throne this trade increased by leaps and bounds till the time of Nero who died in 68 A.D.

1. We may note here the following interesting observations by W.W. Tarn : "I have carefully avoided mentioning the much discussed and variously dated Hippalos, the traditional 'discoverer' of the south-west monsoon, for it matters nothing to me which stage he inaugurated or even whether he was not a man at all but either a sailor's name like Davy Jones or a personification of the monsoon, as Greeks had personified other winds as Boreas or Zephyrus. And I have also not mentioned 'direct' voyages, because the first man who went right through from India to Egypt or *vice versa* could have done it as well coasting as in any other way. One Indian and perhaps a second, who cannot be dated, appeared in Egypt in the Ptolemaic period, but the first man actually recorded to have gone all the way by sea was the Indian captain who in the reign of Ptolemy Euergetes II was picked up half-dead in the Red Sea, having lost his crew (? killed by Arabs); and the first Greek recorded as having gone all the way was Eudoxus of Cyzicus, who sailed under that Indian's guidance to Demetrias or Barygaza. Eudoxus got back to Egypt before Euergetes' death in 116, but his subsequent activity was under that king's successors; his voyage therefore was c. 120 and he presumably coasted. After him a few ships in the late Ptolemaic period went right through from Egypt to India, but the extreme rarity of Ptolemaic coins in India shows that to the end the Ptolemies really relied on their Arab middlemen". (*GBI*, 370)
2. For piracy on the Indian coast see *infra*.

3. In the post-Nero epoch the trade had been gradually declining till the time of Caracalla (217 A.D.) after which it came to a standstill.[1]

It is generally believed that the Roman merchants had possibly a colony and a mint at Madura while the Peutingerian tables locate near Muziris a temple of Augustus.[2] We may note in this connection that the literature of the Śangam age refers to the presence of the Yavanas and seaport towns like Mamallapuram, Puhar and Korkai where possibly many foreign merchants used to live.[3]

The *Periplus* speaks of Barygaza, a Greek corruption of ancient Bhṛgukaccha or Broach at the mouth of the Narmada, which was the port *par excellence* of the kingdom of Nambanus who is certainly no other than Nahapāna, though D.C. Sircar thinks otherwise preferring the variant reading Mambarus or Nambarus.[4] Commodities flowed to Barygaza from the Punjab, North-Western Frontier Province, Kashmir and Eastern Afghanistan through Ozene (Ujjayinī), Paethan (Pratiṣṭhāna) and Tagara (Ter). The merchants of North India could not use Barbaricum, the port of Sind, as the Parthian princes were fighting with one another in this region.[5] 'Under the able rule of Nahapāna North-Western Peninsula evidently saw peace and prosperity and Barygaza, therefore, became the natural outlet for the northerners.

The other important port of Dachinabades was Calliena, the modern Kalyan, on the eastern shore of the harbour of Bombay. 'The name was also applied to the strip of coast on either side of the harbour between 18⁰ and 20⁰ N.' The *Periplus* makes the interesting statement that in the time of elder Saraganus Calliena was a lawful market town, 'but since it came into the possession of Sandares the port is much obstructed, and Greek ships landing there may chance to be taken to

1. *JRAS*, 1904, 591-637
2. cf. R.E.M. Wheeler, A. Ghosh and Krishna Deva : 'Arikamedu : and Indo-Roman Trading Station on the East Coast of India'. (*Ancient India*, No. 2, July 1946)
3. K.A.N. Sastri, *The Colas*, i, 97-103
4. *AIU*, 178-9; cf. contra. *JRAS*, 1946, 170, also *supra*
5. *The Periplus*, ed. Schoff, 37, 41

Barygaza under guard'.[1] Elder Saraganus is evidently Śātakarṇi I, while as we have already seen, the identification of Sandanes with Kaniṣka, as proposed by S. Levi, can hardly be accepted. Who was then this Sandares ?

W. Schoff identifies Sandares with Sundara Śātakarṇi (*Matsya* no. 20; *Vāyu* no. 10 calls simply Śātakarṇi). If we accept this view we shall have to conclude that a branch of the Sātavāhanas had been ruling as subordinate under the Kṣaharāta king Nahapāna. It may, of course, be argued that the Purāṇas do not record the names of subordinate, but of independent, rulers. It should, however, be noted that though this is the *ordinary* system or rule followed by the Purāṇic writers, this is not *always* the case. The Vākātaka king Vindhyaśakti finds a prominent mention in the Purāṇic list of kings, but from the Ajanta inscription of Harisena it is clear that he was not an independent ruler and this view has been accepted by all the historians.

Leaving our topic aside we may deal a little more with this vexed question of the Sātavāhana list of kings. The example of Sundara Śātakarṇi or Sundara Svātikarṇa seems to show that the list of Purāṇic kings from Śātakarṇi I to Gautamīputra (with the exception of Āpīlaka), eighteen names in all, contains names of a few subordinate rulers and also of the different members of the dynasty ruling over different parts of South India. It may also contain a few names that appeared on the scene before Simuka even.[2]

(a) One Kuntala Śātakarṇi is mentioned in the *Matsya* as no. 13, but no such name is found in the *Vāyu* list. If he ruled during this period, he must have his charge over the Banavāsī or the Vaijayantī region, as his designation shows. He is mentioned in the *Kāmasūtra* of Vātsyāyana as a king of Kuntala who killed his wife Malayavatī in course of an amorous play.[3]

1. *The Periplus*, ed. Schoff, 43
2. It is difficult to agree with V.V. Mirashi that during the Kṣaharāta interregnum the Sātavāhanas were living in the Vidarbha region, whatever may be the evidence of the Tarhala hoard. (*JNSI*, ii. 83ff) The account of Kuntala Śātakarṇi and Hāla goes against the theory.
3. *Kāmasūtra*, ii. 7. It may be noted that this Śātakarṇi is called Sāta-

(b) King Hāla (*Matsya* no. 17, *Vāyu* no. 7) is very famous in Indian legends and is credited with the authorship of *Gāthāsaptaśatī*, though the work appears to be a very late one.[1] As we have already seen, the Līlavatī connects him with an expedition in the *Sapta-Godāvarī* region, modern Draksharama, in the Godavari district.[2] The account can hardly be regarded, however, as a piece of sober history. Hemacandra in his *Abhidhānacintāmaṇi* equates Hāla with Sātavāhana. The tradition that Guṇāḍhya, the author of the *Bṛhatkathā* was one of his ministers lacks authenticity.

From the above account it is thus clear that during the period c. 50 A.D.—c. 99 A.D., when the Kṣaharātas dominated over the western part of the Maharashtra region, the Sātavāhanas maintained a precarious existence. It is not easy to determine the cradle of this truncated Sātavāhana power. The evidence of the *Kāmasūtra* shows that some members ruled in the S.W. Maharashtra region. The Purāṇas assert that the Āndhra-Sātavāhanas were divided into five (*pañca*) different branches.[3] The term *pañca* may not be exactly correct, but it seems to throw to some extent light on this confused period, when possibly the different branches of the Sātavāhanas ruled over different principalities.

To return to the account of the *Periplus*. An important market town of the western region was Suppara (modern Sopāra, a few miles north of Bombay and ancient Surpāraka) which along with Calliena played an important part between India and the Western world.

To the South of Calliena were in descending order Semylla (Chaul, about 25 miles South of Bombay), Mandagora (Bankot,

vāhana also. The commentator maintains that he was called Kuntala as he was born in the province of the same name. This may show that the father of Kuntala Śātakarṇi also ruled over the Kuntala country. From Rājaśekhara's *Kāvyamīmāṃsā* it appears that Kuntala Sātavāhana introduced the use of Prakrit by the ladies of the harem.
Hāla is mentioned in *Līlavatī*, *Abhidhānacintāmaṇi* and *Deśīnāmamālā*.

2. *supra*. M. Rama Rao attributes two lead coins in Kaus collection to this king, which, however, seems to be very doubtful. (*JNSI*, xiii, 132f; *List of Published Satavahana Coins*, 7)
3. cf. *Vāyu*, 99, 358

at the mouth of the Savitri river) Palaipatmae (Dabhol), Melizigara (Jaigarh), Byzantium (Vijayadurg), Togarum (Devgarh) and Aurannoboas (Malvan). It is difficult to determine the relative importance of these market towns, but when they are mentioned in a foreign account of trade and commerce it should be assumed that they were of some importance besides others into the interior which might have served mainly the purpose of internal trade.

In the background of the *Kāmasūtra* account noted above it would appear that the market towns of Byzantium, Togarum and Aurannoboas belonged to the kingdom of the Sātavāhanas, who must therefore have patronised the Indo-Occidental trade which evidently saved them from complete eclipse. This trade could not have been a very extensive one in view of the fact that the pirates occupied the small islands nearby.[1] Evidently therefore the Sātavāhanas of the place had to pay more attention to the internal trade with the eastern and southern kingdoms.

The kingdom lying to the south of the principality of the Sātavāhanas was Cerobothra, the Keralaputra of the Aśokan edicts, which along with the Pāṇḍya and the Cola formed the principal political units of Damirica, i.e., Tamilakam. The early history of these kingdoms is disclosed to us by the Śangam literature which, however, can hardly be regarded as fully authentic in the absence of any other corroborative evidence.[2]

1. The *Periplus* states : 'Then there are the islands called Sesecrienae (Vengurla rocks) and that of the Aegidii (Goa), and that of the Caenitae (Oyster rocks, west of and facing the roadstead of Kārwār), opposite the place called Chersonesus (Kārwār) (and in these places there are pirates) and after this the White Island (this is probably the modern Pigeon Island also known as Nitran).' W.H. Schoff thinks that, 'this is probably the same as Nitrias of Pliny (VI, 26), the stronghold of the pirates, who threatened the Roman merchants; and maybe the Nitra of Ptolemy.' He also draws our attention to the observation of Yule to the effect that the 'northern part of Malabar, Kanara, and the Southern Konkan, were a nest of pirates from a very ancient date until well into the 19th century, when their occupation was destroyed by the British arms.' (*l.c.* 203) Suppara and the city of Calliena also felt the pressure of piracy which possibly led to the fall of Calliena and Dounga came to occupy its place. (Ptolemy, ed. L. Renou)
2. Vide, *supra*, ch.

From the *Periplus* it appears that Muziris (Caranganore) of the kingdom of Cerobothra and Nelcynda (Kottyam) of the Pāṇḍyan principality were important centres of trade. In fact, Muziris abounded in ships 'sent there with cargoes from Arabia and by the Greeks'.

On the eastern side of the peninsula, the *Periplus* speaks of many harbours and market towns but only two of them can be located with some amount of certainty, viz., Masalia near Masulipatam and Gange at the mouth of the Ganges. These ports carried on trade mainly with South-East Asia.

The port of Barygaza, the port *par excellence* of the time, imported 'wine, Italian preferred, also Laodicean and Arabian; copper, tin and lead; coral and topaz; thin clothing and inferior sorts of all kinds; bright-coloured girdles a cubit wide; storax, sweet clover, flint glass, realgar, antimony, gold and silver coin, on which there is a profit when exchanged for the money of the country; and ointment, but not very costly and not much. And for the King there are brought into those places very costly vessels of silver, singing boys, beautiful maidens for the harem, fine wines, thin clothing of the finest weaves, and the choicest ointments. There are exported from these places spikenard, costus, bdellium, ivory, agate and carnelian, lycium, cotton cloth of all kinds, silk cloth, mallow cloth, yarn, long pepper and such other things as are brought here from the various market towns.'[1]

Trade and commerce presuppose bank facilities which were provided in ancient India by guild organisations, and there are evidences for believing that they flourished unhampered under the *Kṣaharātas*. Thus Nasik inscription no. 12 records the investment by Ṛsabhadatta, son-in-law of Nahapāna, of 2000 kārṣāpaṇas with the 'western weavers' guild', at the rate of 1% interest per month, with the further condition that the princi-

1. *The Periplus*, 42. The interesting statement that for the king there were brought from outside very costly vessels of silver, singing boys, beautiful maidens for the harem, fine wines, etc. would show at once that king Nahapāna was a man of fashion with tastes of luxury. The singing boys and the beautiful maidens were evidently slaves from Europe and the adjacent countries, but it is difficult to determine their exact status in the Indian society.

pal must remain fixed, and the interest was only to be paid. This is something like the fixed deposit system of the present day banking. The record shows that the Kṣaharātas in India respected the injunctions of the sacred lawgivers, that the guilds were to be respected by the king, if they were not against public interest.[1]

1. *Manu*, viii. 41; *Yājñavalkya*, ii. 187-188

CHAPTER V

RESTORATION OF THE SĀTAVĀHANA EMPIRE

Gautamīputra Śātakarṇi

It has already been shown that Gautamīputra came to the throne in c. 99 A.D., while in 117 A.D. he overthrew the *Kṣaharāta* ruler Nahapāna. The evidence of the Jogalthembi hoard of coins shows that as there is not a single piece in it belonging to any king other than Nahapāna, he must have been the last prince of the *Kṣaharāta* dynasty. We have no details of this fight excepting a veiled allusion in the Nasik inscription of the time of his son Vāsiṣṭhīputra Pulumāyi[1] that Gautamīputra was the destroyer of the Śakas, Yavanas and Pahlavas and the uprooter of the *Kṣaharāta* dynasty. It is not clear whether such statements refer to two separate engagements or to only one against the *Kṣaharāta* who had marshalled in his army the services of the Śaka, Yavana and Pahlava mercenaries. As the same record maintains that he was victorious in many fights against confederacy of enemies (*aneka-samarāvajitasatu-saghasa*) is seems that he possibly fought against other rulers also who offered him a combined opposition. In any case, he was the restorer of the fame of the Sātavāhana dynasty in true sense.

An inscription of Gautamīputra of his regnal year 18, i.e. 117 A.D., records his order to his *amāṭya* at Govardhana regarding the gift of a land which formerly had been bestowed by Ṛsabhadatta to the monks living at mount Triraśmi.[2] The description *ajakālakiyam Usabhadātena bhūtam* shows that till the reaffirmation of the gift by Gautamīputra the region had been under the sway of the *Kṣaharātas*. In other words, this gives us the particular year when Nahapāna was defeated. The question now arises, what was the base of operation of the Sātavahana monarch wherefrom he led his army inasmuch

1. *Select Ins.*, 197
2. *ib.*, 181f

as the order is issued from a *vijayaskandhāvāra* or the camp of victory at Benākaṭaka which was evidently situated in the Nasik district. Now, the record opens with the following words:

> *Siddham senāye Vejayantiye vijayakhadāvarā Govadhanasa Benākaṭakasvāmi Gotamiputo siri Sadakaṇi āṇapayati......*

E. Senart gives the following translation:

> Success! from the camp of victory of the Vejayanti army Siri Sadakaṇi Gotamiputa, Lord of Benākaṭaka of Govardhana commands.........

According to the above interpretation Vaijayantī, Banavāsī, in the Kuntala country may be regarded as the base of operation of the Sātavāhana king against the *Kṣaharātas*. D.C. Sircar and V.S. Bakhle take the expression *senāye vejayantiye* to mean *of the victorious army*, but while Bakhle thinks that the expression 'the lord of Benākaṭaka' has nothing to do with Govardhana,[1] according to Sircar Benākaṭaka formed a part of the *āhāra* of Govardhana itself.[2] Thus for a moment leaving aside this record we may turn our attention to Nasik record of his mother (of the time of Pulumāyi) wherein Gautamīputra Śātakarṇi is described as the king of Asika (Assikas in the valley of the Godavari), Asaka (Aśmaka on the Godavari), Mūlaka (the district round Paithan), Suraṭha (Kathiawad), Kukura (in western or central Madhya Pradesh possibly near the western Vindhyas), Aparānta (north Konkan), Anūpa (district round Māhiṣmatī, on the Narmadā), Vidarbha (Berar) and Ākarāvanti (e. & w. Malwa). All these formed the dominion of the Śaka-kṣatrapas, and thus we may conclude that these were conquered by Gautamīputra after his victory over Nahapāna.

So far we stand on somewhat surer ground. But then the epigraph furnishes us with description the exact significance of which has caused much speculation. Gautamīputra is described as the lord of the Vindhya. Ṛkṣavat, Pāriyātra (all denoting different portions of the present Vindhya range), Sahya (W. Ghats) Kṛṣṇagiri (Kanhagiri), Maca, *Siritana*, Malaya (sou-

1. *JBBRAS*, iii. 86ff
2. *Select Ins.*, 191, fn. 4

thern portion of the W. Ghats), Mahendra (the E. Ghats specially between the Mahanadi and the Godavari), Setagiri and Cakora (s. portion of the E. Ghats). This account is on par with other description in 1.3 that 'his chargers drank the water of the three oceans.'

Two different interpretations have been put on the above account:

(a) A group of scholars hold that the above description is simply a conventional one. Gautamīputra's empire was not certainly so extensive as the description indicates and his sway did not extend over the Andhradeśa where the earliest available Sātavāhana record belongs to the time of his son Pulumāyi.[1]

(b) M. Rama Rao holds, on the other hand, that 'the conventional way is to describe a *digvijayin* as *catussamudrādhipati* and not as *tri-samudratoya-pīta-vāhana*. The mention of three samudras seems to have a purpose and a meaning....The Nasik inscription shows beyond doubt that the entire Dakkan, eastern as well as western, was under the rule of this monarch.'[2]

In discussing the above theories, we should keep in mind the following facts:

(i) that the earliest Sātavāhana record available from the Andhradeśa belongs no doubt to the time of Pulumāyi, but he is nowhere described as a conqueror or as having extended the boundaries of his kingdom.

(ii) that if, on the other hand, we take the whole account in its literal sense, then we have to assume that Gautamīputra's lordship extended over the Cola and the Pāṇḍya countries, of which we have no evidence at all.

From the above discussions it appears that Gautamīputra's mother has stated in detail her son's victory over the Kṣaharātas and the countries that were snatched away by her son from the foreign intruders, while his sway over other parts of the Deccan is alluded to evidently by the specific mention of the Kulācalas of which he is described as the lord. K. Gopalachari

1. *AIU*, 202
2. *PIHC*, 1953, 37

thinks that the mention of Cakora and Mahendra proves the inclusion of Kaliṅga and Andhradeśa in Gautamīputra's empire.[1] M. Rama Rao maintains that Gautamīputra's connection with the Andhradeśa including the coastal region is proved by 'several coins of Gautamīputra Śātakarṇi...... obtained from the coastal Andhra districts in association with the coins of his son, Pulumāyi, and other later Sātavāhana rulers. There are, in the Hyderabad Museum, hundreds of coins of this Śātakarṇi, obtained from the excavations at Kondapuram in association with the coins of Pulumāyi and others. Several hundreds of round and square copper coins of this king are included in the collection from Pedabankurra and the entire collection includes the coins of other later Sātavāhana rulers as well. These coins and the evidence of the Nasik inscription, mentioned above, corroborate my view that Gautamīputra Śātakarṇi's dominions included both Telengana and coastal Andhradeśa.'[2]

The mere find of a few coins from a particular place does not necessarily prove that their issuer held sway over the region, for coins may be carried from one place to another, but in this particular instance when such large discoveries are studied in the background of the epigraphic accounts, they may carry some meaning. As we shall see presently again, Gotamī's inscription is really not silent regarding the suzerainty of her son in eastern direction. This in the background of the circumstantial evidences furnished by the coins can hardly be ignored.

We may now proceed to deal with the problem with which we started:

(1) As thus North Maharashtra and Andhradeśa had been conquered by Gautamīputra, the cradle of his power must have been outside these countries. The *Kāmasūtra* of Vātsyāyana associates the Sātavāhanas with the Kuntala country of which Vaijayantī was the capital.[3] The expression *senāye vejayantiye* should not be taken as meaning the victorious army, for the expression is

1. *CHIN*, 313
2. M. Rama Rao, *Satavahana Coins*, 25-6
3. *supra*.

immediately followed by the word *vijayakhadāvāra* meaning the camp of victory. The simultaneous mention of *vijaya* side by side would hardly carry any meaning. So here we must follow the interpretation of E. Senart and take Vaijayantī, the capital of the Kuntala country, as the base of his operations against the Kṣaharātas.

(2) If thus Maharashtra, Andhra and Kuntala had been under him, we can at once take him as the lords of Mahendra, Sahya, Kanhagiri (Kanheri) and portions at least of Maca, Siritana and Malaya (southern portion of W. Ghats). After his conquests of the Kṣaharāta dominion, naturally he could claim lordship over Vijha, Achhavata (Ṛkṣavat) and Pāricāta. It is difficult to determine the location of Setagiri and Cakora. There is, however, no evidence to prove the inclusion of Kaliṅga within the king's territory. Similarly, we cannot associate him with the extreme south, though it is not unlikely that he led some predatory raids there, which justifies his description as *ti-samudatoya-pīta-vāhana*.

Thus though we may scent some amount of conventionalism in the inscription of Gotami, the statements are more or less based on facts. We should see the epigraph in its proper perspective.

K. Gopalachari draws our attention to a *gāthā* in the *Niryukti*, a commentary on the *Āvaśyakasūtra* which shows that the expedition of the Sātavāhana monarch against Nahapāna was a long-drawn affair and the Scythian capital Bharukaccha was captured after a two-year's siege.[1] If there be any historical truth in it, it seems to show that in his first operation the Sātavāhana monarch captured the Northern Maharashtra region while he had to fight hard to take possession of the Kṣaharāta stronghold at Broach and it is not unlikely that in this Broach fight Nahapāna employed Scythian, Greek and Parthian mercenaries on his side. This possibly explains why Gotamī makes special references to the conquest of the *Kṣaharātas*.

1. *CHIN*, 312

When Malwa, Narmada Valley (Anūpa), Western Rajasthan (Kukura), Surāṣṭra and the adjoining region came under the possession of the Sātavāhana ruler, he naturally found that many foreign hordes (Śaka, Yavana, Pahlava etc.) were already settled in the region and contamination with them was going on in the sense that they were being gradually Indianised. It has already been stated (*supra*) that the Sātavāhanas were living in a period when the caste system in the *jāti* form had not been fully crystallised, and the *varṇa* system was in the forefront through the operation of which, based on qualification and not on birth, many foreigners became admitted into the Indian social fold. A critical study of *ch. x* of the *Manusaṃhitā* will convince the reader that while the *jāti* system prevailed strictly in the Madhyadeśa, the *varṇa* laws operated in other parts of the country. This Madhyadeśa is identical with the Āryāvarta of the early Dharmasūtra writers and is described as the country 'which lies between the Himavat and the Vindhya, to the east of Prayāga and to the west of Vinaśana (the place where the river Sarasvatī disappears in the Hissar district in Haryana[1]). Elsewhere, Manu states that tribes like the Yavanas, Śakas, and Pāradas or Parthians who were originally kṣatriyas 'have gradually sunk in this world to the condition of Śūdras for not consulting the Brāhmaṇas'.[2] In this background we may note Gautamīputra's description as *khatiyadapamānamadana* indicating that the Śakas, Yavanas and the Parthians living in the dominion of Nahapāna were behaving like kṣatriyas and the Sātavāhana monarch had to be on the alert against *varṇasaṃkara* as claimed in l. 6 of the Nasik inscription of Gotamī.

It is difficult to determine when the Yavanas or the Greeks first entered into the peninsular India. According to the *Mahāvaṃsa*[3] Aśoka sent the Yona priest Dhammarakhita as a missionary to the Aparānta country, while the Junagadh inscription[4] of mahakṣatrapa Rudradāman shows that one

1. *supra*.
2. *Manu*, x. 43-4
3. *supra*.
4. *Select Ins.*, 171

Yavanarāja Tuṣāspha was governor of Surāṣṭra under Aśoka. Evidently under the liberal patronage of the great Maurya emperor the Greeks were establishing themselves in Western and peninsular India and in course of time they became merged into Indian Society. Gautamīputra's attempt was directed against this merging.

In the caves at Nasik, Junnar and Karle there are at least eleven inscriptions of Buddhist donors who bear Indian names but call themselves Yavana or Yonaka. While most of the writers take the term Yavana here to mean the Greeks, S. Konow maintains that the Yavana of the Karle records wherever followed by a name in the genitive plural is a personal name, or the name of a family or corporation. E. Senart also maintains a similar view.[1] These interpretations show that the Yavanas were careful in denoting before the public their own nationality though they were Indian by religion and culture and favoured Buddhism. The Yavanas thus had become half-Indianised but had not completely lost their distinct entity. W.W. Tarn maintains that 'the conqueror does not adopt the nomenclature of the conquered', and hence the Yavanas in these records might possibly be 'low-class Greek, broken by circumstances...there is no real doubt that these Yavanas were Indians and what we want to know is why they call themselves Greeks'.[2] He thinks further that they were in fact Indians with Greek citizenship. It is difficult to agree with such view, as most of the Yavanas mentioned in the Karle records were natives of Dhenukākaṭa, identified with Dahanu, near Karle, which was never included in Greek territory. In fact, Indianisation of the Greeks had begun much earlier as evidenced by the famous Besnagar inscription. The South Indian epigraphs mark the next stage in the process.

Like the Yavanas the Śakas too were gradually coming under the influence of the Indian culture. It has already been stated that the name Nahapāna is un-Indian, but his son-in-law Ṛṣabhadatta bore an entirely Indian name. The name of Ṛṣabhadatta's father was Dinika, a term of un-Indian form. Nahapāna's daughter, on the other hand, bears the name

1. In *Indian Culture*, i. 343, O. Stein appears to follow the same view.
2. *GBI*, 255

Dakṣamitrā. Ṛṣabhadatta's gifts were bestowed equally on the brāhmaṇas and the Buddhists. How these Scythians were gradually being Indianised is apparent from Ptolemy's description who locates the Brakhmanoi Magoi or the Maga brāhmaṇas near Mount Bettigo, Podyil, or the Malay mountains.[1] The Epic and the Purāṇas inform us that among the Śakas the Magas were the brāhmaṇas.[2] Evidently, the Magas were the Magai of ancient Iran who entered into India at an early date, then got mixed up with the Scythians and performed the religious duties of the tribe. Though Gautamīputra Śātakarṇi's attempt was directed against mixing of Indian blood with that of these foreigners, yet one of his near descendants, as we shall see presently, married a Scythian girl. From the evidences of the Nāgārjunīkoṇḍa inscription we get another instance of Śaka-Indian marriage. The Ikṣvāku king Vīrapuriṣadāta had as his queen the Mahādevī Rudrabhaṭṭārikā who is described as *Ujanika-mahāra-bālikā*, the daughter of some Śaka *kṣatrapa* of Ujjayinī, while his son Ehuvula Cāntamula married another daughter of a *mahākṣatrapa* (*infra*).

The Nasik inscription of Gautamīputra Śātakarṇi of the regnal

1. The Purāṇas and the Great Epic inform us that the brāhmaṇas of the Śāka-dvīpa or the Śaka country were called Magas. (*Kūrma Purāṇa*, xlviii. 36; *Mbh.*, VI. ii) Ptolemy in his *Geography* speaks of a settlement of the Maga brāhmaṇas in South India.

   "In like manner the parts under Mount Bettigo are occupied by the 'Brakhmanoi Magoi' as far as the Batai with this city...... Brakhme......123 19"

   The 'Mount Bettigo', identical with the Tamil Podegai, Sk. Malaya, ranges in the Pāṇḍya kingdom. Herodotus (i. 101) states that the Magi were one of the six tribes of the Medes. The Magi may be identified with the Magas. In Indian literature, as the Magas are described as the brāhmaṇas of the Śaka land, they seem to have migrated to India in the train of the Śakas and performed the priestly functions of the tribe.

2. The account of the Great Epic, which has incorporated traditions of different ages, that there is full operation of the *Varṇāśramadharma* in the *Śākadvīpa* where the people are honest and devoid of greed and jealousy, could have been composed only after the Śakas of India had been admitted into the fold of the brāhmaṇical society. The Epic and the Purāṇas inform us further that among the Śakas, the *Magas* were the brāhmaṇas; the *Magadhas*, the kṣatriyas; the *Mānasas*, the vaiśyas; and the Mandagas, the śūdras.

year 24 has given rise to some controversy. The record opens with the following words:[1]

1. *Siddhaṃ* [!!] *Govadhane ama* [*ca*]*sa sāmakasa* [*de*]*yo* [*rā*] *jāṇito* [!]

2. *Raño Gotamiputasa Sātakaṇi*[*sa*] *ma*[*hā*]*devīya ca jīvasutāya rāja-mātuya vacanena Govadhane* [*ama*]*co sāmako aroga vatava* [!]

The passages has been interpreted to mean that in the last years of his reign the Sātavāhana monarch became practically invalid and had his mother associated with him in the administration of the country. D.C. Sircar observes that 'the word *jīvasutā* suggests that the king was ill and the people had to be assured against his death. The next king was possibly on his way to the throne, and the queen-mother who might have been in power for some time had to refer to the dying king's name. This illness apparently proved fatal to Gautamīputra.'[2] Such an interpretation appears to be needless, for in the very first line of the record there is reference to the king's order and in this background it is to be noted that the queen-mother was expressing her wish for the dedication recorded in the epigraph. She was wishing health out of courtesy to the *amātya* at Govardhana, though he was nothing but a very subordinate officer. The queen-mother was of course too much courteous on the occasion. We need not dilate on the word *jīvasutā* so much. It was the affectionate expression of a mother.

V.S. Bakhle gives an interesting and ingenious explanation of the queen-mother's gift. In the background of the Nasik record of the year 18 of Gautamīputra's reign it is maintained that as the field in question was not cultivated by the people—it may be perhaps that it was far removed from the headquarters of the Buddhist monks—Gautamīputra had probably confiscated the land. Such a procedure is enjoined by the *Arthaśāstra* of Kauṭilya (*akṛṣatām acchidyānyebhyaḥ prayacchayet*). When such a situation arose the queen-mother intervened and granted another field in exchange five years later. The newly

1. *Select Ins.*, 193
2. *ib.*, fn. 5

granted field 'was on the boundary of the city and although measuring only 100 *nivartanas* enjoyed the same privileges'.[1]

Gautamīputra's inscriptions indicate that he divided the country into *āhāras* each under an *amaca* or *amātya*. We learn further that though himself a staunch Brahmin (*eka bamhana*) Gautamīputra patronised the Buddhist monks also who were divided into three schools, the Bhadāyaniyas, flourishing at Nasik and Kanheri, the Dhammottariyas at Sopara, and the Mahāsānghikas at Karle and nearby places. Gautamīputra was brilliant in war as well as in peace. He felt for the weal and woe of his subjects and taxed them strictly according to the principles of *dharma*. He is given the epithet *āgamāna nilayasa* showing that he was versed in the Vedas and other śāstras. He was indeed one of the greatest kings of South India.[2]

Pulumāyi

In c. 123 A.D., Gautamīputra Śātakarṇi was succeeded by his son Puḷumāyi. His reign is very memorable in the annals of Deccan in many respects. It was during the time of Gautamīputra, that the second family of Śakas of Ujjayinī and Kathiawad, which was destined to rule for centuries and play an important role in the political and the cultural history of the land, came into existence. Caṣṭana, the first ruler of the dynasty, issued *kṣatrapa* and *mahākṣatrapa* coins showing that he first started his career as a subordinate ruler and later on became independent. We have seen that Avanti and Surāṣṭra were conquered by Gautamīputra. Hence the *kṣatrapa* coins of Caṣṭana shows that he was originally a subordinate ruler under the Sātavāhana emperor.[3] His status as an independent ruler, proved by his

1. *JBBRAS*, iii, 72
2. It is not known for certain what was the capital of Gautamīputra, the greatest of the Sātavāhana monarchs. Scholars who maintain the view that the Sātavāhana power started from the Krishna valley hold that either Amaravati or Sri Kakulam was the Imperial city. V.S. Bakhle thinks that Gautamīputra's capital was at Benakaṭaka identified by him with the tract round about Kolhapur.
3. D.C. Sircar thinks that the line of Caṣṭana started as Kuṣāṇa viceroy of the south-western province of their empire in place of the Kṣaharāta rulers 'with instructions to recover the lost districts of satrapy from the Sātavāhanas'. It has already been shown that Bhūmaka and Nahapāna were never subordinate to the Kuṣāṇas. In case of Caṣṭana,

mahākṣatrapa coins, may have been achieved by him in the early years of Pulumāyi, before 130 A.D., for the Andau inscription of that year shows that he had been ruling conjointly as *mahākṣatrapa* with his grandson Rudradāman.[1] As we have coins of Jayadāman, father of Rudradāman, bearing the humbler designation of *kṣatrapa* only[2]—the title of *mahākṣatrapa* has never been used by him—it is clear that before 130 A.D. he was dead. Caṣṭana became independent before this date and issued the *mahākṣatrapa* coins. E.J. Rapson points out that it was the general custom in this family that while the father ruled as *mahākṣatrapa* his son was associated in administration with him as *kṣatrapa* and on the death of the father the *kṣatrapa* son assumed the charge of the higher officer. Jayadāman evidently died

also, there is no proof that he owed allegiance to anybody. G. J.-Dubreuil thinks that Caṣṭana was the founder of the Śaka era of 78 A.D. Prof. Raychaudhuri points out that this cannot be the case for the capital of Caṣṭana (Tiastenes) was Ujjayinī (Ozene of Ptolemy) whereas we learn from the *Periplus* that Ozene was not a capital in the seventies of the first century A.D. The *Periplus* speaks of Ozene as a former capital, implying that it was not a capital in its own time.

1. *Ep Ind*, xvi, 23ff. The inscription, as it stands, is certainly not very lucid and has been a matter of great controversy among the Indologists. It records the erection of private monuments in *Rājña Caṣṭanasa Ysamotika-putrasa rājña Rudradāmasa Jaydāma-putrasav arṣe dvipaṃcāśe* 50,2. Here we find that both Caṣṭana and Rudradāman are mentioned with the honorific *rāja* and the patronymic, a fact which, as R.C. Majumdar has pointed out, clearly proves a case of conjoint rule. Dubreuil and Allan have objected to the view on the ground that there is no '*ca*' in the text, but they would like to supply '*grandson*' in the same. This is, however, more objectionable than the omission of '*ca*'. D.R. Bhandarkar also originally supposed that the term '*pautrasya*' has been omitted, but the construction of the text would hardly allow such an insertion. R.D. Banerjee objected to the theory of conjoint rule on the ground that apart from the possibility of such an event in India, there is sufficient evidence in the Andau inscription itself to prove that the authors of the record were quite ignorant as to the exact relationship between Caṣṭana and Rudradāman. The use of the designation rājā instead of *mahākṣatrapa*, according to Banerjee, shows that in a remote place like Andau on the Rann of Cutch the people were not aware of the new titles of the new dynasty of rulers and the exact relationship between Caṣṭana and Rudradāman.
2. For Jayadāman's coins, E.J. Rapson, *CII*, 76-7

during the lifetime of Caṣṭana and hence he never became a *mahākṣatrapa*. After his death Rudradāman became associated with his grandfather Caṣṭana on equal term as *mahākṣatrapa* and we get such a picture in the Andau inscription. This fact has been interpreted in a different manner by G. Buhler and D.R. Bhandarkar who think that the use of the humbler designation of *kṣatrapa* by Jayadāman shows that *during his reign* the power of the dynasty suffered some diminution probably through a Sātavāhana invasion.[1] The conjecture has further been supported by the statement of the Junagadh record that Rudradāman had 'won for himself the name of *mahākṣatrapa*' (*svyamadhigata-mahākṣatrapa-nāmnā*). As Jayadāman never ruled independently, the question of the diminution of power of the dynasty *during his reign* cannot arise. The statement of the Junagadh record need not be taken seriously. Such boastful empty statements are often found in Indian epigraphs.

It is thus clear that during the early years of his rule, Pulumāyi lost the northern part of his father's empire where a new dynasty arose proving a constant thorn to the empire of the Sātavāhanas.[2] We cannot agree with K. Gopalachari when he states that Pulumāyi 'not only kept his father's empire undiminished but even augmented it',[3] though elsewhere he has taken the view that 'the Andau inscriptions prove that the Śakas had, between 125 and 130 A.D., taken advantage of the preoccupa-

1. *JRAS*, 1890, 646; *Bomb. Gaz.*, I. i, 34, fn 5
2. In point of time, Caṣṭana seems to have been very near to Nahapāna. The head on the obverse of Caṣṭana's coins closely resembles that on the coins of Nahapāna and comes from the same prototype. The coins of Caṣṭana, like those of Nahapāna, again, bear inscriptions in Brāhmī and Kharoṣṭhī character. From the numismatic evidences, we can probably pick up the following facts about him....
   (i) The use of the title of kṣatrapa and the Kharoṣṭhi scripts on the coins show that Caṣṭana was of northern origin.
   (ii) The Caitya symbol on his coins, continued on the coins of his successors also, shows that he must have made some conquests at the cost of the Āndhras or the Sātavāhanas.
   (iii) The well-known Ujjayinī symbol on some of his coins probably shows his connection with that city, proved also by the evidence of Ptolemy's *Geography*. He probably acquired Ujjayinī from the Sātavāhanas.
3. *CHIN*, 315

tion of the Sātavāhana empire elsewhere to recover some of their lost possession'.[1]

Pulumāyi's coins have been found at Gudivada and Amaravati while an inscription found at Amaravati refers to his reign. His coins bearing the picture of 'ship with double mast' evidently shows the maritime activities of the empire on the waters of the Bay of Bengal. The South-East Asia was now gradually coming under India's overseas trade activities and the Sātavāhanas no doubt played an important part in this deal.

In his *Geography*, Ptolemy states that while Siriptolemaios or Sri Pulumāyi had been ruling at Baithana or Paithan, as his capital, Baleokuros had his capital at Hippokura. The precise identification of this place is uncertain, but there can hardly be any doubt that Baleokuros is identical with Vilivāyakura of the coins. According to V.A. Smith, Vilivāyakura was the Sātavāhana king Gautamīputra himself. But this can hardly be possible for Ptolemy makes Baleokuros a contemporary of Pulumāyi.

From the Kolhapur region, we get the coins of three rulers which are distinguishable from other Sātavāhana coins by their types and symbols. The inscriptions on the coins of this class are:—

(i) *Raño Vāsithīputasa Vilivāyakurasa*
(ii) *Raño Māḍharīputasa Sivalakurasa*
(iii) *Raño Gotamīputasa Vilivāyakurasa*

The evidence of re-struck coins, as E.J. Rapson points out, 'seems to prove conclusively that these three kings reigned in the order in which they are placed here, since no. 2 strikes coins of no. 1......and no. 3 coins of both no. 1......and of no. 2.'

It appears that the empire of Gautamīputra did not possibly suffer any loss during his lifetime, and thus the first king, who appears to have been independent may be identified with Baleokuros of Ptolemy. These three independent rulers were probably scions of the Imperial Sātavāhana family, and, after the death Gautamīputra, carved out a kingdom of their own in the South-Western Maharashtra region. D.R. Bhandarkar

1. *EHAC*, 66

thinks that the small kingdom was subordinate under the Sātavāhanas.[1] But the nature of Ptolemy's description shows that it was an independent one. Thus though the reign of Pulumāyi was a glorious one in other respects, the Sātavāhana emperor lost the northern and the south-western part of the empire left by his great father.

1. E.J. Rapson thinks that Vilivāyakura or Baleokuros of Ptolemy is Pulumāyi himself. But as K. Gopalachari points out, the "identification upsets the order in the Purāṇic lists and leaves unexplained the absence on the Kolhāpur coins of the Ujjain symbol employed by all the later Sātavāhanas on their coins. Moreover, as Rapson himself points out, nowhere do the Sātavāhanas employ the Kolhāpur coin device (the bow and arrow) which is nearer to the arrow and thunderbolt of Nahapāna's coins. Przyluski (*JRAS*, 1929) explains 'Vilivāya-kura' as 'horse-town'. To him 'Vilivaya' is a form of Vālavā=horse, and 'Kura' is a non-Aryan word meaning 'town'." (*CHIN*, 314, fn 2)

APPENDIX II

DID GAUTAMĪPUTRA AND PULUMĀYI RULE CONJOINTLY?

R.G. Bhandarkar propounded the theory that Gautamīputra Śātakarṇi and his son Pulumāyi ruled conjointly and on this supposition he built up the whole edifice of his later Sātavāhana chronology. The main reasons that led him to formulate the theory are:

(a) in the Nasik inscription of Pulumāyi of the year 19, Gotamī Balaśrī calls herself mother of the great king and the grandmother of the great king simultaneously showing according to him that she was both at the same time;

(b) in the same record the exploits of Gautamīputra are described in detail but nothing is said about the exploits of Pulumāyi; this could hardly happen unless the former was living at the time;

(c) Nasik inscription of Gautamīputra of the year 24 records a gift of the king with his mother who is described as *mahādevī jivasutā rājamātā* presupposing the gift referred to in the inscription of Pulumāyi showing that Gautamīputra was alive in the 19th year of his son.[1]

D.R. Bhandarkar supported later on the theory of his father that the regnal years 18 and 24 in the Nasik records of Gautamīputra 'pertain to the reign of Pulumāyi and that he reigned

1. K. Gopalachari draws our attention to 'a life-size statue of a person, in the Madras Museum Amarāvati collections, holding a lotus in the left hand, bears the inscription *Gotaminămā* (o). From the dress we can infer that it is not a statue of the Buddha. Even supposing that the inscription records an adoration to Gotamī, the mother of Gotamīputa Siri-Satakarni, it is possible that during the reign of Vāsiṭhīputa sāmi Siri-Pulumāvi (when the Amarāvatī *Stūpa* underwent alterations and perhaps enlargement) a statue of Gotamīputa Siri-Satakaṇi was set up; and from Nasik No. 2 (in which both grandson and grandmother have eulogised Gotamīputa Siri-Satakaṇi) we know that Gotamī Balasirī was living in the 19th year of her grandson's reign.' (*EHAC*, 62, fn. 1)

conjointly with his father, the former over Maharashtra and the latter over the hereditary Sātavāhana dominions'. Such a view, D.R. Bhandarkar holds, 'alone can be correct. For in inscription no. 5, Gautamīputra Śātakarṇi, who is the donor there along with his mother, issues a grant in favour of Buddhist monks, who, it is expressly stated were staying in the cave which was the pious gift of theirs. This cave which was a pious gift of Śātakarṇi and his mother must doubtless be cave no. 3 which,......, was excavated and given over to the Bhadrāyanīyas. But then we have also seen that this cave was presented to these monks in the 19th regnal year, not of Śātakarṇi but, of Pulumāvi'.[1]

The unsoundness of the above theory has been thoroughly demonstrated by G.J.-Dubreuil, H.C. Raychaudhuri, K.A.N. Sastri and others. The pivot of the above theory is the evidences furnished by Gautamīputra's inscription of the year 24 and Pulumāyi's inscription of the year 19. G.J.-Dubreuil has observed: "Indeed, Gautamīputra, in the year 24, states distinctly that the cave was excavated under the orders of his mother and himself: '*Pious gift of ours*'; and in the inscription of queen Balaśrī in the 19th year of Pulumāvi, the queen-mother makes a solemn gift of the cave *in her own name*. This can be explained in only one way: the excavation of the cave was begun under the orders of Gautamīputra and his mother....and was finished only after the death of Gautamīputra and during the reign of his son Pulumāvi; we have proof of it in the fact that it was the latter king that had it embellished with paintings. The cave not having been consecrated officially, this consecration took place only in the 19th year of Pulumāvi. Since the king Gautamīputra was dead, the queen Balaśrī made the gift officially herself".[2]

The above observations clearly show that Pulumāyi ruled after Gautamīputra and this would naturally go against other grounds urged by R.G. Bhandarkar. Gotami was thus the mother of the great king and the grandmother of the great king, not simultaneously, but during the time of her grandson Pulumāyi.

1. *Ind Ant*, 1918, 152
2. *AHD*, 38

When the cave was dedicated during the time of Pulumāyi, Gotami's mind was naturally filled with grief for her departed son and therefore his exploits have been narrated in detail. In fact, 'the inscription of Balaśrī has a clear meaning : it is the funeral oration on the great king delivered by an inconsolable mother.'[1]

The grounds urged by D.R. Bhandarkar for supporting his father's theory that Pulumāyi ruled at Paithan in Maharashtra and Gautamīputra from the hereditary Sātavāhana dominion in the eastern Deccan are more weak. Epigraphic evidences from Nasik clearly show that Gautamīputra had been ruling over the Maharashtra region; in fact, he orders to the officers of Nasik in his records, while the inscription of his mother shows that his sway extended over Surāṣṭra, Aparānta and Vidarbha. Further, had Gautamīputra and Pulumāyi reigned conjointly, we would have found at least one inscription issued in their joint names. In this connection, it may also be noted that the coins of Nahapāna are re-struck by Gautamīputra alone.[2]

1. *AIID*, 39
2. *JRAS*, 1926

Chapter VI

THE LATER SĀTAVĀHANAS

Śivaśrī-Śātakarṇi

Vāsiṣṭhīputra Pulumāyi died in c. 147 A.D. and was succeeded by Śivaśrī Śātakarṇi. He is certainly identical with *raño Vāsithīputa Siva-Siri-Sātakaṃni* of the coins recovered from the Andhradeśa, and Vāsiṣṭhīputra Śrī Śātakarṇi of the Kanheri epigraph. This inscription in Sanskrit 'exhibits the neat characters of Western *Kṣatrapa* inscriptions' and mentions the queen of Vāsiṣṭhīputra Śrī Śātakarṇi, daughter of the *mahākṣatrapa* Ru(dra), who has been identified with *mahākṣatrapa* Rudradāman.[1] Now, in his Junagadh inscription of 150 A.D. Rudradāman states that by his own prowess (*sva-vīryārijitaṃ*), he gained Ākarāvanti (E & W Malwa), Surāṣṭra (Kathiawad), Kaccha (Cutch), Aparānta (North Konkon), Anūpanibhṛt (Māhiṣmatī region), Kukara (probably between Sind and Pāriyātra mountain) etc. Of these Ākarāvanti, Surāṣṭra and Kukura seem to have been conquered earlier during the time of Pulumāyi, as already stated, since Caṣṭana held sway over them. We have now to determine when the rest were conquered. There are two statements in the Junagadh record that are very important for determining this time:—

(a) Rudradāman states that he fought with the Yaudheyas *proud and indomitable*, who had presumably threatened him from the north;

(b) We are informed that the Great satrap twice defeated Śātakarṇi, the Lord of the Dakṣiṇāpatha, but did not destroy him on account of nearness of relationship.[2]

The Yaudheyas originally lived in E. Punjab in the Sutlej region. Later on, however, they moved a little to the south-east as shown by the distribution of their coins. At a place in the neighbourhood of the town of Rohtak large number of coin-

1. Luders, no. 994; G. Buhler, *ASWI*, v. 78
2. *Select Ins*, 172

moulds bearing the legend *Yaudheyānām Bahudhānyaka* have been found.[1] In the *Mahābhārata*, the Yaudheyas are described as Rohitakas showing that Rohitaka or Rohtak was their home.[2] It formed a part of the Kuṣāṇa empire, but the Junagadh inscription is absolutely silent about the Kuṣāṇas. This shows that Rudradāman's conquest was carried out at a time when the Kuṣāṇa power was at a very low ebb. Now, if we turn to the Kuṣāṇa records we find that Huviṣka's reign ended in the year 60 of an era used in the records of the Kuṣāṇas, and for 7 years, i.e., up to the year 67, there is no record of any Kuṣāṇa lord. The recent discovery of the Mathura image inscription of Vāsudeva may reduce this gap by three years if we read the year 64 in it. But D.C. Sircar who edited the record states that the year may be 64 or 67.[3] It was evidently during this period of 4 or 7 years, when the Kuṣāṇa power sank very low, that Rudradāman carried his conquests. There is, however, still great controversy regarding the time of the Kuṣāṇas, and discarding numerous theories, scholars are now divided into two camps, one holding that the Kaniṣka group of kings started their reign in 78 A.D., Kaniṣka, the first king, being the founder of the Śaka era of that year, while the other group believes that Kaniṣka came to the throne some time between 120 and 130 A.D. Recently, R. Ghirshman has proposed the year 144 A.D. as the date of Kaniṣka's accession. His inference is based on the findings at the ancient city of Begram in Eastern Afghanistan. Coins bearing the name of Vāsudeva have been found in the ruins of that city. Vāsudeva, we know, was the last king of Kaniṣka's dynasty to rule into the interior of India, and as the ancient city of Begram was destroyed by Shahpur I, the Sassanid king of Iran, in the period between A.D. 241 and 250, the last year of Vāsudeva, the Indian king, would fall in that period. From the inscriptions it is clear that Vāsudeva I reigned from the year 74 to 98 of the era started by Kaniṣka, and thus the initial year of that era would start from c. 144 A.D., which consequently marks the year of Kaniṣka's accession. On this

1. *EHNI*, 52
2. *Mbh.* II. 32. 4-5
3. *Ep Ind*, xxx, 181ff

view, R. Ghirshman gives us the following chronological table :

Kaniṣka	c. 144-172 (?)
Huviṣka	c. 172-217 (?)
Vāsudeva I	c. 217 (?)-241
Vāsudeva II	
Kaniṣka II	
Vāsudeva III	

As it has been pointed out elsewhere,[1] R. Ghirshman's theory cannot be accepted for the following reasons :—

(a) Vāsudeva, whose coins have been found at Begram, cannot be identified with Vāsudeva I for the provenance of his epigraphic records proves beyond doubt that his empire was confined in the U.P. region with Mathura as its centre, and as the coins attributed by Ghirshman to Vāsudeva have not been found in the U.P., it is clear that the two Vāsudevas are different personages. From the Chinese sources we learn that the king of the Ta-Yueh-chi (Kuṣāṇas) named Po-tiao or Pu-ra-dien (Vāsudeva) sent an embassy to the Chinese emperor in 230 A.D. This king was evidently the Vāsudeva whose coins have been found at Begram and he evidently solicited the help of the Chinese emperor against the Sassanids.

(b) There is no convincing proof that Begram was destroyed by Shahpur I and hence any theory built on the synchronism of Shahpur I with Vāsudeva appears to be a defective one.

The Junagadh inscription of 150 A.D. raises another fact against the above theory. If Kaniṣka ruled from A.D. 144-172, then Rudradāman could hardly conquer the Yaudheyas or the Sindhu-Sauvīra region,[2] mentioned in his epigraph, without

1. *EHNI*, 94ff
2. The Sindhu-Sauvīra country denoted strictly Multan and Jahravar and the adjoining regions. H.C. Raychaudhuri observes : 'The major part of modern Sind was clearly outside the geographical (as opposed to political) limits of ancient "Sin-tu" or Sindhu and was, in the days of Yuan Chwang, included in the countries of A-tien-p'o-chih-lo, Pi to shih-lo, and A-fan-tu. Part of the modern territory of Sind may have been included in Sauvīra whose Southern limits undoubtedly reached the, sea, because the *Milinda-Pañho* mentions it in a list of countries where

coming into conflict with the Kuṣāṇa lord. The silence regarding the Kuṣāṇas in the epigraph speaks evidently for itself. This silence similarly goes against placing the starting point of Kaniṣka's reign between 120-130 A.D., for in that case the Kuṣāṇa empire would have been at its top by c. 150 A.D.

All these difficulties are cleared if we accept the theory that Kaniṣka came to the throne in 78 A.D. and was the originator of the Śaka era starting from that date. This would show that the Kuṣāṇa power sank very low some time between A.D. 138 and 145, and it was during this period that Rudradāman carried his conquest of North India especially of the country of the Yaudheyas and the Sindhu-Sauvīra region. Evidently after thus being secured on his northern frontier, he turned his attention towards the south and defeated Śātakarṇi but did not destroy him because this Śātakarṇi—Vāsiṣṭhīputra Śivaśrī Śātakarṇi—was his son-in-law. This conquest was evidently carried in the early years of Śivaśrī Śātakarṇi's reign, may be in c. 148 A.D.

While we have seen that we can identify Śivaśrī Śātakarṇi with Śātakarṇi mentioned in the Junagadh record, there have been different theories on this point. The unsoundness of many of them would be apparent if we note at the outset that in the Junagadh record the name of the south Indian king is Śātakarṇi and that he is described as *Dakṣiṇāpathapati* or Lord of Dakṣiṇāpatha.

Believing in the theory that the inscriptions of Nahapāna are dated in the Śaka era of 78 A.D. and acting on the synchronism, the last year of Nahapāna=the 18th year of Gautamīputra Śātakarṇi, E.J. Rapson concluded that Pulumāyi ruled up to 154 A.D. and hence he is the Śātakarṇi of the Junagadh record and may have been the son-in-law of Nahapāna. Pulumāyi never assumes the title of Śātakarṇi either in the inscriptions or in the coins, and had he been the son-in-law of Rudradāman, then, as K.A.N. Sastri points out, he would have married Caṣṭana's great grand-daughter whose contemporary

"ships do congregate." We are informed by the author of the *Periplus* that "ships lie at anchor at Barbaricum" (at the mouth of the Indus). But the evidence of Alberuni leaves no room for doubt that the northern limits of Sauvīra reached Multan.' (*PHAI*, 525)

he was according to the evidence of Ptolemy.[1] This proves that the theory is utterly absurd.

J.N. Banerjea holds that 'the Śātakarṇi of the Junagadh record need not be the same as the Vāsiṣṭhīputra Śrī-Śātakarṇi of the Kanheri inscription; he was probably a son of Gautamīputra Śātakarṇi, perhaps much younger than his more important brother Vāsiṣṭhīputra Pulumāyi'.[2] Banerjea does not identify this Śātakarṇi but as he also believes that the inscriptions of Nahapāna are dated in the Śaka era, according to his theory Pulumāyi would be ruling about 150 A.D., and so his brother about this time would not be a king, while in the Junagadh record the Śātakarṇi is described as the Lord of Dakṣiṇāpatha.

G.B. Rao thinks that the Śātakarṇi of the Junagadh record is no other than Yajñaśrī Śātakarṇi who was defeated by Rudradāman with the result that the Sātavāhana empire was divided into two parts, and while Yajñaśrī ruled over the eastern division, the western division was governed by Vāsiṣṭhīputra Śātakarṇi, the mahākṣatrapa's son-in-law, evidently as Rudradāman's viceroy.[3] While the theory is no doubt an ingenious one, we have already indicated that it appears to be impossible that Yajñaśrī Śātakarṇi ruled as early as c. 150 A.D.

Śivaskanda Śātakarṇi

Śivaskanda Śātakarṇi possibly ascended the throne in c. 154 A.D. D.C. Sircar thinks that he is identical with Sivamaka Sāta of an Amaravati record. If the identifications be accepted then it may be assumed that in spite of the Scythian inroad, the Sātavāhana empire remained intact though reduced in glory. He is identical with Khada Sātakani of the coins found from the Akola hoard. As the Purāṇas assign him only seven years it may be presumed that he had a short reign.

Yajñaśrī Śātakarṇi

According to the Purāṇas, the immediate successor of Śivaskanda was Yajñaśrī Śātakarṇi. His relationship with his predecessor is not clear. His inscriptions have been found at Kanheri, Nasik

1. *JRAS*, 1926
2. *CHIN*, 281
3. *EHD*, ed. G. Yazdani, 108ff

and the China in the Krishna district while his coins have been found at Gujarat, Kathiawad, Aparānta, the Chanda district and the Krishna district. This shows that he not only ruled over eastern and western Deccan but also snatched away a considerable portion of the territories once under the rule of the Scythian satraps of Ujjayinī. (The defeat and discomfiture of the dynasty at the hand of Rudradāman was thus fully avenged.) As already stated, from the evidence of the coins it is clear that there was no mahākṣatrapa in the Scythian dominion between the year A.D. 188-90. Evidently the Scythians had to acknowledge the suzerainty of the Sātavāhana king and the office of mahākṣatrapa thus remained in abeyance. As already stated the conquest of the Śaka dominion is proved by the coins of Yajñaśrī issued in imitation of the coins of the Śaka rulers of Ujjayinī.[1] It was evidently after the death of the Sātavāhana king in c. 190 A.D. that the office of the mahākṣatrapa revived again. His coins with the horse device possibly indicates that he performed a horse-sacrifice. K. Gopalachari identifies him with Sātavāhana whom Bāṇa refers to as *trisamudrādhipati* and also with the Sātavāhana monarch who was the friend of the mendicant Nāgārjuna according to Yuan Chwang.[2]

1. We may note here especially the silver coins from Sopara modelled on the issues of the western kṣatrapas. His coins with the horse device show evidently that he performed *aśvamedha* sacrifice to celebrate his victory. (*contra. CII*, xc)
2. *CHIN*, 313. 'The numerous coins of the reign are as varied in type and denomination as they are widely distributed. They come from Gujarat, Kathiawad, Sopara and the districts of Chanda, Akola (Madhya Pradesh), Godavari and Krishna (Āndhradeśa). The Chanda potin coins bear the elephant device, and those of the Sopara fabric bear the portrait head of the king. From Eastern Deccan come sackfuls of lead and copper coins bearing horse, elephant and *chaitya* devices. In addition to 1/16, 1/4, 3/8, 1/2, 3/4, 7/8 and 1 *Kārshāpaṇas* (issued by Pulumāyi II also), Siri-Yaña issued 1-1/8 and 1-3/4 *Kārshāpaṇas*. Wars in the west and a great commercial prosperity in the east explain this plentiful issue of currency.'

Chapter VII

DECLINE OF THE SĀTAVĀHANAS

Yajñaśrī Śātakarṇi appears to have been the last Sātavāhana ruler to exercise control over both the western and the eastern districts of the empire. According to the Purāṇas the following kings ruled after Yajñaśrī:—

Vijaya	6	yrs
Caṇḍaśrī Śātakarṇi	10	yrs (3 yrs according to *Vāyu*)
Pulomāvi	7	yrs

Available evidences indicate that the rule of the above monarchs was confined to the eastern Deccan,[1] as we shall see later on. The question therefore arises, what happened to the Maharashtra region after the death of Yajñaśrī Śātakarṇi about 190 A.D.?

D.R. Bhandarkar maintains that after Yajñaśrī the Ābhīras occupied Western Maharashtra.[2] According to V.V. Mirashi's view the Ābhīra rule could not have started before the middle of the third century, since the so-called Traikuṭaka-Kalacuri era of 249-50 A.D. was started by the Ābhīra king Īśvarasena whose inscription dated in the ninth year has been found at Nasik.[3] G.J-Dubreuil thinks that the Cuṭu-Nāgas occupied the Maharashtra region about this time.[4] But this view is utterly untenable.

In the absence of any positive data we have to fall back upon coins and inscriptions disclosing the names of a few Sātavāhana rulers who are not mentioned in the Purāṇas. The following names, for example, may be noted:—

1. Vāsiṣṭhīputra Catarapana Śātakarṇi mentioned in a Nanaghat record[5]

1. In face of the archaeological finds it is difficult to agree with V.V. Mirashi that the Sātavāhana kings 'continued to hold Maharashtra to the end of the Sātavāhana age.' (*Corpus*, iv, xxiv)
2. *Ind Ant*, 1918, 156
3. *Corpus*, iv. xxii-xxvi
4. *AHD*, 48f
5. Luders, 1120

2. Māḍharīputra Svāmī Sakasena mentioned in Kanheri inscriptions[1]
3. Kauśikīputra Śātakarṇi whose coins have been found in Kaus collection[2]

The sudden withdrawal of the main Sātavāhana house from the Western Maharashtra region really causes somesurprise. We have seen that in 190 A.D. there was a revival of the Śaka house of Western India that has been under the domination of the Sātavāhana king Yajñaśrī. After Yajñaśrī's death, a collateral member of the Sātavāhana house possibly entered into a conspiracy with the Śakas, forced the main line to move to the east and declared himself a king under the Scythian protection. Evidently, in recognition of it, he took upon himself the title of *Catarapana* or kṣatrapa as an expression of gratitude. The name Śakasena, who might have been a son of Vāsiṣṭhiputra Catarapana Śātakarṇi, is also significant for we know that in ancient India kings who entered into subordinate alliance named their son often after the name or the dynastic appellation of the more powerful party. Whether Kauśikīputra Śātakarṇi was the last king of Western Maharashtra is difficult to determine. It is possible that there were one or two more such kings who for the sake of convenience may be called *the Later Sātavāhanas of Western Maharashtra.*

In this connection we may note a Kanheri inscription[3] recording the gift by Nāgamulanikā, wife of a mahārathī, the daughter of a mahābhojī and of the great king, and the mother of Skandanāgaśataka. Who this great king was is rather difficult to determine. This possibly shows that during the post-Yajñaśrī period the mahārathīs and the mahābhojas were gradually coming to the forefront again and were possibly entering into matrimonial alliance with the then kings. Rapson's theory[4] that Skandanāgaśataka is identical with Śivaskandanāgaśrī of the Banavāsī inscription of Hāritīputra—Viṣṇukaḍa—Cuṭukulānanda Śātakarṇi of the year 12, in which the donor (name lost) is also called the daughter of a great king and is associated with the prince

1. Luders, 1101, 1100
2. *JNSI*, xiii, 133ff
3. Luders, no. 1021
4. *CIC*, liii

Śivaskanda can hardly be accepted. On this identification G.J-Dubreuil has concluded that 'there can be no doubt that the Cuṭus succeeded the Āndhras not only in Mysore but also in Aparānta'.[1] It was at a later date that the Cuṭus held their sway in the northern part of the Kanarese and Malayalam speaking area.

II

Of the three kings, Vijaya, Caṇḍaśrī Śātakarṇi and Pulumāvi, mentioned in the Purāṇas, Vijaya's name is found on coins in the Akola hoard. Caṇḍaśrī Śātakarṇi may be identified with Vāsiṣṭhīputra Cadasāta in whose second regnal year an inscription was engraved at Kodavalu near Pithapuram in the Godavari district.[2] The Myakadoni inscription dated in the 8th regnal year of Śrī Pulumāvi of the Sātavāhana family should be ascribed to the last Sātavāhana king of the Purāṇic list. V.S. Sukthankar who edited record in *Ep. Ind.* xiv. p. 155 identified this Pulumāyi with Pulumāyi I, the son of Gautamīputra Śātakarṇi. But the palaeography of the record is clearly against such a theory. The record is a late one and the king is no doubt Pulumāyi II. His coins bearing the name Pulahamavi have been found in the Akola hoard.[3]

F.E. Pargiter has pointed out that the Purāṇic list of the Sātavāhana kings was first prepared during the time of Yajñaśrī Śātakarṇi, as the *Matsya* version would make us believe, but later on three more names were added to it and so it has been maintained that the Sātavāhana dynasty came to an end with Pulumāyi II. The evidence of coins[4] proves however that two or three more kings possibly ruled after Pulumāyi. Thus we get the names of Karṇa, Kuṁbha and Ruḍa Sātakaṇi. Ruḍa Sātakaṇi's coins show that he ruled over the north-eastern part of the Sātavāhana empire and also over the Āndhradeśa. So he possibly ruled after Pulumāyi II. Then the dynasty lost Andhra country to the Ikṣvākus and the other two kings, Karṇa and Kuṁbha, maintained their existence in the Vidarbha region till the family was finally extinguished.

1. *AHD*, 49
2. Luders, 1341
3. *PIHC*, 1945; *JNSI*, ii, 83ff
4. *ib.*

It must of course be admitted that the addition of these three kings to the Purāṇic list is purely a hypothetical one, while the extent of their empire determined on the evidence of the coins is also problematical. Some scholars regard them as the *Collateral Vidarbha line of the Sātavāhanas.*

We are now in a position to trace the different phases in the dismemberment of the Sātavāhana empire:

a. The Ābhīras came to power in Western Maharashtra while the Cuṭus in the northern part of Kanarese and Malayalam speaking areas.
b. The Ikṣvākus and the Pallavas rose in eastern Deccan.
c. The last lingering trace of the Sātavāhana power in the Vidarbha country was wiped away by the Vākāṭakas.

APPENDIX III

NUMISMATIC NOTES

It has already been stated that the list of the Andhra kings in the *Matsya Purāṇa* is quite authentic from Gautamīputra onwards, but for the earlier kings we must be very cautious in utilising the literary evidences. Some scholars, however, take up the *Matsya* list in the background of the evidence of coins, though in most cases the numismatic evidences thus utilised are not very clear. We may note here a few instances :

1. Coins bearing the name Śātakarṇi have been arbitrarily attributed to Śātakarṇi I and Śātakarṇi II, though it has already been shown that the existence of a second Śātakarṇi is not supported by other evidences at our disposal. Thus coins found in E. Malwa (*CIC*, 3, 4, 17) should properly be attributed to Śātakarṇi who conquered Malwa and whose coins have been found from Nasik, Tewar and other places (*JNSI*, xiii, 35; xv, 205). (*supra*)
2. Coins bearing the legend *gha sadasa* have been attributed to Meghasvāti, the ninth king of the *Matsya* list (*CIC*, 28). Another coin recently found with the legend *ha ta me ka sa* has been taken as *Śātameghasa* and ascribed to the same king. It is rather curious that on the evidence of this single coin, though showing Southern Brāhmī letters, it has been inferred that the 'Sātavāhana dominions in the second century B.C. included the Krishna valley and probably came down to the Pennar line'. (*JNSI*, xxvii, 94) When the very attribution is doubtful it is rather risky to draw such inferences.
3. There is absolutely no ground to attribute two lead coins to king Hāla as has been done by M. Rama Rao. (*List*, 7)
4. V.V. Mirashi's attempt to identify the kings known exclusively from the Tarhala hoard (*JNSI*, ii, 83ff) with one or other kings of the Purāṇic list is open

to objection in many cases. It is better to think that they represent the Vidarbha line of the later Sātavāhanas.

It may be noted in this connection that the *Mahārathis* also issued coins in their own names. From a close study of such coins it has been inferred that those who flourished in western Deccan issued coins of *bull* type, the *Mahārathis* of eastern Deccan issued coins of *caitya* type, while those in the central Deccan issued coins of *lion* or *elephant* type along with *Ujjayin* symbols evidently following their masters. (*JNSI*, xxviii, 57-9)

In conclusion we may note that the coins of Yajñaśrī Śātakarṇi cover not only Andhra state, Maharashtra but also Baroda and Kathiawad regions of Gujarat. The find of a coin of the same king with the ship motif from Poona district shows, as already pointed out by Mirashi, that such issues were not exclusively current in the eastern coastal districts. (*JNSI*, xxiv, 174-5) Though we are not in favour of attaching any importance to the find spots of a few coins of any king, still Yajñaśrī's coin from Baroda tends indirectly in the background of other evidences to support the view that he possibly brought the Śaka *kṣatrapas* under control during 188-190 A.D. (*supra*)

Appendix IV

GLIMPSES OF SĀTAVĀHANA ADMINISTRATION

Epigraphic evidences show that the Sātavāhana empire was roughly divided into two parts, not from the point of view of geography but from the nature of administrative arrangements, one under the royal officers and the other under the feudatory chieftains. This reminds us of the British days when the Indian empire was divided into provinces under the governors and the states under native princes. Such feudatory rulers, known as *mahārathīs* and *mahābhojas*, were mainly confined to Western Maharashtra. The kings entered into matrimonial alliances with them and this often strengthened their hands as we find it in case of Simuka. (*supra*) Whether the office of *mahārathī* and *mahābhoja* was a hereditary one is difficult to determine, though Kuda inscriptions nos. 1 and 9 seem to indicate that in some cases it might have been so. There has been some controversy whether a *mahābhoja* was superior to a *mahārathī* or vice versa. E. Senart maintains that *mahārathī* cannot imply a nobility superior to that of *mahābhoja*.[1] K. Gopalachari, on the other hand, points out that a Kuda inscription (no. 23) is dated 'almost' in the years of a *mahābhoja* but there are no records of this nature belonging to any *mahārathī*.[2] From such evidences however we cannot make out a general case. Some time a *mahārathī* or a *mahābhoja* might have been bold enough to defy his overlord while under a strong king like Gautamīputra they would remain docile and subservient. However, as among the native princes of the British days there were different grades of honour, so it was possibly the case in the Sātavāhana age. G.J-Dubreuil assigns the feudatory status only to the *mahārathīs* when he states that

1. Senart observes: 'the occurrence of the feminine *Mahāraṭhinī* in Bēḍsā No. 2 also indicates rather that the term does not imply the actual office of governor of a district or province, but an honorific or nobiliary title'.
2. *EHAC*, 80

'the Āndhra empire was governed by feudatories who bore the title of Mahārathīs and were called "Nāgas" as they belonged to a race of serpent-worshippers'.[1] From a critical study of the epigraphs it appears however that *mahārathī* and *mahābhoja* were feudatory titles prevailing in two distinct geographical regions. The *mahābhojas* exercised power in northern Konkan and the *mahārathīs* above the Western Ghats. Both the feudatories were superior in rank to the royal governors or *amātyas* inasmuch as while the latter made grants of lands only under the orders of the kings, the former could make the same under their own authority.

The royal state proper was divided into *āhāras* or *rāṣṭras* each under an amātya. The āhāra or rāṣṭra again was subdivided into *nigama* (town) and *grāma*. In the Jangli Gundu inscription we find the mention of a *gāmika*.[2] Among the other officers of the state mention may be made of the following :

mahāmātra, who was possibly in charge of a specified task

bhaṇḍāgārika, the superintendent of stores

lekhaka, the royal scribe

nibandhakāra, officer in charge of the registration of documents

heranika, treasurer

With regard to two offices, *rājāmātya* and *mahāsenāpati*, we do not get any clear light. *Rājāmātya* was possibly officer attending the king like his private secretary. *Mahāsenāpati* denoted the commander in chief. But in the Jangli Gundu inscription we find him in charge of an *āhāra*. In such cases, they were possibly military governors akin to the *Strategos* of the Indo-Greek days.[3]

1. *AHD*, 47
2. *Ep Ind*, xiv, 155f
3. D.C. Sircar thinks that under the Sātavāhanas, the *Mahāsenāpatis* were feudatory chieftains in charge of *rāṣṭras*. (*Suc Sat*, 15)

PART II

MINOR DYNASTIES OF EAST AND WEST

Chapter VIII

EASTERN DYNASTIES

On the ashes of the Sātavāhana empire two dynasties arose in the eastern part of South India—the Ikṣvākus with their capital at Dhānyakaṭaka and the Pallavas centring round Kāñcī. *Another* dynasty came into existence after the fall of the Ikṣvākus in the Guntur region and it played a rival role with the Pallavas. The Guntur monarchs were not the members of the Pallava dynasty as it has been supposed to be.

There are still several controversies that engulf unfortunately the history of the dynasties; *first*, about the origin; *secondly*, whether the Pallavas rose simultaneously with the Ikṣvākus or a little later, and *lastly* whether there was a break between the time of the Pallava kings known from the Prakrit charters and that of the later kings known from the Sanskrit records. Diverse views may be expressed on all the above points; before we proceed to discuss them we may note the following genealogies :

I

(*Ikṣvāku*)

Cāṃtamūla I
|
Vīrapuruṣadatta
|
Ehuvula Cāṃtamūla II
|
Hārītīputra Vīrapuruṣadatta — Rudrapurisadāta

(The spelling of the names follows as they are given in the epigraphs.)

II

Kāñcī kings (Pallavas)	*Guntur kings* (Pallavas ?)
Mahārāja-bappasvāmī	Siṃhavarman
|	|
Śivaskandavarman	Skandavarman
|	|
Viṣṇugopa	Buddhavarman
	|
	Buddhyaṅkura

Epigraphic and numismatic evidences prove beyond doubt the rule of the Sātavāhanas in the Kistna-Godavari region where the Ikṣvākus who served under the Sātavāhanas ultimately came to supreme power. There is, on the other hand, no epigraphic evidence connecting the Sātavāhanas with Kāñcī. G.J-Dubreuil observes that "coins containing the image of a 'ship with two masts' are found almost exclusively on the coast between Madras and Cuddalore and they represent the moneys of Toṇḍai-Maṇḍalam of which Kāñchī is the capital. According to Prof. Rapson, these coins bear the legend 'Śrī Puḷumāvi'. The Ujjayin symbol indicates the rule of the Sātavāhana dynasty. So this dynasty reigned over the territory of Kāñchīpuram. Further, an inscription of Pulumāvi, the last king of that dynasty, shows that the prince Skanda-Nāga was his great general; there is no doubt that the Nāgas were very powerful when the Sātavāhana dynasty came to an end".[1] The Nāgas might have been powerful as subordinates under the Sātavāhanas, and the Pallavas evidently captured power by overthrowing them. D.C. Sircar is inclined to connect the lead coins with '*ship with two masts*' and the Ujjayin symbols with the Nāgas and observes that 'before the middle of the second century therefore not the Pallavas but the Nāgas were ruling the coast country'.[2] In support of his contention he cites the evidence of Ptolemy that the *Coast Country* of the Soringoi = Colas was ruled by Sornagos and Arouarnoi was ruled by Basaronagos. From this description it is clear no doubt that the district to the south

1. *AHD*, 47
2. *Suc Sat*, 149

of Masulipatam to the Pāṇḍya country was under the rule of the Nāgas. Ptolemy composed his *Geography* about 140 A.D., when the Sātavāhanas were in the full swing of their power over the Andhrāpatha region and the Nāga rulers of that age were thus not independent potentates, and we have no evidence to determine what position the Nāgas enjoyed nearly ninety years after the days of Ptolemy. The Valurpalaiyam plates contain the tradition that the Pallavas acquired royal power 'on marrying the daughter of the lord of serpents, i.e., the Nāgas.' The account is a very late one and this may be an echo of the Pallava conquest of the Cuṭus who came to power in the western part of the Sātavāhana empire.[1]

So far we had been treading on uncertain path. For studying the history of the Guntur and the Pallava kings we have the following fixed points:

1. The Prakrit inscription of Siṃhavarman has been discovered in the Guntur district.
2. The Gupta emperor Samudragupta who set out on his Dakṣiṇāpatha expedition about 350 A.D. refers to Viṣṇugopa of Kāñcī.

As the Guntur region had been under the sway of the Ikṣvākus the discovery of Siṃhavarman's record from the place seems to indicate that he came to power after overthrowing the Ikṣvākus. According to the chronology of the Sātavāhanas followed in these pages the rule of the Imperial dynasty came to an end c. 213 A.D.[2] when consequently came the Ikṣvākus. Allowing an average of 25 years for each of the Ikṣvāku kings, the first three Ikṣvākus would rule up to 290 A.D. and then naturally Rulupuruṣadatta, the last king overthrown by Siṃhavarman, would have a short reign. According to this calculation then the Guntur dynasty came to power at the close of the third century. The history of the Kāñcī region on the other hand from the fall of the Sātavāhanas to the rise of the Pallavas still remains blank. The Pallavas of the Prakrit record in any case ruled before Viṣṇugopa whose relationship with the former still remains a matter of conjecture.[3]

1. Sastri, *A History of South India*, 98
2. *supra*
3. *infra*

Different theories have been maintained regarding the origin of the Ikṣvākus and the Pallavas. In a letter written by S. Konow to J. Ph. Vogel the learned professor observed, 'I would therefore be inclined to define the dialect of your inscriptions (Prakrit inscriptions from Nāgārjunikoṇḍā) as follows: We are faced with a normalised semi-literary Prakrit, used by people whose home tongue was Draviḍian, and probably Kanarese. If I am right, we should *a priori* be inclined to infer that the Ikkhākus had come to the Kistna country from the West. But all such conclusions are bound to be uncertain'.

According to E. J. Rapson the Ikṣvākus were of northern descent, being an offshoot of the great Solar dynasty of Ajodhya.[1] If the Purāṇic accounts are to be believed Ikṣvāku, the progenitor of the Solar race, had a hundred sons of whom forty-eight were entrusted with charges of different states in the south and one of them might have been the founder of the Ikṣvāku line of the Āndhradeśa.

All such accounts are however myths recorded in later works which can hardly be used for historical purposes without proper scrutiny. The dynastic accounts of the Purāṇas have no doubt historical value, but it will be an idle speculation to hold that each and every Purāṇic account is historical.

K. Gopalachari draws our attention to a Kanarese work entitled *Dharmāmṛta* affording 'evidence of an early drift. In the time of the 12th *Tīrthaṅkara* Vasupūjya (third or second century B.C.), Ikṣvāku Yaśodhara of Aṅga carved a kingdom for himself in the Vēṅgī country, to use the later designation of the heart of the *Āndhradeśa*, and founded the town of Pratipālapura identified by Mr. M.S. Sarma with *Bhaṭṭiprōlu*'.[2] It is quite evident that the work is based on myths and religious stories.

Bp. Caldwell seems to be hitting at the truth when he states that the Aryan immigrants to the south appear to have been generally brāhmaṇical priests and instructors who taught the South Indian, especially the Draviḍian chiefs, to imitate and emulate the grandeur and taste of the Solar, Lunar and Agnikūla

1. *CIC*, xliv
2. *EHAC*, 129

races of kings of the north.[1] Similar examples we find with the various Rajput chiefs of the early medieval ages. This is what the anthropologists call the Sanskritisation of the different groups of Indian cultures and ultimately reducing them into one pattern. In case of the Mahāmegha dynasty of Kaliṅga referred to before we find an entirely different strain (*supra*) inasmuch as the Cedis were an Aryan people and a branch of them settled in the so-called Outer Band of the Aryan region.

The same process of Sanskritisation can be found in case of the Pallavas of the Toṇḍaimaṇḍalam region. Earlier scholars identified them with the Pahlavas or the Parthians. But a foreign origin for the tribe is negativated by the fact that the Pallava kings performed the Aśvamedha sacrifice. The obnoxious practices centring round the ceremony was naturally abhorred by the foreigners and we know of no foreign king having ever performed this sacrifice. The claim in the records of the Pallavas that they belonged to the Bhāradvāja *gotra* is another instance of this process of Sanskritisation. Non-brāhmins generally accept the *gotra* of their preceptors and spiritual directors. The Pallavas were evidently Sanskritised by the brāhmaṇical leaders having Bhāradvāja *gotra*. The Pallava territory was on the outskirt of the Cola janapada where the Nāgas had also been living and hence the tribe seems to have been of Cola-Nāga origin. It may be noted in this connection that the term *toṇḍai* which was the name of the land means a creeper. This was evidently Sanskritised into Pallava as the name of the people of the region also.

The Ikṣvākus

According to the epigraphic records the founder of the Ikṣvaku dynasty was mahārāja Vāsiṭhīputa Cāṃtamūla. If we accept the view that the Ikṣvākus came to power after the fall of the Sātavāhanas we may place Cāṃtamūla some time between c. 213 and 235 A.D.

K.P. Jayaswal has identified the Ikṣvākus with the Śrīpārvatīyas of the Purāṇas.[2] These Śrīpārvatīyas are also called Āndhrabhṛtyas and as consisting of seven kings. According to

1. Bp. Caldwell, *Comparative Grammar of Dravidian Languages*, 115
2. *JBORS*, 1933, 171

the *Matsya* account the dynasty ruled for *dvi pañcaśatam* years which may mean fifty-two or one hundred. The *Vāyu* text gives us the reading *dve'rdhaśata* which of course means fifty-two.[1] There are however some difficulties in accepting the theory of K.P. Jayaswal, for though we know that the Ikṣvākus were originally the *bhṛtya* of the Āndhra-Sātavāhana kings, epigraphic records supply us with the names of only four rulers and not seven. Further, it is still a moot question whether the Ikṣvāku citadel was at Śrīśailam. Scholars generally think that their capital was either at Nāgārjunikoṇḍā or at Dhānyakaṭaka. E.J. Rapson identifies the Āndhrabhṛtyas with the Cuṭus, 'who rose to power in the western and southern districts after the reign of Śrī-Yajña'.[2]

Cāṃtamūla, the founder of the dynasty, has left no record. In the inscriptions of his successors he is given the epithet Vāsiṭhīputa or Vāsiṣṭhīputra and as the performer of Agniṣṭoma, Agnihotra, Aśvamedha and Vājapeya sacrifices. As in the Ikṣvāku records no mention is made of his father it may be presumed that he was the first king of the dynasty. Aśvamedha etc. was performed by a king after his victories in battle. It is not unlikely that Cāṃtamūla fought against the last Sātavāhana king in the Andhra region and after driving away his lord performed the sacrifices. To celebrate his victory he might have made gifts of lumps of gold, ploughs of land, cows and oxen, though J. Ph. Vogel is inclined to think that the description *go-satasahasa-hala-satasahasa padāyisa* occurring in the Nāgārjunikoṇḍā records is merely a conventional one.[3] His warlike activities are further alluded to in his description 'Mahāsena parigahitasa', protected by Lord Mahāsena, the lord of warfare, and we know that in ancient India kings often worshipped this god before going to a warlike expedition. Cāṃtamūla was also a statesman of farsight and evidently to make his hand strong against the Sātavāhanas or their supporters he contracted several matrimonial alliances. Thus one of his sisters was married to a *mahāsenāpati-mahādaṇḍanāyaka* of the Pūkiya family flourishing in the Pungi district on the banks of the Guṇḍlakamma

1. *DKA*, 46, fn. 34
2. *CIC*, lxix
3. *Ep Ind*, xx, 6

river[1] while his daughter Cāmtasiri was married to another *mahāsenāpati-mahādaṇḍanāyaka* of the Dhanaka family.[2] If these marriages had been contracted before Cāṃtamūla ascended the throne, then it may be assumed that the Sātavāhana power came to an end in the eastern Deccan under the pressure of a military *coup* organised by Cāṃtamūla with other feudatories. We are, however, in the dark regarding the position held by Cāṃtamūla himself before he became king. K. Gopalachari thinks that 'the ancestors of the Ikṣvākus were *Mahātalavaras* under the Sātavāhanas'.[3] But of this there is no evidence, though in view of the military coup referred to above, it is natural for us to assume that he must have been a military officer of considerable importance. Cāṃtamūla's son Vīrapurisadāta is not credited with any conquests in the epigraphs. It may be assumed therefore that the Kistna-Guntur districts were conquered by Cāṃtamūla himself. According to some scholars the fifth memorial panel at Nāgārjunikoṇḍā represents his figure and he appears there to be a middle-aged man.[4]

Vīrapurisadāta

Cāṃtamūla was succeeded by his son Vīrapurisadāta whose reign marks a glorious epoch in the history of Buddhism in South India. The monastery of Nāgārjunikoṇḍā was developed in this period with the addition of Cetiya hall and *stambhas* or pillars mostly donated by the ladies of the royal family. Additions were also made to the Buddhist establishments at Amarāvatī and Jaggayyapeta. One of the Nāgārjunikoṇḍā epigraphs state that holy men from different countries used to visit the place at that time, while an inscription of the year 14 contains a list of the countries that had contact with the sacred shrine. These countries were Kāśmīra, Gandhāra, Kirāta in the Himalayas (possibly Tibet), Cīna, Tosali, Aparanta, Vaṅga, Vanavāsī, Damila or the Tamil country, Palura and Yavana or the 'Greek colony of North-west or South India or Southern Anam'.[5] Thus during the time of Vīrapurisadāta, the Ikṣvāku

1. B.V. Krishna Rao, *Early Dynasties of Āndhradeśa*, 45
2. *Ep Ind*, xx, 18
3. *EHAC*, 131
4. *ib.*, 134
5. *Select In.*, 226, fn. 1

kingdom of the Āndhradeśa attained an international status through Buddhism and this might have effected the economic prosperity of the country.

In considering the above list we may note that while we find mention of the countries lying to the south, west and north of the Ikṣvāku kingdom, the region lying immediately to the north of the territory, *the janapada of Mosala*, is significantly omitted, though the Kaliṅga region e.g. Palura = Dantapura finds there a place. Was Mosala included within the Ikṣvāku kingdom? It formed a part of the Sātavāhana territory and when Cāṃtamūla effected the *coup* it evidently came under his sway. Thus the Ikṣvāku kingdom was possibly larger in area than it has been supposed to be.

Like his father, Vīrapurisadāta appears to have contracted matrimonial alliances that strengthened the hands of the dynasty. The Nāgārjunikoṇḍā inscription of his 6th regnal year speaks of *mahādevī* Rudradharabhaṭārikā who is described as *Ujanikā-mahārabālikā*, which has been emended by J. Ph. Vogel as *Ujenikā-mahārāja-bālikā*.[1] Rudradharabhaṭārikā was thus evidently a Śaka princess of the house ruling over Ujjayinī. As her name is mentioned in an inscription of the year 6, we may presume that Vīrapurisadāta married the Śaka girl either immediately after his accession to the throne or this Śaka-Ikṣvāku alliance was contracted by his father Cāṃtamūla. D.C. Sircar observes that 'though there is no name like Rudradhara (of whom the queen might have been supposed to have been a sister or a daughter) in the genealogy of the Śakas of Ujjayinī, two kings having names beginning with Rudra reigned in the third century A.D.—(1) Rudrasena I, circa Śaka 122-135 (A.D. 200-213); (2) Rudrasena II, circa Śaka 176-196 (A.D. 254-274). It is not altogether impossible that the Ikṣvāku queen was related to one of these kings.'[2] It is not however necessary for us to find a Śaka king of Ujjayinī with a name beginning with Rudra so that he may be a father or brother of the queen. In a Basarh seal we find the name of (a Muruṇḍa queen) Prabhudamā who was sister of the king, the

1. *Ep Ind*, xx, 4
2. *Suc Sat*, 23

mahākṣatrapa svāmī Rudrasena, and daughter of the king, the mahākṣatrapa svāmī Rudrasiṃha.[1] In the present state of our knowledge it is impossible to determine the exact place of Rudradharabhaṭārikā in the Śaka family of Ujjayinī.

The Śaka-Ikṣvāku marriage was undoubtedly of some political significance. It may have checked the advance of the Ābhīras towards eastern Deccan, and thus a threat to the Ikṣvāku dominion was averted once for all. Evidently as a result of this marriage the Śakas came to be favoured in the new kingdom. Thus a Nāgārjunikoṇḍā record registers the gift of a pious Śaka girl and a Nāgārjunikoṇḍā pillar bears the sculpture of a Śaka warrior.[2]

Another such diplomatic marriage is hinted at in the epigraph of the son of Vīrapurisadāta, Ehuvula Cāṃtamūla, which records a donation of mahādevī Kodavalisiri, the daughter of Vīrapurisadāta and the wife of a king of Banavāsī (*Vanavāsaka mahārāja*).[3] Banavāsī, with its capital Vaijayantī, was a part of the Sātavāhana empire, and after the death of Yajñaśrī Śātakarṇi it passed ultimately under the rule of the Cuṭu dynasty. The Vanavāsaka mahārāja who was the son-in-law of the Ikṣvāku monarch might have been a member of the Cuṭu dynasty.

Besides Rudradharabhaṭārikā, Vīrapurisadāta appears to have other queens, three of whom were the daughters of his father's sisters. The system of cross-cousin marriage had been a feature of South Indian social life, and it was a recognised custom as early as the time of Bodhāyana (c. 400 B.C.). Kumārila Bhaṭṭa also refers to this custom.

From the epigraphic evidences it is clear that Vīrapurisadāta must have ruled at least for 20 years. Buddhism flourished in his kingdom, but there is no evidence to show that he himself became a Buddhist. It should, however, be noted that unlike his father, he did not claim to be protected by the god Mahāsena nor did he perform any Vedic sacrifice.

1. *ASIR*, 1913-4, 136
2. *Ep Ind*, xx, 37
3. *ib.*, 24

Ehuvula Cāṃtamūla

Vīrapurisadāta was succeeded by his son Ehuvula Cāṃtamūla. The first part of the name is possibly a Tamil one, *ehu* meaning steel, 'a very old Tamil word'.[1] Nothing practically is known about his reign excepting that Buddhism flourished further during his time.

Rudrapurisadāta

An inscription found at Nāgārjunikoṇḍā speaks of a king named Rudrapurisadāṭa who, from the find spot of the inscription, the palaeography of the record, and the form of the name, appears to have been an Ikṣvāku monarch, and may be identified with Rudapurisadāta of Gurzala record.[2] The step-mother of the king is named in inscription as Varambhaṭā and 'as the wife of *Mahārāja* Ehavala Chāntamūla, as the daughter-in-law of *Mahārāja* Vīrapurushadatta and as grand daughter-in-law of *Mahārāja* Chāntamūla. She is further stated to have belonged to the Bahapala (i.e., Bṛihatphala or Bṛihatphalāyana) *gotra* and to have been the daughter of a *Mahākhatapa* (*Mahākṣatrapa*). Thus the record supplies us with a second instance of the relations of the Ikṣvāku family of the Kṛṣṇa-Guntur region with that of the Śaka *Mahākṣatrapas* of Western India, the first being that of Māṭharīputra Vīrapurusadatta's marriage with *Mahādevī* Rudradhara-bhaṭārikā described as the *Ujanikā-mahāra*[*ia*]*-bālikā* (*Ujjayinikā-mahārāja-bālikā*, i.e., daughter of the *Mahārāja* of Ujjayinī) known from an inscription from the same place. The discovery of a big hoard of the coins of the Śaka rulers at Pēṭlūripālem in the Guntur district is also interesting to note in this connection. The presence of Śakas at the Ikṣvāku capital is also indicated by the epigraphic and sculptural records discovered at Nāgārjunikoṇḍā. Though the identity of the *Mahākṣatrapa* who was the father of queen Vaṁmabhaṭā is not disclosed, a very interesting information supplied for the first time by the inscription under study is that the Śaka *Mahākṣatrapas* of Western India claimed to have belonged to the Bṛhatphala or Bṛhatphalāyana *gotra*. While the Hinduization of these Śakas is clearly indicated by the records of Ṛshabha-

1. *EHAC*, 143, fn
2. *Ep Ind*, xxvi, 23ff

datta and Rudradāman, the Śakas in general were regarded in ancient India either as clean Śūdras or as degraded Kṣatriyas.' (*Ep. Ind.* xxxiv, 21)

It would thus appear that Rudrapurisadāta was a step-brother of Hārītīputra Vīrapuruṣadatta. It is however not known to us which of the two step-brothers ruled first. We have got an inscription of Hārītīputra Vīrapuruṣadatta commencing with the expression *siddham* followed by an invocation to the god Mahādeva Puṣpabhadrasvāmī and records the construction of a *devakula* and a *dhvajastambha* for the same god. The expression *devakula* is interesting. He is further stated to have created an endowment of a village evidently for the maintenance of the temple.

Prince Vīrapuruṣadatta is also styled as *mahārāja-kumāra* and *mahāsenāpati*. He was evidently the commander-in-chief of his father, Vāsiṣṭhīputra Ehavula Cāṃtamūla. Possibly Rudrapurisadāta succeeded him.

We do not know exactly how the rule of the Ikṣvākus came to an end. Rulupurisadāta was possibly overthrown by Siṃhavarman in the Guntur area while the Bṛhatphalāyana king Jayavarman occupied the Masulipatam region.

The Nāgārjunikoṇḍā records show how the Ikṣvāku kingdom had its relationship with the island of Ceylon. Thus inscription F mentions Sīhala-vihāra which, as J. Ph. Vogel states 'must have been a convent founded either by a Singhalese or, more probably, for the accommodation of Singhalese monks. This "Ceylonese convent" appears to have contained a shrine with a Bodhi-tree (Bodhi-rukhapāsāda = Skt. *Bodhi-vṛkṣaprāsāda*) which is, indeed, a necessary adjunct of the Buddhist monasteries of Ceylon up to the present day. Not only the mention of a Sīhala-*vihāra*, but also the dedication of a *chetiya-ghara* to the *theriyas* or "fraternities" of Tambapaṁṇi point to relations which must have existed between the Buddhist community of Dhaññakaṭaka and their co-religionists in the Isle of Ceylon. The existence of such relations can be easily accounted for from the sea-borne trade which was carried on between the ports of the Island and Kaṇṭakasela, the great emporium on the right bank of the Kistna river.'[1] J. Ph. Vogel makes the following observations in connection with Buddhism of the period which is really very interesting:

'This trade (between India and Ceylon) was, no doubt, also largely responsible for the flourishing state of Buddhism in this part of India. The devotees of the Good Law were largely recruited from the commercial classes and it was their wealth which enabled not only the merchants themselves, but also their royal masters, to raise monuments of such magnificence as the great *stūpa* of Amarāvatī. Both Amarāvatī and Nāgārjunikoṇḍā are situated on the right bank of the Kistna, the former being situated at a distance of some 60 miles from the mouth of the river. Nāgārjunikoṇḍā lies considerably higher up the river, the distance between this place and Amarāvatī being another 60 miles as the crow flies, but considerably longer by river. On the opposite side of the river we have Jaggayyapeta, containing another monument of the reign of the Ikhākus. The village of Allūru in the Nandigāma *taluk* of the Kistna district has yielded a fragmentary Prakrit inscription, referred to above, which appears to record a donation to a Buddhist monastery. At the village of Gummaḍiduru in the Kistna district the remains of a large *stūpa*, adorned with marble reliefs in the Amarāvatī style, have recently come to light together with the remnants of monastic buildings. All these monuments attest to the piety and the wealth of the Buddhist community in these parts during the second and third centuries of our era. In the days of Hiuen Tsiang the monasteries were mostly deserted and ruined. The collapse of Buddhism on the lower Kistna may have had various causes; besides the general wane of that religion all over India, there may have been economic agents at work, like the decline of the sea-borne trade with the West, which had caused vast quantities of Roman gold to pour into the Peninsula. There was also the conquest of Southern India by the Gupta Emperor Samudragupta and the rise of powerful dynasties devoted to Brahmanism like the Pallava in the South and the Chālukya in the West.'[2]

1. *Ep Ind*, xx, 10
2. *ib*.

The Guntur kings and the Pallavas

It has already been stated that the early history of the Pallava dynasty that ruled in Kāñcīpuram and is supposed to have been originally subordinate under the Sātavāhanas is shrouded in mystery. Siṃhavarman of the Guntur record has been supposed to be the first king of the dynasty.[1] As however no record of him has been found in the Kāñcī region we shall have to think before we rush to such a conclusion. It is not unlikely that when Jayavarman, the Bṛhatphalāyana king,[2] revolted against the Ikṣvākus in the Masulipatam region, Siṃhavarman became independent in the Guntur valley. On this assumption both Jayavarman and Siṃhavarman might have been originally governors under the Ikṣvākus. In any case, the conjecture that Siṃhavarman was the father of Śivaskandavarman lacks any direct evidence in its support.

The Pallavas were maintaining their precarious existence, of course independently, after the fall of the Sātavāhanas. The Mayidavolu grant issued from Kāñcīpuram by the Pallava Yuvamahārāja in the tenth year of the reigning Pallava king records the gift of a village named Viripāra situated in the Andhrāpatha, while the order was sent to the *vāpaṭa* i.e., the governor, of Dhaṃñakada (Dhānyakaṭaka) showing that the Ikṣvāku kingdom lying to the south of the river Kistna had passed under the Pallavas.[3] Unfortunately, the name of the father of the crown prince is not mentioned in the record. In the Hirahadagalli grant Śivaskandavarman refers to his father as Mahārāja-*bappasāmi*.[4] G. Bühler thinks that Bappasāmi is a proper name referring to the Yuvamahārāja's father, but recently the view has been challenged on the ground that kings often describe themselves as *bappabhaṭṭāraka-pādabhakta*, 'devoted to the feet of the lord, the father,' where *bappa* can hardly be construed as a personal name. The argument has no doubt some force but the use of the word Mahārāja-bappasāmi is somewhat on a different *par*. D.C. Sircar who rejects G. Bühler's view, himself points out, '*cf* Bappa, the name of the

1. *Ep Ind*, xxxii, 87-90
2. *ib.*, vi, 315
3. *ib.*, vi, 84-91
4. *ib.*, i. 2-10

progenitor of the Guhilots of Mewar, and also the names Bappa-sarman in the Birur grant of Kadamba Viṣṇuvarman and Bappasvāmin in the Nidhanpur grant of Bhāskaravarman.'[1]

While thus not pressing for any of the views centring round the word *bappasvāmi* we refrain from identifying him with Siṃhavarman of the Guntur record. In any case, Śivaskanda-varman's father's sway extended over Andhrāpatha. The Hirahadagalli grant credits Śivaskandavarman with Agniṣṭoma, Vājapeya and Aśvamedha sacrifices, signifying that he made fresh conquests before the eighth year of his reign when the grant was issued. He is also adorned with the title of *dharma-mahārājādhirāja*. What these fresh conquests were is difficult to determine. D.C. Sircar thinks that his sway was acknowledged by the Gaṅgas of Mysore and the Kadambas of Banavāsī. It is pointed out that the Penukonda plates of the Gaṅga king Mādhava refer to the suzerainty of the Pallavas of Kāñcī, while according to the Talgunda inscription the early Kadambas of Banavāsī also acknowledged the supremacy of the Pallavas.[2] But in no case it can be said with certainty that this suzerain was Śivaskandavarman.

It is very difficult to determine who succeeded Śivaskanda-varman. The British Museum plates of Cārudevī,[3] issued during the reign of *Sirivijaya* Khandavamma (Śrī-vijaya-Skandavar-man) record a gift to the god Nārāyaṇa of the *Kuli-mahātaraka-devakula*. Cārudevī is described as the wife of the Yuvamahārāja Buddhavarman and the mother of a prince whose name has been tentatively read as Buddhyaṅkura. From the epigraph it is not clear whether Buddhavarman was a son of Skandavarman nor there is any other evidence to show that Buddhavarman ever ascended the throne. As the British Museum grant was originally found in the Guntur district it is not unlikely that he belonged to the line of Siṃhavarman. After Siṃhavarman was overthrown by the father of Śivaskandavarman the former's line went temporarily into oblivion but revived again under Skandavarman, who is not known at all to have ruled at Kāñcī.

1. *Suc Sat*, 183, fn. 2
2. *ib.*, 184f
3. *Ep Ind*, viii, 143-6

Viṣṇugopa of Kāñcī who came into conflict with Samudragupta appears to have been a Pallava king though his relationship with Śivaskandavarman cannot be determined.[1]

The materials at our disposal for writing the history of the early Pallavas of Kāñcīpuram are very meagre. Three facts seem to come out of them:

a. that the main Pallava line ruled at Kāñcīpuram and the suzerainty of the dynasty extended from the river Palar in the south to Krishna in the north and the Bellary region in the west.

b. that the Krishna valley often changed hands. After the fall of the Ikṣvākus it passed under Siṃhavarman, then under the Kāñcī line and again under a descendant of Siṃhavarman.

c. that Viṣṇugopa who fought against Samudragupta had as a feudatory under him Ugrasena of Palakka ruling somewhere in the Nellore district.

1. D.C. Sircar thinks that Viṣṇugopa was a son of Skandavarman. T.V. Mahalingam, on the other hand, holds that Viṣṇugopa was the elder brother or son of Skandavarman and never ascended the throne on the main line. (*Kanchipuram*, 27)

Chapter IX

WESTERN DYNASTIES

It has already been stated that the Sātavāhana king Yajña-śrī Śātakarṇi died in c. 190 A.D. and after him there was a partition of the empire. The eastern branch ruled up to 213 A.D., while three kings at least, if not more, ruled in the west.[1] It is difficult to determine how long the western line survived, but when fresh light comes we find the Ābhīras occupying a considerable portion of the Marathi speaking area, while the Kanarese region passed under separate dynasties whose history is far from clear as yet. The Ābhīras were no doubt very strong and although their advance in the eastern Deccan was checked by the Ikṣvākus, it is really a mystery what prevented them from pushing towards the Kanarese area. In this connection it may be noted that Ptolemy (c. 140 A.D.) in his *Geography* refers to the Ariake of the Pirates who held Byzanteion or Vaijayantī.[2] The *Periplus* also refers to piracy in this region, but simply states that three islands on the western coast were under their control.[3] So some time after the days of the *Periplus* the pirates occupied a portion of the Kanarese district and brought the region round Vaijayantī under their control. Vaijayantī was the base of Gautamīputra's attack against the Kṣaharātas and it is not unlikely that it was lost to the Sātavāhanas either during the time of Pulumāyi or his successor who was involved in a life and death struggle against mahākṣatrapa Rudra-dāman.[4] Was Muḍānanda one of these pirate kings whose coins have been found in this region and by overthrowing whom the Cuṭus occupied the coastal district regions ? Thus in dealing with the western successors of the Sātavāhanas we have to take into account the history of the following dynasties:

1. The Ābhīras

1. *supra*
2. *Ptolemy*, ed. L. Renou, 4
3. *supra*
4. *surpa*

2. The dynasty of Muḍānanda (the pirate king ?)
3. The dynasty of the Cuṭus

The Ābhīras

The Ābhīras who succeeded the Sātavāhanas in the western Deccan were originally an alien people who, according to Tarn, entered into India during the confusion caused by the invasion of Alexander the Great.[1] It is difficult to determine what the original home of the tribe was, but the name of the country Abiravan, in eastern Iran, reminds us of one of their settlements before they entered India. The earliest mention of the Ābhīras is to be found in the *Mahābhāṣya* of Patañjali where they are classed as śūdra.[2] One of their settlements is referred to in the Great Epic near the Vinaśana region, the present Hissar in Haryana.[3] Another colony is mentioned as Abiria in the *Periplus* and Aberia in the *Geography* of Ptolemy, according to which it formed a part of the Indo-Scythia or the Lower Indus Valley.[4]

Epigraphic evidences show the gradual movement of the

1. *GBI*, 712
2. *Mahābhāṣya*, i. 2.3
3. *Mbh.*, ix.37.1; 'The Mahābhārata mentions three divisions of the Ābhīras dwelling in the north-west of India, viz., those who lived on the bank of the Sarasvatī, fisherman and mountaineers. (Sabhāparvan, ad. 32, v. 10) In another passage the Epic states that the *tīrtha* Vinaśana lay in the country of the Ābhīras as the sacred river Sarasvatī disappeared at the place through hatred of the Śūdras and the Ābhīras living there. (Śalyaparvan, ad. 37, v. 1) Elsewhere, Pañchananda, the land of the five rivers, is described as the stronghold of the Ābhīras. (Mauṣalaparvan, ad. 7, vv. 45ff) We are told that while Arjuna was encamped in that fertile country together with the women of the Vrishṇis and the Andhakas, whom he was escorting from Dvārakā to Hastināpura after the internecine fight amongst the Yādavas, he was attacked by the Ābhīras. All these references indicate the eastern part of the Panjab between the Satlaj and the Yamunā as the original home-land of the Ābhīras'. (*Corpus*, iv, xxxi) V.V. Mirashi however thinks that 'the Ābhīras were probably the aboriginal inhabitants of the country who were gradually admitted to the Hindu fold.' (*ib.*)
4. From the *Geography* of Ptolemy it appears that the lower Indus Valley was known as Indo-Scythia and it consisted of three countries, Patalene or the Indus delta, Aberia or the Ābhīra country and Surastrene or Kathiawad.

tribe into Madhya Pradesh and then into Maharashtra where after the Sātavāhanas they founded a kingdom of their own. The Gunda inscription of 181 A.D. shows the Ābhīra general Rudrabhūti referring to Rudrasiṃha as kṣatrapa, ignoring the existence of any mahākṣatrapa altogether.[1] This shows that though not assuming any higher title, the Ābhīra general was the *de facto* ruler in the state. General Rudrabhūti is described as the son of general Bāpaka.[2] It appears that the Ābhīras first entered into service under the Śaka rulers of Ujjayinī and then gradually came to the forefront. D.R. Bhandarkar thinks that when during the period 188-190 A.D. there was no *mahākṣatrapa* in the Śaka kingdom of Ujjayinī, one Ābhīra king Īśvaradatta ruled over the realm. E.J. Rapson has, however, no doubt that Īśvaradatta 'reigned some time between A.D. 236 and A.D. 239'.[3] Īśvaradatta's silver coins have been found in Malwa, Gujarat and Kathiawad. We fully agree with the view of E.J. Rapson. Yajñaśrī Śātakarṇi's coins show his victory over the Śakas of Ujjayinī and on all accounts his rule appears to have spread over the last quarter of the second century A.D. Further from the history of the Śaka *kṣatrapas* of Ujjayinī we know that whenever there was any foreign rule over the Śaka dominion, the office of the *mahākṣatrapa* remained in abeyance and so we can only connect the period 188-190 A.D. with Sātavāhana rule over the Śaka realm.[4]

An inscription dated in the 9th regnal year of an Ābhīra king named Māḍharīputra Īśvarasena has been found at Nasik.[5] Māḍharīputra Īśvarasena is described as the son of Śivadatta. It records the gift of Śakānī Viṣṇudattā, daughter of Śaka Agnivarman, wife of the *Gaṇapaka* Rebhila and mother of *Gaṇapaka* Viśvavarman, of three investments of 2000, 1000 and 500 kārṣāpaṇas in the trade guilds of Govardhana for the purpose of providing medicines for the sick Buddhist monks living at the monastery on mount Triraśmi. The epigraph points to the following interesting facts:

1. *Ep Ind*, xvi, 233
2. *Ind Ant*, x, 157; *Ep Ind*, xvi, 235
3. E.J. Rapson, *CIC*
4. *supra*
5. *Ep Ind*, viii, 88

(i) that Śivadatta is not given any royal honorific showing that Īśvarasena became the first king of his line;

(ii) that the record follows the Sātavāhana mode of dating;

(iii) that the Śakas had been living in the Western Maharashtra region possibly in the service of the Ābhīra lord.

Now, about one thing we are almost sure. The Ābhīra rule in Western Maharashtra started after the rule of three or more kings in succession to Yajñaśrī Śātakarṇi.[1] Thus it is quite possible that Īśvarasena might have begun his rule in 248-9 A.D., and he started an era from that year to commemorate his accession. From the later use of the era, we may infer that the empire of Īśvarasena comprised the region of Western Maharashtra, including Nasik and the adjoining areas, Aparānta and Lāṭa.

An inscription has been found at Nāgārjunakoṇḍā of the time of Ābhīra Vasuṣena of the year 30. It is difficult to determine whether Vasuṣena actually ruled over the Guntur region, but in the present state of our knowledge we may maintain this much that the Ābhīra king ruled over the Nasik region and extended his sway over the Krishna-Guntur area about 278 A.D. From the internal evidences of the record it does not appear that it is a record of pilgrimage. (*Ep. Ind.* xxxiv, 202ff)

The above instance seems to indicate that the Ābhīra kingdom in South India was far more extended than we are apt to think. It is not unlikely that the Muṇḍas and the Cuṭus were originally subordinates to the Ābhīras but later on managed to regain their independence. The *Viṣṇu Purāṇa* maintains that thirteen Muṇḍa kings ruled after the Andhras. Large lead coins bearing the legend *raño Mudanaṃdasa* have been found from the district of Karwar. Muḍa is evidently identical with Muṇḍas. The coins clearly belong to one of the members of the subordinate dynasty.

1. As the Traikūṭaka era is associated with the Ābhīras it is apparent that several kings ruled in Western Deccan between Yajñaśrī Śātakarṇi's death in 190 A.D. and 248-9 A.D., the initial year of the Traikūṭaka era.

The Cuṭus also possibly started as subordinates to the Ābhīras but later on became independent. We have several lead coins bearing the legend *raño Cuṭu-kulānandasa*. The fact that the Muḍānanda coins and these coins have been found in the same region practically proves nothing, for such pieces often travel from one place to another. We have at least two inscriptions referring to the Cuṭu kings. Thus a Banavāsī stone inscription mentions Hārītīputra Viṣṇukaḍa Cuṭu-kulānanda Śātakarṇi who in the twelfth year of his reign made a gift of a *nāga*, a tank and a *vihāra*. The Mallavalli inscription refers to the same king Mānavyasagotra Hārītīputra Viṣṇukaḍḍa Cuṭu-kulānanda Śātakarṇi who in the first year of his reign made the grant of a village. The king is described as the *rājā* of the city of Vaijayantī.

On the same pillar there is an inscription of an early Kadamba king referring to Mānavya-sagotra Hārītīputra Vaiyayantīpati Śivaskandavarman who is stated to have ruled in the same locality. This Śivaskandavarman has been supposed to be a member of the Cuṭu dynasty which, however, seems to be quite unconvincing since he does not adopt title like Cuṭu-kulānanda.

According to the Purāṇas, the Ābhīras ruled for 67 years.[1] In other words, the Ābhīra rule continued from 248-9 A.D. to 315-6 A.D. V.V. Mirashi, however, maintains that 'this is abnormally low. Perhaps the expression *sapta-shashṭi śatān = īha*, stating the period of Ābhīra rule, which occurs in a manuscript of the *Vāyu Purāṇa*, is a mistake for *sapta-shashtim śatañ = ch = īha*. In that case the Ābhīra rule may have lasted for 167 years or till 415 A.C.'[2] In support of this view it may be pointed out that the Kadamba king Mayūraśarman who ruled from c. 340 to c. 360 A.D. refers to his fight with the Ābhīras and (their subordinates) the Traikūṭakas.

V.V. Mirashi further maintains that the Ābhīras had the following feudatories under them[3] :

a. the *mahārājas* of Valkha (Vāghli) in Chalisgaon *tāluka* of East Khandesh

1. *DKA*, 46
2. *Corpus*, iv, xxvi
3. *ib.*, xxvff

b. Īśvararata ruling in Central Gujarat
c. the kings of Māhiṣmatī
d. the Traikūṭakas

The above scheme of feudatories rests *firstly* on the emendation of 67 to 167 years for the duration of Ābhīra rule and *also* on the supposition that the inscriptions of the first three feudatories at least are dated in the Ābhīra or the Traikūṭaka era. Otherwise, the whole account falls through.

Epigraphic records disclose the names of following Valkha rulers, *mahārāja* Svāmidāsa (year 67), *mahārāja* Bhuluṇḍa (year 107), *mahārāja* Rudradāsa (year 117). As these grants do not mention any royal genealogy but simply describe each of the three *mahārājas* as *paramabhaṭṭārakapādānudhyāta* it is clear that they were subordinate rulers but the relationship of one with the other is not known.[1]

Īśvararāta, who meditated on the feet of a lord paramount, 'appears to have ruled over a fairly extensive territory; for, among the persons to whom he addressed his order are 'included such high officers of the state as *kumārāmātya* and *uparika*.' He appears to have held Central Gujarat and some portions of the Khandesh district.

V.V. Mirashi's view that the kings of Māhiṣmatī were subordinates under the Ābhīras will not be readily accepted by scholars. Two coins discovered from the region give the legend *raño Sagamānamahasa* (*sa*). Palaeographically, the coins would belong to the period 200-300 A.D. It has been suggested that Saga-Māna was a Śaka or Scythian king 'who may previously have been an officer or perhaps a feudatory of the Sātavāhanas, but he later on declared his independence in token of which he issued his own coinage. He had evidently a fairly extensive dominion, for he is one of the few kings of the historic period, to be named in the Purāṇas.' If we accept the reading of the Purāṇic text as amended by Mirashi *Śakya-Māno — bhavad rājā Mahiṣinām mahīpatiḥ* then it is possible to some extent to agree with the view that there was really a Śaka king of the name of Māna, though we have to admit at the same time that the account is hopelessly a corrupt one.

1. *Corpus*, iv, xxvff

Mirashi thinks that (a) Māna was 'the founder of a dynasty which may have continued to flourish for some generations'; (b) that Śaka Śrīdharavarman of the Kanakhera record, was a member of the dynasty; (c) that the Śaka who submitted to Samudragupta, as mentioned in the Allahabad Pillar inscription, should be identical with this Śaka dynasty of the Anūpa country. All these are possible theories, but have yet to be proved.

In *CII*, iv, xxxvii ff, V.V. Mirashi maintains that Śrīdharavarman, the *mahādaṇḍanāyaka*, the son of Śaka Nanda, whose stone inscription, recording the excavation of a well, has been found at Kanakhera near Sanchi in Bhopal, was a subordinate ruler under the Ābhīras. It is maintained that the inscription is dated in the thirteenth year of Śrīdharavarman's reign and also in the year 102, which being referred to the Ābhīra era becomes equivalent to 351-52 A.D......... This view, however, is not shared by other scholars. According to N.G. Majumdar, the inscription is dated in the Śaka year 241 = 319 A.D. There was no *mahākṣatrapa* in the Śaka dominion from A.D. 295 to c. 340 A.D., when apparently the Śaka kingdom was passing through some crisis.[1] Probably, taking advantage of this adverse situation, Śrīdharavarman, originally an official of the Śaka house of Malwa, declared his independence. The inscription seems to be dated in his own thirteenth regnal year. The view of R.D. Banerjee that the regnal year refers to Jīvadāman's rule can hardly be accepted, because the latter never ruled. Like so many other cases, Śrīdharavarman used his original official or subordinate titles, even after he had assumed independence.[2]

Thus it is difficult to agree with the view that the Ābhīras extended their rule to Anūpa (the country round Māhiṣmatī) and Ākarāvanti or the Malwa region.

About the Traikūṭakas who are supposed to have been subordinates under the Ābhīras we have no early records. As already stated, they are mentioned in the Chandravalli inscrip-

1. Chattopadhyaya, *The Śakas in India*, 85
2. *ib.*, 79

tion of Mayūraśarman along with the Ābhīras. Bhagavanlal Indraji propounded the theory that the Ābhīras and the Traikūṭakas were identical.[1] But this seems to be disproved by their separate mention in the Kadamba record.[2]

1. 'In recent times, R.B. Hiralal, who identified the Traikūṭakas with the Kalacuris, has expressed the view that Trikūṭa is identical with the Sātpurā mountain which was so called on account of its three prominent peaks, viz., the Āmrakūṭa or Amarakaṇṭaka in the former Rewa State, Sālakūṭa in the Balaghat district and Madhukūṭa in the Chhindware district. (*A.B.O.R.I.*, Vol. IX, pp. 283-84) As shown below, the inscriptions and coins of the Traikūṭakas have been found only in South Gujarat, North Konkan and Maharashtra. Traikūṭa, from which they derived their name, cannot, therefore, be located in the north, east, south or centre of India, but must be looked for in the west. Kālidāsa's description, which, as already stated, is supported by a lexicon, clearly indicates that it was situated in Aparānta or North Konkan'. (*Corpus*, iv, xl-xli)
2. 'Kadaṃbānam Mayūraśammaṇa vinimmiaṃ taṭākam [kuṭa]-Tekuḍa-Abhira-Pallava-Puri-yotik-Sakastha [na]-Sayinthaka-Punda-Mokari [na]'. (*Select Ins.*, 449)

PART III

THE VĀKĀṬAKAS OF MAHARASHTRA

Chapter X

SOURCES

Our chief sources for studying the history of the Vākāṭaka dynasty are the following :—

(a) the Purāṇas

(b) the *Daśakumāracarita* of Daṇḍin

(c) the charters left by the Vākāṭaka sovereign themselves and their feudatories.

A

The Purāṇic account of the Vākāṭakas is a hopelessly confused one. Thus it is stated :—

(a) '*Then after the Kilakilas Vindhyaśakti will reign. He will enter after it has known those kings* 96 *years*.'[1]

(b) '*Vindhyaśakti's valiant son, named Pravīra, will enjoy the city Kāñcanakā* 60 *years, and will sacrifice with vājapeya sacrifices replete with choice largesse. His* 4 *sons will be kings*.'[2]

The first account quoted above is given in connection with 'various local dynasties' that ruled after the fall of the Āndhras or the Sātavāhanas. The family name Vākāṭaka is never mentioned in the sacred lore. From the Ajanta inscription of Hariṣena, we learn that Vindhyaśakti was the founder (*vaṃśa-keta*) of the Vākāṭaka dynasty.[3] We know nothing about the Kilakilas. The *Viṣṇu Purāṇa* states that they were Yavanas, and Vindhyaśakti is also called a Yavana in that work,[4] though we learn from the inscriptions that the Vākāṭakas were brāhmaṇas of the Viṣṇuvṛddha gotra. From the account, K.P. Jayaswal has inferred that the Purāṇas connect Vindhyaśakti with the Kilakila country, i.e., the region ruled over by the Kilakilas, and that it is the territory drained over by the river of the same

1. *DKA*, 72
2. *ib.*, 73
3. *Select Ins.*, 425
4. *Viṣṇu Purāṇa*

name in Punna in Bundelkhand,[1] M.P. The Purāṇic passages in question have jumbled up the accounts of *ten* different dynasties that ruled after the fall of the Āndhras or the Sātavāhanas.[2] These dynasties did not always rule over the same kingdom. So the expression 'after the Kilakilas' may simply have reference to time not to territory, but this is also very doubtful in view of the nature of the Purāṇic description. The second part of the statement '*he* (*Vindhyaśakti*) *will enter upon the earth after it has known those kings* 96 *years*' is somewhat ambiguous. F.E. Pargiter remarks that "this seems to be the meaning, but literally, 'he after having known 96 years will enter upon the earth'; but evidently finding that this also carries no 'meaning', he remarks that the sentence then would be 'after having known the earth 96 years, he will come to his end'."[3]

Let us now turn to *b* above. It has been generally taken to mean that here Pravīra and his father Vindhyaśakti are associated with the Vidiśā region since this section opens with the line: 'Hear also the future kings of Vidiśā'. A perusal of the section shows that it should be divided into three parts: *ll.* 1-6, speaks of the Nāga kings of Vidiśā; *ll.* 7-10, the kings who will reign (possibly in Purikā), 'when the family of the Śuṅgas ends,' while, the last four lines of the passage describe Vindhyaśakti's son Pravīra who ruled in Kāñcanakā.[4] This Kāñcanakā cannot at once be connected with the Vidiśā region; in fact, it has not yet been identified.

So by combining the two Purāṇic passages we get the following:

Vindhyaśakti was the founder of the dynasty and he lived for 96 *years. His son was Pravira who ruled for* 60 *years and performed vājapeya and other sacrifices. His four sons became kings.*

A critical study of the Purāṇic traditions in the background of the available epigraphs will show at once their unhistorical character. If Vindhyaśakti lived for 96 years and then died evidently as a king, then it appears to be impossible that his son would rule for 60 years in succession. It may be noted here that

1. K.P. Jayaswal, *History of India*, 66-8
2. *infra*
3. *l.c.*, 72, fn. 21
4. *ib.*, 49-50

Vindhyaśakti's name is mentioned only in the Ajanta record among so many Vākāṭaka epigraphs, and even there he is not mentioned as a king. Again, the Purāṇas maintain that four sons of Pravīra (Pravarasena) became king i.e., the Vākāṭaka kingdom became divided into four parts after his death. The epigraphs, on the other hand, show that the Vākāṭaka kingdom became divided into two parts, and this division took place not after the death of Pravarasena, but possibly after the death of his son Sarvasena, as we shall see later on. Thus the only sober information that the Purāṇas supply is that Vindhyaśakti had a son named Pravīra who performed many sacrifices and that Pravīra ruled in Kāñcanakā, and not in Vidiśā or Purikā as it has been supposed by scholars from a wrong understanding of the Purāṇic account.

The *Daśakumāracarita* of Daṇḍin is regarded as a romance and a didactic work 'an attempt to teach the doctrines of the Nītisāra in narratives of attractive character',[1] V.V. Mirashi maintains that it is an important source for studying the history of the Vākāṭakas.[2] If Mirashi's interpretation of the account be accepted, then we get in it reference to a Vākāṭaka king, not mentioned in the epigraphic records, who ruled after Hariṣena.

The charters left by the Vākāṭaka emperors themselves and their feudatories are the most important source for the history of the dynasty. In case of the feudatories, however, we are often in difficulty, for as it has been observed, the Vākāṭakas 'do not seem to have insisted on their feudatories specially mentioning their suzerainty in records',[3] and we are often left to guesswork on the basis of other evidences. Only in a few cases, this suzerainty is specifically noted, e.g., the Nachna-ki-talai and the Ganj inscriptions which mention prince Vyāghradeva as meditating on the feet of the Vākāṭaka Pṛthivīsena', and Bamhani plates of Pāṇḍava king Bharatabala which indirectly refer to Narendrasena.[4]

1. A.B. Keith, *History of Sanskrit Literature*, 299
2. *ABORI*, xxvi, 20-31
3. *Ep Ind.*, xxiii, 173
4. *ib.*, xxvii, 137

In conclusion, we may refer to the views of K.P. Jayaswal who has attributed the coins bearing the legend *Pravarasenasya* with the date 76, (?) and another having the legend *Rudra*, and the date 100, (?) to the Vākāṭakas. According to him, the dates refer to the Kalacuri-Cedi era which was started by the Vākāṭakas in the year 248.[1] The view has already been refuted by A.S. Altekar who pointed out that the legend read by Jayaswal as Pravarasena is Vīrasena, while the symbols taken as 76 are really the branches of a tree in railing. Again, what has been read as Rudra is only a *triratna* symbol and the date 100 a *svastika*.[2] M.G. Pai advocates that the Kalacuri-Cedi era was started by the Vākāṭaka king Pravasena I in 248 A.D. to mark the assumption of his title of *samrāṭ*, after his aśvamedha sacrifice.[3] We have already seen that the era was started by the Ābhīras.

Original Home

As already stated, scholars have generally sought for the original home of the dynasty on the north of the Vindhya in Vidiśā or the adjoining regions on a wrong understanding of the Purāṇic account regarding Vindhyaśakti and Pravīra (*supra*). Attempts have again been made to confirm this misconception by other evidences of doubtful character. Thus K.P. Jayaswal maintains that Bundelkhand was the original home of the dynasty, and makes the following suggestions in support of his theory :—

(a) there is a village called Bajaur—Bagat in Bundelkhand, and Bagat is to be connected with the name Vākāṭaka.

(b) a pillar at Durcha, four miles south of Jaso in Bundelkhand, bears the inscription *Vākāṭakānām*.

(c) an inscription of Vyāghradeva, a feudatory of the Vākāṭaka king Pṛthivīsena, has been found at Nachna which is in Bundelkhand,[4] and this Nachna should be identified with *Chanakā* where Pravīra ruled according to the Purāṇas.[5]

1. *l.c.*, 52ff, 108ff
2. *JNSI*, v, 130ff
3. *JIH*, xiv, 184ff
4. *Corpus*, iii, 234ff
5. K.P. Jayaswal, *l.c.*, 66-8 & App. A

It is really difficult to accept any of the above arguments. There is nothing but only phonetic semblance between Bagat and Vākāṭaka, while what has been read as Vākāṭakānām is really *Vaṅkattrikanam*, 'which cannot be interpreted'. (A.S. Altekar) As we shall see later on, Bundelkhand region was conquered by Pṛthivīsena I, and then Vyāghradeva became his vassal. Further the reading of the Purāṇas is clearly Kāñcanakā, as the name of the capital of Pravīra, which Jayaswal emends as Canankā. Even if we accept it, then it can hardly be identified with Nachna, for as A.S. Altekar says, 'how can we explain the presence of a feudatory ruler at the same place as his sovereign ?'[1]

There is no definite evidence that the Vākāṭakas were of northern origin. Hence it is difficult to agree with V.A. Smith when he states that 'if Vindhyaśakti and Pravarasena are the same person as Vindhyaśakti and Pravīra of the Purāṇas, the origin of the family might be sought somewhere in the area now known as Central India (M.P.)'.[2] On the other hand, we meet for the first time with the name Vākāṭaka in an inscription on a pillar at Amarāvatī. There it is the name of a person and no definite conclusion can be drawn from it regarding the original home of the tribe; but at the same time it is not possibly without significance that the first mention of the name comes from South India. It should further be noted in this connection that all the charters, excepting one, of the dynasty have been found in the region lying to the south of the Vindhya, and that *one* also—the Indore plates of Pravarasena II[3] —might have been carried to the place, as assumed by V.V. Mirashi, who observes that 'these plates were found in the collection of the late Pandit Vamanasastri Islampurkar. It is well-known that the Pandit was engaged in collecting old Sanskrit manuscripts and historical records from different parts of the country. I have shown elsewhere that the two other grants found in his collection at Indore were originally from Khandesh and the places mentioned in them can also be located in Khandesh. As all other copper-plate grants of the

1. *EHD*, ed. G. Yazdani, 154
2. *JRAS*, 1914, 329
3. *Ep Ind.*, xxiv, 52ff

Vākāṭakas discovered so far originally came from Vidarbha, the Indore copper-plate grant also, in all probability, belongs to the same part of the country. None of the places mentioned in it have been located in North India.' (*CII*, V, XIII). Even if Indore be considered to be the original site of the record, it cannot go against the South Indian origin theory of the Vākāṭakas, for as we have already indicated, Pṛthivīsena I appears to have conquered a portion of the Madhya Pradesh region, which may thus have formed a part of the empire of Pravarasena II. It should, however, be noted in this connection, that immediately after Pṛthivīsena I the M.P. region passed under the rule of the Gupta Mahārājādhirāja Candragupta II.

While writing on the Basim plates of Vindhyaśakti II, V.V. Mirashi made the following interesting observations :—

(a) there are several Prakrit technical terms common to this plate and the Hirahadagalli and the Mayidavalu plates of the Pallava king Śivaskandavarman;

(b) the titles Hārītīputra and Dharmamahārāja given to Pravarasena I, Sarvasena and Vindhyaśakti II in the above grant are on a *par* with the use of such titles in the grants of the early southern dynasties like the Cuṭus, Pallavas, Kadambas and the early Cālukyas.[1]

It has further been pointed out that 'the patronage that the Vākāṭakas extended to a ministerial family of South India for several generations may also indicate their southern origin. This family was named Vallūra after the village Vallūra in the southern region which was its original place of residence. This place has not yet been definitely identified, but it may be the same as modern Velūr, which lies 30 miles north by east of Hyderabad in the Yelgandal district of the former Hyderabad state.' (*CII*, VXVf).

In view of the above discussions we may possibly infer that the Vākāṭakas were of southern origin and their homeland might have been in the Vidarbha country. From this base they expanded towards the north and west and brought a portion of the Madhya Pradesh region also under their control. G. J-Dubreuil has very aptly observed, 'When trying to compile

1. *Ep. Ind.*, xxvi, 137ff

the ancient history of the Deccan, I have come to the conclusion that the Vākāṭakas must be classed among the dynasties of the Deccan; and what is more, I can affirm that of all the dynasties of the Deccan that have reigned from the III to the VI century, the most glorious, the most important, the one that must be given the place of honour, the one that has excelled all others, the one that has had the greatest influence on the civilisation of the whole of the Deccan, is unquestionably the illustrious dynasty of the Vākāṭakas."[1]

V.V. Mirashi has observed : 'The Vākāṭakas were one of the most glorious dynasties that flourished in South India in ancient times. Their empire at one time extended from Malwa and Gujarat in the north to the Tuṅgabhadrā in the south and from the Arabian Sea to the west to the Bay of Bengal in the east. They were great patrons of literature. The liberal patronage they gave to Sanskrit and Prakrit poets soon brought the Vaidarbhī and Vachchōmī *ritis* into prominence and induced great poets like Kālidāsa to adopt them for their works. They themselves composed *Kāvyas* and *subhāshitas* which have evoked praise from famous poets and rhetoricians like Bāṇa and Daṇḍin, Kuntaka and Hemachandra. The temples they erected are no longer in existence, but the sculptures found in their ruins have attracted the notice of art-critics, who rank them among the best specimens of ancient times. The magnificent *vihāra* and *chaitya* caves which their ministers and feudatories excavated out of solid rock at Ajanta and Gulwāḍa still excite the admiration of the world.' (*CII*, v, i)

Our inference regarding the original home of the Vākāṭakas is confirmed to some extent by the evidence of the Sassanid Paikuli inscription. It mentions the Ābhīras and the kṣatrapas of Malwa as subordinates under the then ruler of Iran, but is absolutely silent about the Vākāṭakas. Had Indore or Vidiśā been the home of the dynasty, we may expect that they would have been brought under the Sassanid yoke and mentioned in that epigraph. In fact, the Vākāṭaka expansion began from south towards the north and not *vice versa*.

It may of course be pointed out that the Paikuli inscription has got no direct bearing on the evidence of the early home of

1. *AHD*, 71

the Vākāṭakas, since it does not preclude the existence of the dynasty in the eastern Madhya Pradesh region. But still we may use it as an indirect evidence corroborating other sources of information. We have to bring in the evidence since it has been supposed that Vindhyaśakti and Pravīra ruled not far from Vidiśā, modern Besnagar near Bhilsa. Such a wrong idea arose from a misunderstanding of the Purāṇic account quoted before and herein the Paikuli record comes to our help.

Genealogy and chronology of the Vākāṭakas

The genealogy and chronology of the Vākāṭakas are still in a very unsettled state. R.C. Majumdar has presented us with the following table :[1]

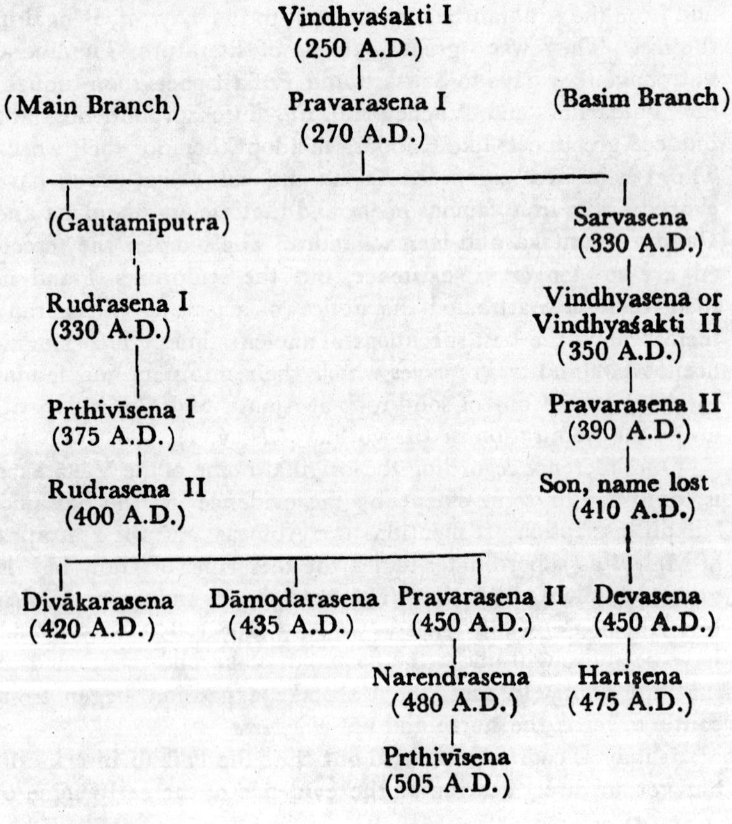

1. *JRASB (L)*, xii, 1-5

V.V. Mirashi rejects the table of R.C. Majumdar and suggests the following one in its place :[1]

Vindhyaśakti
(250 A.D.)
|
Pravarasena I
(270 A.D.)
|

Main Branch
|
(Gautamīputra)
|
Rudrasena I
(330 A.D.)
|
Pṛthivīsena I
(350 A.D.)
|
Rudrasena II
(400 A.D.)

- Divakarasena (405 A.D.)
- Pravarasena II (420 A.D.)
  |
  Narendrasena (450 A.D.)
  |
  Pṛthivīsena (470 A.D.)

Basim Branch
|
Sarvasena
(330 A.D.)
|
Vindhyasena
(355 A.D.)
|
Pravarasena II
(400 A.D.)
|
Son (unnamed)
(410 A.D.)
|
Devasena
(450 A.D.)
|
Hariṣena
(475 A.D.)
|
Son (Name unknown)
(500 A.D.)

Genealogy

We have to enquire at the outset how many sons did Rudrasena II leave after his death. The Poona C.P. inscription of Prabhāvatī Gupta[2] describes her as the daughter of the Gupta king Candragupta, son of Samudragupta, and as the chief queen of the Vākāṭaka mahārāja Śrī Rudrasena and as the mother of *yuvaraja* (crown prince) Divākarasena. The inscription on the

1. *IHQ*, xxiv, 148-55
2. *Ep Ind.*, xv, 30ff

seal of the record shows that the charter was issued in the thirteenth year of her regency. This shows that at the time of the epigraph king Rudrasena was dead and Prabhāvatī Guptā was acting as the regent of her minor son Divākarasena, who was, however, not less than thirteen years of age. The Rithpur C.P. inscription[1] of Prabhāvatī Guptā of the nineteenth regnal year of Pravarasena II, on the other hand, describes her......... as '*Vākāṭakānāṃ mahārāja Śrī-Dāmodarasena-Pravarasena-jananī*' and as '*sāgra-varṣa-śata-divaputra-pautrā*.' It has been maintained that *diva* is a mistake for *jīva*.[2] It means that Prabhāvatī Guptā lived for hundred years at the time of the execution of the epigraph and she was *jīva-putra-pautrā* at that time.

V.V. Mirashi, however, gives an entirely different interpretation of the line observing that the expression *diva-putra-pautrā* means 'having living sons and grandsons.' 'Similar expressions *jīva-sutā* or *jīva-putrā* occur in the Ṛgveda, the *Mahābhārata* and the *Rāmāyaṇa* as well as in some old inscriptions. To have living sons and grandsons is regarded as a sign of good fortune and is therefore often mentioned in the description of women. The preceding expression *s-āgra-varsha-śata* indicating long life must evidently be connected with *jīva*. The expression, therefore, refers to the long life of the sons and grandsons of Prabhāvatī and not to her own. Besides, to a widow like Prabhāvatī Guptā a long life of a hundred years is most distasteful. No Indian widow is likely to boast of it in her own record. The long life mentioned in the expression must therefore be taken to refer to that of the sons and grandsons of Prabhāvatī. The expression cannot, of course, be taken literally, but must be interpreted like the epithets *dīrghāyuḥ* or *āyushmat* applied to small children. The intention in such cases is to express the wish that they would be long-lived. The expression therefore means "who has sons and grandsons who (it is hoped) will live for a full hundred years." ' (*CII*, v, 34-5)

All such criticisms and interpretations hinge on the term *jīvaputrapautrā*. The record, as it stands, contains the expression *diva* meaning *heaven*. Can we change it to *jīva*, which would show that all the sons and grandsons of Prabhāvatī Guptā

1. *Select Ins.*, 415ff
2. *ib.*, 416, fn. 8

were living at the time of the execution of the epigraph ? R.C. Majumdar's chart shows that two of her sons were already dead, while according to Mirashi's account the number would be one. The plate was issued from the holy place of Ramagiri where evidently the dowager queen's mind was filled with grief and emotion. Here we may scent rather the funeral oration of a lamenting lady. In this background R.C. Majumdar's division of the expression into two parts sāgravarṣaśatā, as referring to Prabhāvatī Guptā herself, meaning, who was full hundred years of age, seems to be more reasonable. In that case, the other expression *divaputrapautrā* would mean one whose few sons and grandsons were already dead.

We should now study the Poona plates in the background of the above accounts :

(a) The non-mention of Divākarasena together with the description of Prabhāvatī as *sāgravarṣaśatā divaputrapautrā* shows that he was already dead at the time of the execution of the epigraph.

(b) The description of the dowager queen as *mahārāja-Śrī Dāmodarasena-Pravarasena-janani* has caused some difficulty with scholars. Two different theories have been put forward : *first*, that Dāmodarasena and Pravarasena were one and the same person and, *secondly*, that actually Dāmodarasena was dead at the time of the execution of the epigraph and the epithet *mahārāja* is added before his name to show that he also ascended the throne and was ultimately succeeded by his younger brother, Pravarasena II.

R.C. Majumdar has pointed out the defect of the first theory on two grounds : *first*, 'in that case it would be somewhat unusual to mention the two names together'; *secondly*, 'as noted above Prabhāvatī Guptā was more than hundred years old in the nineteenth year of Pravarasena II. If this king had ascended the throne immediately after he had become a major, as his identification with Dāmodarasena would imply, then he would have been forty years of age at the time of the Rithpur grant. As his mother was more than 100 years old, she must have been more than sixty when Dāmodarasena alias Pravarasena was born. This must be regarded as very unusual.'[1] Thus we cannot accept the theory of A.S. Altekar

1. *JRASB (L)*, xii, 3

that 'Divākarasena died while yet a minor, that his younger brother Dāmodarasena, another minor succeeded him and that Prabhāvatī continued to be the regent till the latter came of age and assumed full power of administration under the name of Pravarasena II.[1]

So on the basis of the above accounts we can draw the following conclusions :—

1. After the death of Rudrasena II, Prabhāvatī Guptā became the regent of her minor son Divākarasena. This regency lasted at least for 13 years, and then Divākarasena died and his brother Dāmodarasena succeeded him.
2. When Prabhāvatī Guptā was nearly 100 years of age, both her sons Dāmodarasena and Pravarasena had been alive. R.C. Majumdar's table seems to indicate that Pravarasena began his rule after the death of Dāmodarasena. The Rithpur C.P. is dated in the 19th year of Pravarasena, and as in *l.* 10 of the record the name of Dāmodarasena is preceded by the word *mahārāja* the natural inference is that there was a partition of the Vākāṭaka empire between the two brothers. The land granted evidently fell within the kingdom of Pravarasena and hence his regnal year has been mentioned in the record.

We now turn to the *Vatsagulma* or *Basim* branch. The above genealogy possibly needs some modifications in two respects. *First*, according to the Basim record, Sarvasena, the first king of the branch was succeeded by his son Vindhyaśakti or Vindhyasena. In the Ajanta inscription of the time of Hariṣena, however, the name of the son of Sarvasena is read as Pṛthivīsena by G. Bühler, while V.V. Mirashi reads the name as Vindhyaśakti. G. Bühler's reading seems to be the correct one.[2] If this view be accepted then it naturally appears that Sarvasena had two sons, Vindhyaśakti and Pṛthivīsena, and both of them became kings, evidently one after the other.

Secondly, from a study of the *Daśakumāracarita* as already stated, V.V. Mirashi points out that Hariṣena left a son who evidently succeeded him.[3] Hariṣena left a vast empire, as we

1. *l.c.*, cf. *EHD*, ed. G. Yazdani, 177; *NHIP*, vi, 104
2. *Select Ins.*, 427, fn.
3. *ABORI*, xxv, 20 ff

shall see later on, and the dynasty did not come to an end with his death.

Before we turn to the vexed problem of chronology we may note two broad facts about the dynasty :

1. Both Sarvasena of the Basim branch and Rudrasena of the main branch have been assigned to 330 A.D.; in other words, both of them became king at the same time. It is not unlikely that Pravarasena I was succeeded by his youngest son Sarvasena, because his eldest son Gautamīputra died during his lifetime. The question now arises, whether according to the law of primogeniture Rudrasena could legally succeed Pravarasena I. The Mitākṣarā on Yājñavalkya states that a son gets right to his father's property as soon as he is born. But Mitākṣarā is later than 4th century A.D. Manu, on the other hand, seems to indicate that a son could get a right to property after the death of his father only (ix. 104). So Gautamīputra had not the privilege of getting any right to the property of Pravarasena I and hence his son Rudrasena, strictly speaking, had no claim to the throne. So after the death of Pravarasena I, Sarvasena evidently became king and during his time the Vākāṭaka kingdom had not evidently been partitioned. (*infra*) When Sarvasena's son Pṛthivīsena I or Vindhyasena became king, Rudrasena of the main branch, son of Gautamīputra, challenged the authority of his cousin Pṛthivīsena or Vindhyasena and with the help of his maternal relatives, the Bhāraśivas, partitioned the Vākāṭaka kingdom and forced him to the Basim region.
2. R.C. Majumdar thinks that 'Narendrasena of the main branch and Hariṣena of the Basim branch were both sixth in descent from Pravarasena I. As such they may be regarded as contemporaries or very nearly so.'[1] V.V. Mirashi, however, objects to this view: 'We cannot however be certain about the contemporaneity of princes by counting generations, as the reign-periods of kings

1. *l.c.*, 4

vary greatly. Besides, Narendrasena was sixth in descent from Pravarasena I, one of his ancestors, viz., Gautamīputra did not reign. Narendrasena was therefore probably a contemporary of Devasena. Consequently, Pṛthivīsena and Hariṣena may have ruled in the same period.'[1] A critical study of the available records, however, shows that R.C. Majumdar's view is the correct one. We shall see later on that Narendrasena ruled from 475 to 500 A.D., while Hariṣena from 480 to 505 A.D , and thus they were contemporaries.

Chronology

The Main Branch—Epigraphic records prove beyond doubt that Rudrasena II, the fifth king of the main line married Prabhāvatī Guptā, the daughter of the Gupta king Candragupta II, who ruled from c. 375 A.D. to 414 A.D. Thus the two rulers were contemporaries at least for some time. On the basis of this contemporaneity R.C. Majumdar has made two interesting observations :—

(a) 'We can hardly believe, in the absence of clear and positive evidence, that Candragupta II was more than 40 in 375 A.D. (the year of his accession) for he ruled till 413 A.D., and personally carried on military expeditions in Western India about 400 A.D. Even if we regard his age as 40 when he ascended the throne, he would have led an active military life at 65 and ruled till 78. The probability therefore is that he ascended the throne at about 30 and his daughter Prabhāvatī was born about 365 A.D.'[2]

(b) Prabhāvatī Guptā did not become a widow till after the death of her father Candragupta. The period of her regency could not be earlier than 417 to 436 A.D.[3]

The first theory is a very reasonable one and we may hold that the date of the Rithpur plates, which were issued when

1. *IHQ*, xxiv, 153
2. *l.c.*, 3
3. *ib*,, 2

Prabhāvatī was 100 years of age, as we have already seen, would approximately be 465 A.D.

There may, however, be some difficulty in accepting the second theory. Candragupta II's conquest of the Śakas must have been achieved in the first decade of the 5th century, and V.A. Smith has very aptly observed that in this Śaka-Gupta struggle, the Vākāṭakas held a position of strategic importance and a Vākāṭaka king 'could be of much service or disservice to the northern invaders of the dominions of the Śaka satrap of Gujarat and Surastra.'[1] The Udayagiri cave inscription of 401 A.D. shows that Candragupta II made elaborate preparation for this campaign and he also must have taken the Vākāṭaka factor under consideration. It is therefore very likely that this campaign which came to a successful close not earlier than 410 A.D., was carried on when the Vākāṭaka kingdom was under the control of his daughter. This seems to show that the regency of Prabhāvatī Guptā continued in the first one and half decade of the 5th century. It may, of course, be argued that the campaign against the Śakas might have been carried during the time of Rudrasena II who was the son-in-law of Candragupta II and who was under a certain amount of Gupta influence as proved by his acceptance of Vaiṣṇavism in preference to Śaivism which was the religion of his ancestors. We shall see later on that this Gupta-Vākāṭaka matrimonial alliance was concluded to check the hostilities between the two families and Candragupta II could hardly be sure of the Vākāṭaka factor until her daughter came to power.

On the basis of the above discussions we may tentatively come to the following dates with a margin of few years :—

c. 390-400 A.D. —Reign of Rudrasena II: the short reign of the monarch is evidenced by the fact that he left minor sons.

c. 400 A.D.-415 A.D. —Regency of Prabhāvatī Guptā

c. 465 A.D. —The 19th regnal year of Pravarasena II. The kingdom was therefore partitioned between the two brothers Dāmodarasena and Pravarasena in c. 446 A.D.

1. *JRAS*, 1914, 324

We have already seen that the Poona C.P. inscription of Prabhāvatī Guptā was issued in the 13th year of her regency when her son Divākarasena, it has been held, was possibly 5 or 6 years of age.[1] R.C. Majumdar has pointed out that princes attained majority in ancient India generally at the age of 21. It may then be assumed that Prabhāvatī's regency ended about 415 A.D., when Divākarasena ascended the throne. D.C. Sircar, on the other hand, quotes several śāstric injunctions to show that in ancient India majority was attained at the age of 16 and then observes : 'If Divākarasena was the eldest of the three sons (Divākarasena, Dāmodarasena and Pravarasena II, there being no reason to believe that two of the three names indicated a single individual) of the Vākāṭaka king Rudrasena II, as he seems to have been, it is not unnatural to believe that he was at least about five years old, when his father died. Consequently, it is probable that he had already attained majority before the time when the Poona grant was issued about 13 years after the death of his father. This would suggest that the cause of Divākarasena not being installed as *mahārāja* even as late as the 13th year of his *yauvarājya* was probably something other than his minority. It may have been due to his mother's love of power, or to some defect or deformity of the prince, or to some unknown political problem.'[2]

If we accept the above view it would be difficult for us to determine the time when Divākarasena ascended the throne. But there is no difficulty in assuming that Pravarasena II became king in 446 A.D. and the Vākāṭaka kingdom was partitioned about that time.

Rudrasena II's father Pṛthivīsena I evidently enjoyed a fairly long reign as in the Vākāṭaka records he is described as being surrounded by sons and grandsons. V.V. Mirashi attributes to him a reign of 50 years.

As already stated all the Vākāṭaka records while speaking of Pṛthivīsena categorically asserts that the military and the fiscal power of the dynasty had been continuing steadily to increase and prosper for about a hundred years at the time of his rule. This shows that the Vākāṭaka dynasty came to power

1. *IHQ*, xxiv, 151-2
2. *Select Ins.*, 416

about 265 A.D. The question now arises how we should divide these 100 years among the predecessors of Pṛthivīṣena I. It may be noted in this connection that the Vākāṭaka records of the main line which speak of these 100 years with reference to Rudrasena I never mention the name of Vindhyaśakti. According to these records the line starts with Pravarasena I. So the beginning of this '100 years' should synchronize with the accession of Pravarasena I on the throne. In this connection we may note again the following Purāṇic account regarding Pravarasena I and his father Vindhyaśakti :

(a) That Vindhyaśakti 'after having known 96 years will enter upon the earth'.

(b) That Pravarasena I 'will reign for 60 years.'[1]

It is really difficult to determine what is exactly meant regarding Vindhyaśakti I in the above statement. He certainly could not have ruled for 96 years which is by itself impossible. If it means that he lived for 96 years and if at the same time we believe in the Purāṇic statement that Pravarasena I ruled for 60 years then we have to assume that Pravarasena I became a king during the lifetime of his father who never ascended the throne. In the Ajanta record, Vindhyaśakti is described as *vaṃśaketu* and equal in prowess to Purandara and Upendra but he is never given any royal title, rājā or mahārāja. The statement *svavāhuvīryārijitasarvaloka* by itself carries hardly any meaning besides showing that he was a powerful man. In the face of all these evidences it is quite apparent that Pravarasena I was the first independent king of the dynasty and he came to the throne about 265 A.D., while his father Vindhyaśakti has been in all probability a subordinate ruler of some importance.

In this connection we should note another fact ignored by many previous writers. When Pravarasena died about 325 A.D. he was succeeded very naturally by his son Sarvasena, his eldest son Gautamīputra having predeceased him. Sarvasena appears to have been much older than Rudrasena I, his nephew, and there was evidently no partition of the empire during his lifetime. It was evidently after his death when his successor came to the throne that Rudrasena I rose in revolt and the empire

1. *DKA*, 48 & 72

was partitioned. (*supra*) Thus the 100 years before Pṛthivīsena I may be divided as follows :—

Pravarasena I —60 years (265-325 A.D.)
Sarvasena —15 years (325-340 A.D.)
Rudrasena I —25 years (340-365 A.D.)

As Pravarasena I ruled for 60 years his son naturally appears to have a short reign. The division of the two houses took place thus between 340 and 365 A.D.

Let us now turn to Pravarasena II of the main line and his successors. We have already seen that in c. 445 A.D. he came to the throne while his charters range from the years 2 to 27. So his reign-period would cover c. 445 A.D. to 475 A.D. His son Narendrasena and grandson Pṛthivīsena II may each be allotted 25 years in the absence of other evidences.

The Basim Branch—Sarvasena died c. 340 A.D. He left two sons Pṛthivīsena and Vindhyaśakti II. The Basim plate of Vindhyaśakti II is dated in his 37th regnal year. He therefore appears to have ruled for 40 years if not more and in that case Pṛthivīsena, evidently his elder brother might not have ruled for more than 15 years. In determining the chronology of the successors of Vindhyaśakti II we shall follow the maxim set forth by R.C. Majumdar: 'In all cases where nothing definite is known, we should proceed on the basis of a reasonable and probable state of things', with two observations of our own:—

(a) Vindhyaśakti II's grandson ascended the throne when he was a boy of mere 8 and so we can accept a period of 48 years of reign in his case as assumed by Majumdar and Mirashi.

(b) In the Chikkulla plates Vikramendravarman I, son of Mādhavavarman I, is called *Viṣṇukuṇḍi-Vākāṭa-vaṃśa-dvay-ālaṅkṛta-janmā*.[1] Vākāṭa is evidently the same as Vākāṭaka and the statement shows that Mādhavavarman I had a Vākāṭaka princess as his wife. According to V.A. Smith the Vākāṭaka father-in-law of Mādhavavarman Viṣṇukuṇḍin was king Hariṣena,[2] the last king of the Basim branch mentioned in the

1. *Ep Ind.*, iv, 193ff
2. *JRAS*, 1914, 137

epigraphic records, and this view has been accepted by almost all the later writers. D.C. Sircar thinks that Mādhavavarman I ruled from c. 535-585 A.D. while according to K. Gopalachari the period is 553-593 A.D., and according to M. Rāma Rao 525-575 A.D.[1] We shall see later on that Gopalachari's view cannot be accepted. Mādhavavarman I possibly began his reign about 530 A.D. He ruled for a period of nearly 50 years and thus when he ascended the throne he could not have been more than 30. According to the scheme of chronology we have adopted here Harişena cannot be dragged down beyond 505 A.D. R.C. Majumdar thinks that Harişena became king in 475 A.D. V.V. Mirashi's view on this point is somewhat self-contradictory. In *IHQ*, xxiv, p. 155 and *Ep. Ind.*, xxvii, p. 315, Mirashi accepts Majumdar's date, while in *Ep. Ind.*, xxii, p. 22, the same scholar says : 'the reign of Harişena, the last known Vākāṭaka king came to an end about 530 A.D.'. In his *Corpus* v, he again adopts the date 475-500 A.D. As we have already seen from the evidence of the *Daśakumāracarita* it appears that Harişena left a son who might have been the father-in-law of the Vişṇukuṇḍin king Mādhavavarman I.

1. *JIH*, xl, 580

On the basis of the above discussions, the Vākāṭaka genealogy and chronology may be stated as follows :

(Vindhyaśakti) (1)

Pravarasena I (2)
(265-325 A.D.)

(Gautamīputra) (4)

Sarvasena (3)
(325-340 A.D.)

Rudrasena I
(340-365 A.D.)

Pṛthivīsena I (5)
(340-355 A.D.)

Vindhyasena
or
Vindhyaśakti II
(355-395 A.D.)

Pṛthivīsena II
(365-390 A.D.)

Pravarasena I
(395-415 A.D.)

Rudrasena II
(390-400 A.D.)

= Prabhāvatī Guptā
(Regency—400-415 A.D.)

Son (name lost) (6)
(415-455 A.D.)

Divākarasena (7)
(acc. 415 A.D.)

Pravarasena II &
Dāmodarasena (?)
(445-475 A.D.)

Devasena
(455-480 A.D.)

Narendrasena
(475-500 A.D.)

Hariṣena
(480-505 A.D.)

Pṛthivīsena II
(500-525 A.D.)

(?) Son (505-) (8)

NOTES

1. According to the epigraphic records of the main branch, the hundred years before the time of Pṛthivīṣena I when the Vākāṭaka rule is supposed to have begun, as we have already seen, does not include the period of Vindhyaśakti. It is really doubtful whether he ever assumed any independent status. The Purāṇic account here is hopelessly corrupt and is often contradicted by epigraphic evidences.
2. As already indicated, the Purāṇas attribute to him a long reign of 60 years which may only indicate that he ruled for a long period. In the absence of any other evidence, we have no other alternative but to take the statement only tentatively.
3. He should be included within 'the period of hundred years' before Pṛthivīṣena I, and the partition of the empire evidently took place during the time of his successor. As his father ruled for a very long period, his reign period naturally was short.
4. Gautamīputra died before his father and did not reign.
5. As his younger brother ruled for nearly 40 years, his reign period appears to have been short. The Basim plate of his brother is dated in 37th regnal year.
6. As this prince ascended the throne at the age of eight only, he evidently had a long reign.
7. The dates of Divākarasena and Pravarasena II have already been discussed.
8. From a critical study of the *Daśakumāracarita*, V.V. Mirashi concluded that Hariṣena left a son who came to the throne. We shall discuss this topic later on.

Chapter XI

POLITICAL HISTORY

On the basis of the Purāṇic accounts noted above,[1] Vindhyaśakti I has been considered to be the founder of the dynasty. The Ajanta inscription of Hariṣena no doubt calls him *vaṃśaketu* but does not adore him with any royal title. He was possibly a subordinate ruler though described as equal to Purandara and Upendra in power and as the conqueror of the earth by his valour—vague descriptions practically carrying no significant meaning. In the epigraph, he is described as a brahmin of *Viṣṇu-vṛddha-gotra*.[2]

Vindhyaśakti I was succeeded by Pravarasena I (265-325 A.D.) the first independent king of the dynasty. He possibly put an end to the rule of the later Sātavāhanas in the Vidarbha region. In the Vākāṭaka records, he is given the title of *mahārāja* and *samrāṭ* and is credited with the performance of four *aśvamedhas*, *vājapeya*, sixteen *atirātra* and other Vedic sacrifices. He evidently undertook extensive military conquests which earned for him and his dynasty an important position among the royal families of South India. A.S. Altekar makes two sweeping statements regarding this monarch that need consideration :—

(a) 'In his father's time his principality consisted of a few districts in the western Madhya Pradesh and in Berar. At the end of his career the Vākāṭaka empire included the whole of the Madhya Pradesh and Berar, Malwa, Northern Maharashtra, a considerable portion of the modern Hyderabad (State) and portions of (South) Kośala or Chhattisgarh.'[3]

1. For the Purāṇic account, *supra*
2. A.S. Altekar thinks that Vindhyaśakti is a *biruda*, the real name of the king being something else. He adopted it when his power extended up to the Vindhyas.
3. *EHD*, ed. G. Yazdani, 159

(b) 'The patrimony which Pravarasena had inherited included only a few districts; he expanded it into an empire which covered practically the whole of the Deccan between the rivers Narmada and Krishna. The northern Maharashtra, Berar, the Madhya Pradesh and Hyderabad (State) were certainly included in his empire. His sphere of influence extended over Malwa and Gujarat, Andhradeśa and Southern Kośala.'[1]

Pravarasena I was no doubt a great king but it is very doubtful whether his kingdom was such an extensive one.

It is contended by several scholars that the Śaka satraps of Malwa and Gujarat acknowledged his supremacy. A study of the kṣatrapa coins shows that there was no mahākṣatrapa in the Śaka realm from A.D. 295 to c. 340 A.D. Thus during this period the Śakas evidently acknowledged the supremacy of some other power. E.J. Rapson points out that the Sassanids of Iran extended their sway over India while the Paikuli inscriptions mention the chiefs of Paradan (Paradas), Makuran (Makran), the Ābhīras and the kṣatrapas of Avanti [Avandikan xvat(a)vya] as vassals under Varhran III. It is difficult to believe that this Sassanid lordship over the satraps continued for long and there must have been other factors that prevented the revival of the office of mahākṣatrapa. Altekar thinks that after 340 A.D. the Scythians acknowledged the suzerainty of Pravarasena. But of this there is absolutely no proof. The big hoard of 633 kṣatrapa coins found at Chhindwada district of Madhya Pradesh has been supposed to be tribute paid by the Scythians to Pravarasena I. It is very doubtful whether the district was included within the empire of Pravarasena at all.

From the tradition recorded in the *Śrīśailasthalamāhātmya* that 'the princess Candrāvatī, a daughter of the Gupta king Candragupta conceived a passion for the God on the Śrīśaila hill and began offering everyday a garland of jasmine (mallikā) flowers to him,' it has been inferred that the Vākāṭaka territory in the east extended round about the mouths of the Krishna; i.e., Andhradeśa was conquered by Pravarasena I. We know that Prabhāvatī Guptā, the daughter of the Gupta monarch, was married to Rudrasena II, fifth in descent from

1. *EHD*, ed. G. Yazdani, 161

Pravarasena I. Even if we identify Candrāvatī with Prabhāvatī Guptā there is no reason to assume that Andhradeśa came under the influence of the first Vākāṭaka emperor. The historical value of the *Śrīśailasthalamāhātmya* is very doubtful. Prabhāvatī Guptā was a staunch follower of the Vaiṣṇava faith, while Mallikārjuna on Śrīśaila is a form of God Śiva.

Barring the Purāṇic tradition which has been wrongly interpreted as associating Pravarasena with the Madhya Pradesh[1] there is no evidence that the Vākāṭaka monarch's sway extended over that region or over Southern Kośala. The Nachna-ki-talai and the Ganj records are the earliest evidences showing Vākāṭaka suzerainty over Bundelkhand but they belong to the time of Pṛthivīsena I, the great grandson of Pravarasena I. Pravarasena I's sway over the western Maharashtra region also is incompatible with the rule of the Ābhīras in the same place in the same period.

It is difficult to agree with V.V. Mirashi that Pravarasena I conquered Purikā which was, according to the Purāṇas, it is maintained, under the domination of the Nāgas at this time. We have already noted that a critical study of the Purāṇic accounts, on the other hand, seem to indicate that a branch of the later Śuṅgas had been ruling over there. If he really conquered Purikā and made it his capital it was at the cost of the later Śuṅgas. Similarly, there is no evidence, whatsoever, that some smaller kings of the Kaliṅga region acknowledged his sway, though the performance of four *aśvamedhas* by him proves that he made some conquests.

The Vākāṭaka epigraphs are eloquent over the marriage of Pravarasena's son Gautamīputra with the daughter of Bhavanāga, the king of the Bhāraśivas, 'who were besprinkled on the forehead with the pure water of (the river) Bhāgīrathī (Ganges) that had been obtained by their valour.'[2] K.P. Jayaswal has tried to show that in the so-called *dark age* intervening between the fall of the Imperial Kuṣāṇas and the rise of the Guptas the Bhāraśivas became the most important power of India and they extended their rule over almost the whole of North India as well as a large tract of South India including the Andhradeśa.[3] Jayaswal's theory has already been refuted[4] and here we only want to note

1. *supra*
2. *Corpus*, iii, 241
3. *History of India*, 48ff, 174
4. *EHNI*, 138f

the fact that there is no evidence to show that the Vākāṭakas were originally subordinates under the Bhāraśivas, as maintained by Jayaswal.

According to the Purāṇas, Pravarasena I had four sons and all of them became kings. This statement, as already stated, can hardly be accepted; for the epigraphs clearly show that the Vākāṭaka empire became partitioned into two parts, and not into four as the Purāṇic statements would suggest, and this partition again took place possibly after Sarvasena, the son of Pravarasena. (*supra*)

Pravarasena I was succeeded by his son Sarvasena (325-340 A.D.) on the Vākāṭaka throne, his other son Gautamīputra, the son-in-law of Bhava-nāga, having predeceased him.

Partition of The Empire

Main Branch—Sarvasena was succeeded by his son Pṛthivīsena. *Rudrasena I* (340-365 A.D.), son of Gautamīputra, challenged the authority of his cousin which ensued ultimately into a civil war and Pṛthivīsena was forced to retire to the Basim region where he founded a new kingdom. Here we may note that as Samudragupta is described in the epigraphs as a *Licchavi dauhitra*, which has been interpreted by historians to mean that he owed much to the Licchavis for his power and conquest, Rudrasena I is similarly described as '*Bhāraśivānāṃ mahārāja-śrī-Bhavanāgadauhitra*', which evidently shows that in his struggle against his cousin, he was helped by his maternal grandfather's family and this help evidently enabled him to seize the throne.

This Vākāṭaka-Bhāraśiva *entete* produced an indirect result. The Guptas were rising to power in North-Eastern India and Candragupta I, the first Gupta *mahārājādhirāja* came to the throne of Magadha in c. 319-20 A.D. It appears that his kingdom extended from Allahabad to W. Bengal. When Samudragupta succeeded Candragupta he undertook extensive military campaigns as proved by his Allahabad record. It was formerly believed that Samudragupta conquered the Maharashtra region and brought the Vākāṭakas under control. The theory was based on the wrong identification of Devarāṣṭra, mentioned among the countries of Dakṣiṇāpatha conquered by the great Gupta monarch, with Mahārāṣṭra. G. J-Dubreuil has pointed out, that 'it (Devarāṣṭra) must be identified with the province of Devarāṣṭra (=Yellamanchili tract) mentioned in a copper-plate grant found in the district of Vizagapatan'.[1] But even after this, K.P. Jayaswal maintains that Samudragupta attacked the kingdom of the Vākāṭakas and killed Rudrasena I. The basis of this theory is the identification of Rudradeva conquered by Samudragupta with the Vākāṭaka king. But here we should remember the fact that Rudradeva conquered by Samudragupta is called the king of Āryāvarta, while Rudrasena I was the king of Dakṣiṇāpatha. Rudradeva should be identified with the king of the same name whose coins have been found at Kosam and this would explain why he is mentioned first among the Āryāvarta monarchs in the Allahabad record. S.K. Aiyangar postulated the view that as in the Vākāṭaka records Pravarasena I only is called *samrāṭ* while his successors are given the title of *mahārāja*, the Vākāṭakas after Pravarasena I entered into a subordinate alliance with the Guptas evidently being frightened by the great *digvijaya* of Samudragupta. This theory, curiously enough, has been accepted by some recent scholars[2] like D.C. Sircar who maintains that if not during the time of Samudragupta, during the time of his son Caṇdragupta II at least the Vākāṭakas became subordinate under the Guptas. In support of this theory, it is pointed out that in the records of Prabhāvatī Guptā we find the use of the term *mahārājādhirāja* with reference to the Gupta monarch while the Vākāṭaka kings are given the simpler title of *mahārāja*. It is no doubt a fact that during the regency of Prabhāvatī Guptā the Gupta influence reigned supreme in the domain of the Vākāṭakas but there is no evidence that these South Indian monarchs played a subordinate role at this time. In this age, while with the Guptas generally the title of *mahārājādhirāja* denoted an independent status and *mahārāja* a subordinate one, with the kings of South India the title of *mahārāja* was quite a loftier one. Pravarasena I was given the title of *samrāṭ* evidently because he performed *aśvamedha* and other sacrifices, for, according to the

1. *AHD*, 60
2. *The Classical Age*, 180

śāstric injunctions such kings only could take that title. So when in the epigraphs of Prabhāvatī Guptā we find a distinction between the titles of the Guptas and the Vākāṭakas, we may assume that she was only following the then customs of the two countries lying on two sides of the Vindhya. It should be noted further that in the records of Prabhāvatī Guptā the Gupta era has not been used.

The main result of the Vākāṭaka-Bhāraśiva *entete* was that it stirred up Samudragupta to take steps against the further increase of the Vākāṭaka power and influence which could hinder him in his campaigns both in the Uttarāpatha and the Dakṣiṇāpatha. Evidently with this aim Samudragupta conquered the *forest country* (*l.*21 of the Allahabad record). Two inscriptions dated in the years 199 and 209 of the Gupta era from the Baghelkhand region describe king Hastin as ruling over Ḍabhāla together with the 18 forest kingdoms. The Āṭavikarājya or the forest country therefore denoted Ḍabhāla and the adjoining wild region corresponding to the territory round present Jubbulpore. As a result of this conquest the Narmada became the southern boundary of the Gupta empire. The conquest of Āryāvarta together with the Āṭavikarājya thus put a strong barrier against the expansion of the Vākāṭakas towards the north.

In the epigraphic records Rudrasena I is described as a devotee of the God Mahābhairava, the terrific aspect of Śiva. The Bhāraśivas were worshippers of Śiva and it is not unlikely that the Vākāṭaka king developed his devotion for the god through the influence of his maternal grandfather's family which helped him in his war against the son of Sarvasena of the Basim branch.

Rudrasena was succeeded by his son Pṛthivīsena I (365-390 A.D.) who is described in the epigraphic records as *dharmavijayī*. From the Allahabad inscription we learn that *dharmavijaya* was marked by three distinct features, viz., *grahaṇa* (capture of the enemy), *mokṣa* (liberating him), and *anugraha* (favouring him by reinstating him in the kingdom). In this connection we may note two records, one from Nachne-ki-talai in the old Jaso state and the other at Ganj, both in the Bundelkhand region. The records belong to a king named Vyāghradeva who calls himself a vassal of the Vākāṭaka king Pṛthivīsena. Some scholars hold that this Vākāṭaka monarch should be identified with Pṛthivīsena II, the last king of the main branch but as D.C. Sircar points out, the palaeographical peculiarities, e.g., the triangular form of *v* and the old form of *t* and *j* of the Nachne-ki-talai and Ganj records are certainly older than those of the Basim plates of Vindhyaśakti II and hence Pṛthivīsena of the records should be identified with Pṛthivīsena I.[1]

If we accept the above view, it will at once raise some interesting issues. From the Allahabad record it is clear that the Bundelkhand region passed under the rule of Samudragupta, while there is an inscription of the emperor at Eran in the Saugar district, to the south-west of Bundelkhand. Samudragupta lived up to c. 375 A.D.,[2] while Pṛthivīsena I appears to have been a younger contemporary of Samudragupta because he ruled from c. 365-390 A.D. The question now arises, who conquered the Bundelkhand region and from whom? Was it conquered by Samudragupta from Pṛthivīsena I or did Pṛthivīsena conquer the region from the Guptas? Here we should make a very critical study of the available epigraphs, especially the Allahabad record. Incidentally it should also be noted that the old view that Samudragupta carried on his digvijaya some time between 340 and 350 A.D. is a mere surmise not supported by any positive evidence.[3]

Let us now turn to the Allahabad record. J.F. Fleet thought that the record was incised after the death of Samudragupta inasmuch as *ll.*29-30 describe the fame of Samudragupta as reaching the abode of Indra[4] (i.e. he was dead). This theory has been controverted by G. Būhler and others who pointed out that the epigraph contains no reference to the *aśvamedha* sacrifice of Samudragupta, the performance of which by the king is proved by the evidence of

1. *JRASB (L)*, xii, 72-3
2. This is proved by the Mathura inscription of Candragupta II, Regnal year 5; Gupta year 61 = 380 A.D., *Select Ins*, 269
3. *EHNI*, 179
4. *ib.*, 180

the coins, and hence the record must have been executed before that event. Further, *ll*.29-30 really mean that the king's fame reached heaven and this cannot be interpreted as meaning that he was dead.[1]

From the above discussions we can possibly conclude that Samudragupta's conquests were not undertaken in the later part of his reign, but before his *aśvamedha* sacrifices. Now, in the Poona plates of Prabhāvatī Guptā, he is given the epithet *anekāśvamedhayājin*[2] while his *aśvamedha* type of coins can clearly be divided into two groups according to the legend on the obverse[3]. He therefore must have performed at least two *aśvamedha* sacrifices when the two groups of coins were issued. Such costly sacrifices could not have been performed in quick succession and thus we must allow a margin of some years between the execution of the Allahabad record and his death. Now, there is another record of the king at Eran, as already stated. Lines 1-6 of the record are entirely broken and lost and an indefinite number at the bottom is damaged.[4] What, however, remains of it shows that it could not have contained in the broken part a detailed account of his *digvijaya* as described in the Allahabad record.[5] The find spot of the record shows thus that he extended his conquest upto Eran in the early part of his reign and before he undertook his campaigns in south-eastern Dakṣiṇāpatha and his second digvijaya in North India. Evidently in his first Āryavarta campaign he attacked the Nāgas of Mathurā-Kāntipura-Vidiśā region and then swooped down upto Eran. Military Strategy also points to his conquest of Baghelkhand and Bundelkhand regions prior to his conquest of Dakṣiṇāpatha, for, he could not undertake such campaign leaving his western rear exposed to the attack of the rising Vākāṭaka power, now in alliance with his enemies.

Thus we are naturally inclined to think that Pṛthivīsena conquered the Bundelkhand region from the Guptas, possibly from Candragupta II who came to the throne in 375 A.D. as

1. *EHNI*, 180
2. *Select Ins*, 411
3. *EHNI*, 197
4. *Select Ins*, 260
5. *ib.*, 254ff

proved by the Mathura inscription of his time. The territory, however, did not remain long under Pṛthivīsena I and was retaken by Candragupta as proved by latter's inscriptions at Udayagiri and Sanchi. Thus a trial of strength went on between the two dynasties and ultimately a peace was cemented by matrimonial alliance resulting in the marriage of Pṛthivīsena I's son Rudrasena II with Prabhāvatī Guptā, the daughter of Candragupta II. This marriage was of great political importance for both the dynasties. Like his father, Pṛthivīsena I was a devotee of Lord Maheśvara or Śiva and it was evidently for his honest character that he has been compared to Yudhiṣṭhira in the Vākāṭaka epigraphs.

Pṛthivīsena I was succeeded by his son Rudrasena II (390-400 A.D.), the husband of Prabhāvatī Guptā. The predecessors of Rudrasena II were all Śaivas, as we have already seen, but the new king became a devotee of Cakrapāṇi-Viṣṇu evidently under the influence of his wife. His reign thus saw the beginning of the introduction of Gupta influence in the trans-Vindhyan region. This influence became stronger when Rudrasena II died a premature death about 400 A.D. and Prabhāvatī Guptā became the regent of her minor son *yuvarāja* Divākarasena. The Poona C.P. inscription of the queen, issued in the 13th year of her regency throws interesting light on the history of the Vākāṭakas of the age. The inscription opens with an account of the Gupta dynasty upto Candragupta II and then mentions Prabhāvatī Guptā, the *agramahiṣī* of Rudrasena and mother of the crown prince Divākarasena. The absence of the names of the predecessors of Rudrasena II evidently shows how Candragupta II, exercised tremendous influence in the affairs of the kingdom through his daughter. The grant was issued by the queen from Nandivardhana which was the capital of the kingdom at that time. The mention of Nāgapura-Nandivardhana in the Deoli grant of the Rāṣṭrakūṭa king Kṛṣṇa III shows that the place was very near Nagpur, possibly in the Nagpur district itself.

Candragupta II selected this period for his expedition against the Śakas of Western India. The Gupta king realised that his southern rear was now quite safe and through his daughter help would also come from that quarter, if necessary. The conquest of the Western *kṣatrapas* by Candragupta II is proved by his rare silver coins which are more or less direct imitations of those of the latest Western *kṣatrapas*. As E.J. Rapson states : 'Like their prototypes, the coins of the latest *mahākṣatrapas*, which they closely resemble in style and fabric, they have on the *obv* the date accompanied by some equivalent of the word *varṣe*, being the king's head, and retain some traces of the old inscription in Greek characters, while on the *rev* they substitute the Gupta type (a peacock) for the *caitya*, with crescent and star.'[1] The latest date on the coins of the Western *kṣatrapas* is 310 or 31X (Saka) = 388+X A.D., while the earliest date on the silver coins of the Gupta monarch struck in imitation of the former is G.E. 90 or 90X = A.D. 409+X. Thus it was during this period that the Gupta conquest of Malwa and Gujarat took place. It is possible to limit the period further, for the Udayagiri inscription of the year 401 A.D. shows the occupation of the Eastern Malwa by the Guptas and it is improbable that the Western *kṣatrapas* were able to resist for long the victorious progress of Candragupta II.[2]

Thus it is evident that the conquest of the Śakas by Candragupta II which earned for him the immortal titles of Śakāri and Vikramāditya was achieved while his daughter had been ruling over the Vākāṭaka territory. This coincidence can hardly be accidental. It is not unlikely that the Vākāṭakas also had some contributions in the achievement of this stupendous task. This part of Vākāṭaka history cannot be properly assessed for want of direct evidence.

We have already indicated that the Rithpur inscription of Prabhāvatī Guptā was issued about 415 A.D.[3] It proves that Divākarasena ascended the throne while about 445 A.D. Pravarasena II, became king after a partition of the empire. (*supra*) After Divākarasena's death, Pravarasena II appears to have captured a part of the kingdom as proved by the find spot of his epigraphs. His charters range from the year 2 to 27 and the fact that he appointed *senāpati* governors in

1. *CIC*, cli
2. *EHNI*, 205
3. *Select Ins*, 415

different parts of his empire is also very significant. This seems to show that Dāmodarasena, his another brother, who became king in other part of the empire, possibly left an heir whose cause was upheld by a section of the people. Pravarasena II evidently set aside the claim and there was trouble in the country when military governors had to be appointed. From the epigraphic records we get the names of some such *senāpati* governors, such as Citravarman, Namidāsa, Kātyāyana, Vappadeva etc. Of these Chitravarman was placed to look after the affairs of the Bhojakaṭa rāṣṭra (?) then ruled over by Śatrugnarāja and Koṇḍarāja. It is not unlikely that the Bhojas, who were an important factor in the Maharashtra politics, took the side of the son of Dāmodarasena and so a military governor was placed in the region.

There was also another factor that induced Pravarasena II to keep the country under military rule. The Bhitari inscription of Skandagupta shows that about 455 A.D. the Puṣyamitras who, 'had great resources in men and money' attacked the Gupta kingdom then ruled over by the aged king Kumāragupta I, maternal uncle of Pravarasena II, and Skandagupta, the son of Kumāragupta, had to fight hard with them 'to restore the fallen fortunes of his family' and had to pass a whole night on bare earth.[1] Ultimately Skandagupta became victorious but the aged king Kumāragupta died before he could get news of this victory. The Purāṇas associate the Puṣyamitras with the Mekala country lying to the north-eastern frontier of the Vākāṭaka kingdom. Pravarasena II might have apprehended some danger from this tribe, which like the nomads of Central Asia, suddenly became infused with warlike activities. Under such circumstances, which appeared to be an abnormal one, military governors had to be appointed for the protection of the country.

The epigraphs of Pravarasena II have been found in Wardha, Chhindwara, Nagpur, Balaghat, Siwani, Amaraoti, Betul and other districts. Thus he kept intact the kingdom ruled over by his grandfather and the territory appears to have suffered no loss since the time of Pṛthivīsena I.

1. *Select Ins*, 312

The early charters of Pravarasena II were issued from the city of Nandivardhana while his later charters were issued from Pravarapura. It is not unlikely that Pravarapura was another name of Nandivardhana itself. Narattaṅga-vāri-sthāna, from where his Tirodi plates were issued, was evidently a place of pilgrimage which the king visited. Unlike his parents, who were Vaiṣṇavas, Pravarasena II became a Śaiva. This shows that he freed his country from the influence of the Guptas.

The commentator of the Prakrit kāvya *Setuvandha* informs us that Pravarasena II lived some time in the court of his maternal grandfather Candragupta II and once composed a poem which was later on corrected by the great poet Kālidāsa. The prince must have composed the same in the later days of the Gupta monarch, and in this connection we may note further that in his *Śṛṅgāraprakāśa*, Bhoja has quoted a verse written by the great poet who is said to have reported to the Gupta monarch Vikramāditya on the luxurious life at the court of the Lord of Kuntala, who has been identified with Pravarasena II.[1] It is difficult to determine the authenticity of such statements. In any case, the Kuntala region at this time was under the rule of the Kadambas. V.V. Mirashi points out that the Pattan plates of Pravarasena II of the year 27 refer to a Kālidāsa as the writer of the charter.[2]

At this stage we may make a short *resume* of the history of the Basim branch, for after the death of Pravarasena II we enter into a confused period of Vākāṭaka history when the cousin dynasties entered into a bitter rivalry with each other.

The Basim Branch—We have already seen that after the death of Sarvasena there was a war of succession and Sarvasena's son moved to the Basim region and founded a new dynasty there. Sarvasena had two sons, Pṛthivīṣena and Vindhyaśakti II. Pṛthivīṣena was possibly the eldest one in whose time, as we have already seen, Rudrasena I started the so-called main branch with the help of his maternal relatives, the Bhāraśivas. In this connection it may be noted that in the Ajanta inscription, as restored by D.C. Sircar, Pṛthivīṣena is des-

1. *EHNI*, 207
2. *Ep Ind*, xxiii, 81ff

cribed as having defeated the king of Kuntala.[1] According to the scheme of chronology accepted in these pages Pṛthivīsena I (340-355 A.D.) would be a contemporary of the Kadamba king Mayūraśarman who was the first ruler to establish his dynasty in the Kuntala country. In his Candravalli stone inscription[2] Mayūraśarman claims to have conquered Trikūṭa, Ābhīra, Pallava, Pāriyātra, Śakasthāna, Sendraka, Punnādu and the Maukharis. It is very difficult to determine how far the claims can be regarded as authentic. He possibly made an attempt to extend his territory towards the north and formed alliances with the Traikūṭakas and the Ābhīras of the Aparānta region and the Śaka kṣatrapas of Malwa and Gujarat. This alliance might have been directed against the new Vākāṭaka power and the statement of the Ajanta record may be interpreted to mean that Pṛthivīsena I thwarted the attempt of the Kadamba king. The war, however, weakened his position and Rudrasena I, son of Gautamīputra, utilised this opportunity to drive him into the Basim region. Pṛthivīsena was succeeded by his brother Vindhyaśakti II whose Basim record is dated in the 37th year of his reign showing that he possibly ruled from 355 to 395 A.D.[3] Very likely he left no son and so after his death the throne passed on to his nephew, the eldest son of Pṛthivīsena, Pravarasena I. In 415 A.D. Pravarasena's minor son of eight years of age ascended the Basim throne. His name cannot be traced in the Ajanta record. He may, however, be allowed a tentative period of 40 years. The next king Devasena was a contemporary of Pravarasena II of the main branch. He was a pleasure loving ruler but was fortunate in getting the services of an efficient minister named Hastibhoja who looked after the affairs of the state.

1. *Select Ins*, 425f
2. *ib.*, 449
3. *Ep Ind*, xxvi, 137f

CHAPTER XII

TUSSLE BETWEEN THE TWO BRANCHES

After the death of Pravarasena II of the main branch in 475 A.D. and the end of the rule of Devasena of the Basim branch c. 480 A D., we enter into a very confused period of Vākāṭaka history and often it becomes difficult for us to follow the course of events. A critical study reveals, however, the following characteristics that began to orient the life of both the main and the Basim branches :

(a) Both the dynasties contracted matrimonial alliances for political purpose with different ruling houses of the Deccan.

(b) While after the partition the two houses had been living independently without intervening in the affairs of the other, there arose gradually a bitter rivalry between the two and this ultimately proved disastrous for both, especially for the main branch.

(c) The Vākāṭakas began to intervene in the affairs of other Deccan states and also in Malwa, Kośala and Mekala where new dynasties appeared. Such imprudent policies became ultimately another factor of their ruin.

III

Pravarasena II of the main branch was succeeded in 475 A.D. by his son Narendrasena while in 480 A.D. Devasena was succeeded on the Basim throne by Hariṣena. Narendrasena and Hariṣena thus appear to have been contemporaries. Narendrasena's son Pṛthivīsena II ascended the throne in c. 500 A.D. while Hariṣena ruled up to c. 505 A.D. Thus for 5 years extending from 500 to 505 A.D. Hariṣena also was his contemporary. Now we have to make a comparative study of the achievements of Narendrasena and Pṛthivīsena II on the one hand and of Hariṣena on the other. This will bring forth at once the bitter rivalry that had been going on between the two houses :

(a) The Balaghat record informs us that the command of Narendrasena (475-500 A.D.) was honoured by the kings of Kośala, Mekala and Malwa;[1] that he married Ajitabhaṭṭārikā, the Kuntala princess;[2] he is further described as *apahṛtavaṃśaśriyaḥ* suggesting that the fortune of his family had for a time been in the possession of another and he retrived this fallen fortune.

(b) In the Ajanta inscription, on the other hand, Hariṣena (480-505 A.D.) of the Basim branch is described as subjugating Kuntala, Avanti, Kaliṅga, Kośala, Trikūṭa, Lāṭa, Andhra and other countries. The inscription is partly damaged and so the full sense of the account cannot be precisely determined.

Now, if we make a comparative study of the above details we find that both Narendrasena and Hariṣena claim suzerainty over Kośala and Malwa regions (Avanti), showing that a rivalry was going on between the two families. This rivalry possibly originated when Narendrasena married the Kuntala princess Ajitabhaṭṭārikā for the Kadambas appeared to have lived in bad terms with the Basim house, since Pṛthivīsena I thwarted the northern advance of the first Kadamba king Mayūraśarman. (*supra*) Narendrasena's Kuntala wife was evidently a daughter of the Kadamba king Śāntivarman who ruled from 450 to 475 A.D.

Now, let us see what is meant by *apahṛtavaṃśaśriyaḥ*, an expression used in connection with Narendrasena in the Balaghat plates, and then we shall try to determine how far his command was respected by Mekala and Malwa. A study of the history of the Traikūṭakas at this stage would throw welcome light on our problem, and so we propose to go a little bit off the track here.

As we have already seen the Traikūṭakas are mentioned for the first time in the Candravalli inscription of Mayūraśarman. The name of the dynasty is evidently derived from the Trikūṭa

1. *Ep Ind*, ix, 267ff
2. A.S. Altekar thinks that 'the identification of the family of this princess is not yet satisfactorily settled, but very probably she was a daughter of the Kadamba king Kākustha-varman, who is known to have married his daughters in Gupta and other royal families.' (*NHIP*, vi, 106)

mountain which is placed by Kālidāsa in the Aparānta region.[1] It started as a subordinate under the Ābhīras and in the first quarter of the fifth century assumed an independent status, but used the era started by their former master which was evidently prevalent in the region. The independent existence of the dynasty is revealed to us by three C.P. inscriptions[2] and coins. From these we get the following genealogy :—

mahārāja Indradatta
mahārāja Dharasena (K.E. 207 = 456-57 A.D.)
mahārāja Vyāghrasena (K.E. 241 = 490-91 A.D.)

The existence of *mahārāja* Indradatta is known to us from the inscriptions on the coins of his son Dharasena which reads as '*maharaja-Andradattaputra-paramavasnava-sri maharaja-Dharasena*'. V.V. Mirashi assigns him to the period 415-440 A.D.[3]

Dharasena, who appears to have ruled from c. 440 A.D. to 465 A.D., was a contemporary of the Vākāṭaka king Pravarasena II. From his Pardi plate of the year 207 we learn that he performed an *aśvamedha* sacrifice and he takes the title of *mahārāja* both in the inscription and coins.

Dharasena was succeeded by his son Vyāghrasena who is known from coins as well as his Surat plate of the year K.E. 241. He thus may be assigned to the period 465 A.D. to 495 A.D A Kanheri inscription of the year 245 = 494-95 A.D. refers to the increasingly victorious reign of the Traikūṭakas. It, therefore, belongs to the time of Vyāghrasena.[4]

1. *Raghuvaṃśa*, iv, 58-9
2. Pardi plates of Dharasena: year 207; Surat plates of Vyāghrasena; year 241; Kanheri plate of the Traikūṭakas: year 245. (*Corpus*, iv, 22-32)
3. *Corpus*, iv, xlii
4. 'One more inscription, consisting of a single plate was found inside a Buddhist *stūpa* at Kaṇhēri in North Konkan. It records the construction of a *chaitya* (i.e., the *stūpa* in which the inscription together with some relics was found) dedicated by a pilgrim from Sindh to the venerable Śāradvatīputra, the foremost disciple of the Buddha. The inscription mentions only the increasingly victorious reign of the Traikūṭakas, but does not name any reigning king. It is dated in the year 245 (494-95 A.C.). As a period of as many as 36 years intervenes between the date of the Pardi plates of Dharasena and that of the Surat plates of his son Vyāghrasena, it seems that the latter were pro-

After Vyāghrasena, we get no inscription or coin of the dynasty. On the other hand, as we have already stated, we find that Hariṣena of the Basim branch who ruled at this period claims to have conquered the Traikūṭakas in the Ajanta record. The Vākāṭaka king Narendrasena of the main line might have been in alliance with the Traikūṭakas, and this episode is hinted at by the expression *apahṛtavaṃśaśriyaḥ* in the Balaghat record.[1] If that be so then ultimately Narendrasena managed the affairs in his favour and his prestige suffered no loss.

Another interpretation is also possible, Hariṣena's suzerainty extended over Kośala and other regions. But epigraphs indicate that Kośala and Mekala had been under the influence of the main branch and this evidently shows the tussle between the two houses. The Bamhani plates of the Pāṇḍava king Bharatavala refer to a dynasty of four rulers of Mekala :—

Jayavala
|
Vatsarāja = Droṇobhaṭṭārikā
|
mahārāja Nāgavala = Indrabhaṭṭārikā
|
mahārāja Bharatavala or Indra = Lokaprakāśā, a princess of Kośala

While editing the epigraph, Chhabra observes : 'The contents of the eleventh stanza......are ambiguous. In natural sequence, it speaks of the royal donor Bharatavala, represented, as an Emperor (*sārvabhauma*) honoured by his vassals, but, at the

bably issued towards the close of Vyāghrasena's reign. The Traikūṭaka king during whose reign the Kaṇheri plate was issued may, therefore, have been the successor of Vyāghrasena. During his reign the Trikūṭa country was invaded by Hariṣena, the last known Vākāṭaka king who flourished in *circa* 475-500 A.C. In the inscription in the Ajantā cave XVI, Hariṣena is credited with a victory over Trikūṭa, but it is not known if he supplanted the ruling dynasty. He was possibly content with exacting a tribute from it as he must have done from the other countries mentioned in the same inscription, viz, Kuntala, Avanti, Kaliṅga, Kośala, Lāṭa and Andhra.' (*Corpus*, iv, xliii) We cannot agree with the view that the inscription was issued by a successor of Vyāghrasena.

1. *Corpus*, v

same time it contains a veiled reference to his overlord, Narendra, that is the Vākāṭaka monarch Narendrasena. There is obviously a pun upon the word Narendra, which, when construeted with Bharatavala, means 'king', while otherwise it stands for the personal name of the Vākāṭaka sovereign concerned. There is another word in the verse, which has likewise double meaning, and that is *saumya*. It qualifies *vaṃśa*. When it refers to Bharatavala's *vaṃśa* it means 'lunar', and when it adverts to Narendrasena's *vaṃśa*, it simply denotes 'auspicious'. The implication is quite obvious. The Pāṇḍavas, the avowed ancestors of Bharatavala, belonged to the lunar race, while the Vākāṭakas were Brāhmaṇas and as such their family could aptly be described as auspicious."[1]

This shows that Bharatavala[2] was a subordinate ally of Narendrasena. His marriage with a Kośalan princess is also significant. The dynasty of Kośala appears to have been not in enmity, but rather under the influence of Narendrasena, for otherwise a subordinate ruler would not have dared marry a princess of the family. In this sense it may be contended that Kośala also obeyed the command of the Vākāṭaka king. It is not unlikely that the marriage was arranged by Narendrasena himself. Thus the Kośalan affair was another cause of tussle between the two houses, but Narendrasena somehow maintained his prestige.

Narendrasena's claim over Malwa is indeed an interesting one. We have seen that the Malwa region (Avanti) was conquered by Candragupta II during the regency of Prabhāvatī Guptā. During the time of Kumāragupta, Ghaṭotkaca Gupta was appointed a viceroy in eastern Malwa with jurisdiction over Tumbavana, modern Tumain about 50 miles to the north-west of Eran. The position of western Malwa was somewhat peculiar. The Mandasore inscription of Kumāragupta I and Bandhuvarman refers to Kumāragupta as ruling the earth (Kumāragupte pṛthivīṃ praśāsati) and Bandhuvarman as ruling at Daśapura evidently as a feudatory under the

1. *Ep Ind*, xxvii, 137
2. The assumption of the title of *mahārāja* by Bharatavala and his father proves that they were practically independent though obeying the command of the Vākāṭaka monarch.

former. The record, however, is dated in the Malwa year 493 = A.D. 436.[1] The absence of any reference to the Gupta era is very significant. It shows that though Kumāragupta I was recognised as the nominal overlord, Bandhuvarman, the ruler of Daśapura, was practically independent so far as the internal affairs of the territory was concerned. In this connection we may note the evidence of another Mandasore record of the Malwa year 524. The record is a posthumous one and mentions Govinda Gupta while Indra is represented as being suspicious of Govinda's power. Govinda Gupta is evidently identical with mahārāja Govinda Gupta known from the Vaisali seal as the son of mahārājādhirāja Candragupta II and the queen Dhruvasvāminī. D.R. Bhandarkar thinks that as in this record 'Indra is represented as being suspicious of Govīnda Gupta's power the latter seems to have been in supreme power.'[2] If we accept the view then we have to infer that Govinda Gupta, brother of Kumāragupta I, revolted and became independent in the western Avanti region. Some scholars find in the term Indra an indirect reference to Kumāragupta I, on account of the latter's title of *Śrī Mahendra* and *Mahendraparākrama* on the coins. As the Mandasore record of 435 A.D., referred to before, describes Kumāragupta I as ruling the earth, it may be presumed that this revolt possibly occurred after that date. This supposition is strengthened by the fact that in the second part of the above Mandasore record, which bears the date M.E. 529 = 473 A.D. there is no reference to any Gupta king. Possibly, after this revolt western Malwa region became an independent unit, though it had already been autonomous in internal matters, as shown by the use of dates in the records in the Malwa era and not in the Gupta era.

We have sketched at some length the history of the western Malwa country to show that when Narendrasena Vākāṭaka had been ruling it was not strictly a part of the Gupta empire, as it has been supposed by many scholars, and so it might have entered into an alliance alternately with Narendrasena and Hariṣena.

1. *Select Ins*, 288
2. *ASIR*, 1922-3, 187

About c. 500 A.D. Narendrasena was succeeded by his son Pṛthivīsena II. For five years he was thus a contemporary of Hariṣena of the other branch. In the Balaghat record Pṛthivīsena II is described as the restorer of the fortune of his family which had fallen twice. A.S. Altekar makes two observations in this connection :—

(a) 'The first misfortune mentioned above probably refers to the invasion of Mānamātra, the king of Śarabhapura in Chhattisgarh, who succeeded temporarily in occupying Berar and the Southern Madhya Pradesh. He was, however, soon expelled from these territories by the exertion of Pṛthivīsena.'

(b) 'The Vākāṭaka seems to have fallen on evil days again during the reign of Pṛthivīsena following an attack by the Traikūṭakas in the west.'[1]

None of the above views can be accepted. We have already seen that the Traikūṭaka power came to an end with the death or defeat at the hand of Hariṣena of the Traikūṭaka king Vyāghrasena during the time of Pṛthivīsena's father and therefore the question of Traikūṭaka attack referred to above cannot arise.

As regards the invasion of Mānamātra, the king of Śarabhapura, it may be noted that the theory is based on the wrong identification of the Śarabhapurīya king Mānamātra with Mānāṅka, the Rāṣṭrakūṭa monarch, originally suggested by Sten Konow[2] and accepted by many later scholars. We shall see later on that a branch of the Rāṣṭrakūṭas of which Mānāṅka was one really occupied a considerable portion of the Vidarbha region after the fall of the Vākāṭakas, but the Śarabhapura king Mānamātra never came into collision with Pṛthivīsena II.

From several epigraphs we can draw out the following genealogy of the dynasty of Śarabhapura to which Mānamātra

1. *EHD*, ed. G. Yazdani, 184
2. *Ep Ind*, ix, 171

belonged :—

Prasannamātra
- Mahājayarāja
- Mānamātra[1]
  - Mahāsudevarāja
  - Mahāpravararāja

Thus we find the presence of a new dynasty in Kośala. Hariṣena, as we have already seen, claims to have conquered the country and he might have overthrown the dynasty of Śarabha that had been ruling there and that was subordinate to the other branch. He installed a new dynasty headed by Prasannamātra under his own suzerainty. Prasannamātra had a short reign and was succeeded by his eldest son Mahājayarāja. Mahājayarāja died without leaving any issue and was succeeded by his nephew Mahāsudevarāja. All the charters of Mahājayarāja and Mahāsudevarāja were issued from Śarabhapura. When Mahāpravararāja came to the throne he began issuing his charters from Śrīpura, where evidently he had transferred his capital. In the seal of his Thakurdiya plates he is described as having won the earth by his own arms. If he really made some new conquests and assumed an independent status it must have been long after the fall of the Vākāṭakas. There is nothing to show that the Śarabhapura kings threatened Pṛthivīsena II in any way as asserted by A.S. Altekar.

The dangers to the dynasty of Pṛthivīsena II referred to in his Balaghat plates came possibly from Hariṣena who had been meddling in the affairs of the eastern Maharashtra since the time of Narendrasena.

The second danger threatened him directly and it came from the Nala dynasty whose existence is disclosed to us by the Rithpur C.P. inscription and the Podagarh record.[2] The Rithpur plates were discovered along with a set of copper plate of the Vākāṭaka queen Prabhāvatī Guptā. The inscription refers to *mahārāja-Bhaṭṭāraka-arthapati* Bhavaṭṭavarman of the

1. Some scholars maintain that the successor of Mahājayarāja was his younger brother Mānamātra. But there is no proof to substantiate the assertion. The identification of Mānamātra with Mahādurgarāja also appears to be untenable.
2. *Ep Ind*, xix, 100ff; xxi, 153ff

Nala dynasty and records the grant of a village called Kadamba-giri-grāma (Kalamba in the Morsi taluk of Amraoti where the plates were discovered). The grant is dated in the eleventh regnal year of the king and was issued from Nandivardhana, but actually made at Prayāga or the confluence of the Ganges and the Jumna. It does not follow, however, that Prayāga formed part of the dominion of Bhavaṭṭavarman for grants of distant villages were often made at holy places like Prayāga and Benares. We have seen that Nandivardhana was the capital of the main line of the Vākāṭakas and the Rithpur record thus shows unmistakably that it was conquered by the Nalas. Pṛthivīsena, however, was able to drive the invader out. This is proved indirectly by the Podagadh inscription of prince Skandavarman, son of king Bhavaṭṭavarman, informing us that the prince recovered the lost sovereignty and repopulated the capital. In the background of the Balaghat record stating that Pṛthivīsena II overcame all his dangers, this can only mean the defeat of either Bhavaṭṭavarman or his son Skandavarman, who had to acknowledge the suzerainty of the Vākāṭaka monarch. Later on prince Skandavarman managed to regain his independence somehow, though ruled evidently as a subordinate ally of Pṛthivīsena II.

From what has been stated above it will appear that both Pṛthivīsena II of the main branch and Hariṣena of the Vatsagulma house were great conquerors. Hariṣena possibly gave a death blow to the Traikūṭaka house of Aparānta and also threatened the main line by establishing a dynasty of his own choice in the Dakṣiṇa-Kośala region. He might have also helped the Nala king in occupying a portion of the Vidarbha country. But Pṛthivīsena II withstood successfully the danger created by his relative. In the Ajanta record, Hariṣena further claims his suzerainty over Kuntala, Lāṭa, Andhra and other countries. He might have remained satisfied by exacting tributes from these kingdoms, as Mirashi suggests.[1]

We have no record of any Vākāṭaka king after these two monarchs. From a critical study of the *Daśakumāracarita*, Mirashi has inferred that Hariṣena left a son who was weak and led a dissolute life and the feudatories began to show signs

1. *Corpus*, iv, xliii

of revolt. This ultimately led to an invasion of the kingdom by the Kadambas and the king suffered a serious defeat and was killed in the fight.[1] The suggestion is no doubt very interesting but the account of the *Daśakumāracarita* is a confused one. In this connection we may note that Vikramendravarman II, son of the Viṣṇukuṇḍin mahārāja Mādhavavarman I who came to the throne about 535 A.D., is described in the Chikkulla plates, as *Viṣṇukuṇḍi-Vākāṭa-vaṃśa-dvayālaṅkṛta-janmā*.[2] This shows that Mādhavavarman I was the son-in-law of a Vākāṭaka king. This king has been identified with Hariṣena, which, however, becomes chronologically impossible. He may have been the son-in-law of Pṛthivīsena II who ruled up to c. 525 A.D. It is not unlikely that after the death of Hariṣena, Pṛthivīsena II occupied the territory of the collateral branch to avenge the troubles created by Hariṣena himself. If Hariṣena left any heir he was possibly killed.

1. *ABORI*, xxvi, 30
2. *Ep Ind*, iv, 193f

CHAPTER XIII

FALL OF THE VĀKĀṬAKAS

It is difficult to determine how the Vākāṭaka dynasty which played such a glorious part in the annals of ancient Deccan came to an end in such on abrupt manner. Two theories have been put forward by scholars :

(a) that the Viṣṇukuṇḍin king Mādhavavarman I became too powerful and occupied the kingdom of the Vākāṭakas.

(b) that the Vākāṭakas met their end under the pressure of a Rāṣṭrakūṭa dynasty in the sixth century A.D.

Mādhavavarman

The first theory is based on the evidence of the Khanapur plates edited in Ep. Ind. xxvii, pp. 312ff. It maintains one Mādhavavarman who has been sought to be identified with Mādhavavarman I of the Viṣṇukuṇḍin dynasty who claims to have performed eleven aśvamedhas and thousand agniṣṭomas etc. On the basis of this identification it is claimed that Mādhavavarman I conquered Maharashtra and gave a death blow to the Vākāṭaka dynasty. The history of the Viṣṇukuṇḍin Mādhavavarman is still far from clear and so any speculation centring such a figure will remain always inconclusive. In any case, there are difficulties in identifying the Viṣṇukuṇḍin Mādhavavarman I with the king of the same name in the Khanapur plates :

(a) There is no other definite Viṣṇukuṇḍin records from the Maharashtra country nor there are any other references to his supremacy in later records.

(b) As already stated, the son of the Viṣṇukuṇḍin mahārāja Mādhavavarman I, Vikramendravarman II, who came to the throne about 535 A.D., is described in the Chikkulla plates as *Viṣṇukuṇḍi-Vākāṭa-vaṁśa-dvayālaṅkṛta-janmā*, showing that Mādhavavarman I was the son-in-law of a Vākāṭaka king.

Had Mādhavavarman I put an end to the rule of the Vākāṭakas, Vikramendravarman's statement becomes meaningless.

Mādhavavarman of the Khanapur plates was possibly a local king and cannot be identified with his namesake of the Viṣṇukuṇḍin dynasty.

Early Rāṣṭrakūṭas

Let us now turn to the second theory that the Vākāṭaka kingdom came to an end under the pressure of the Rāṣṭrakūṭas and in the sixth century there rose up a Rāṣṭrakūṭa kingdom in the Deccan. The main plank of the view is the Kauthem plates of the later Cālukya king Vikramāditya which state that the early Cālukya ruler Jayasiṁha defeated the Rāṣṭrakūta king Indra, son of Kṛṣṇa, who had a mighty force of 800 elephants and thereby established the Cālukya sovereignty.[1] This account has further been worked out on the basis of the following two records :

(a) The *Undikavatika grant* which describes Mānāṅka as 'the ornament of the Rashtrakutas' and then speaks of his son Devarāja whose son was Bhaviṣya who was succeeded by Abhimanyu.[2]

(b) The *Pandurangapalli plates* which speaks of Mānāṅka as the conqueror of Aṅga, Aśmaka and Vidarbha. His son Devarāja appears to have three sons, Jayarāja, Bhaviṣya and Abhidheya.[3]

We can thus draw up the following genealogy of the Rāṣṭrakūṭa family :

Mānāṅka
|
Devarāja
|
Bhaviṣya | Abhidheya | Jayarāja
|
Abhimanyu

So far we stand on somewhat sure ground. But the account has been complicated by several identifications. *First*, Mānāṅka

1. *Ind Ant*, xvi, 151ff
2. *Ep Ind*, viii, 63
3. *MASR*, 1929, 197

has been identified with the Śarabhapurīya king Mānamātra and his son Devarāja with Mānamātra's son Mahāsudevarāja. Thus it has been held that the dynasty ruled over an empire extending from the Kolhapur region, proved by the discovery of the Pandurangapalli plates, to the Kośala country where the charters of the Śarabhapurīya kings have been found. It is further believed that the empire after Devarāja became divided into three parts, Jayarāja ruling in Chattisgarh, Bhaviṣya in Western Madhya Pradesh and Abhidheya in Southern Maharashtra region. Abhimanyu succeeded his father Bhavīṣya and the three parts formed a loose federation.

The identification of Mānāṅka and his son Devarāja with Mānamātra and Mahāsudevarāja has no basis. It was first suggested by Sten Konow, then accepted by G.J-Dubreuil and later on became an obsession with most writers. The unsoundness of the theory has been ably demonstrated by D.C. Sircar on the following grounds :—

(a) 'that none of the Śarabhapurīyas ever claimed to be a Rāṣṭrakūṭa;
(b) that the two families apparently ruled over different territories from different capital cities;
(c) that the seal of the Śarabhapurīyas bears the representation of the Gaja-Lakshmī, while that of the Mānapura kings (the dynasty of Mānāṅka) the figure of a lion; and
(d) that the charters of the kings of Mānapura are not written in the box-headed script like those of the Śarabhapura kings.'

The above observations would shake up the theory of an *early big* Rāṣṭrakūṭa empire and there is no basis for thinking that king Indra, son of Kṛṣṇa, who is stated to have been defeated by the Cālukya ruler Jayasiṃha in c. 530 A.D., according to the Kauthem Plates of Vikramāditya, was a grandson of king Abhidheya of the Pandurangapalli plates. Even the Aihole inscription[1] which describes in minute details the achievements of all the predecessors of Pulakeśin II is silent over this feat of Jayasiṃha. On the other hand, the Aihole record informs us that Kīrtivarman had to conquer the Nalas of Bastar, the Mauryas

1. *Ep Ind*, vi, 4ff

of Konkan, the Kadambas of Karṅataka while his successor Maṅgalīśa annexed the kingdom of the Kalacuris.

The Undivatika and the Pandurangapalli records prove, however, the existence of the kingdom of Mānāṅka in the Maharashtra region, possibly after the fall of the Vākāṭakas. In these records the royal house of Mānāṅka is said to have its headquarter at Mānapura, which has been identified by V.V. Mirashi with Man in the Satara district.[1] The Pandurangapalli grant makes the interesting statement that Mānāṅka conquered Vidarbha, Aśmaka and Aṅga. The mention of Aṅga seem to indicate only that the king of the country entered into some sort of relationship with the ruler, while the kingdoms of Vidarbha and Aśmaka may have been actually conquered by him. Vidarbha was the kingdom of the main branch of the Vākāṭakas while Aśmaka which included Mūlaka, i.e., the district round Pratiṣṭhāna, modern Paithan on the Godavari in the Aurangabad district, was under the Vākāṭakas of the Basim branch and later on came under Pṛthivīsena II. Thus the rise of Mānāṅka might have been one of the causes of the downfall of the Vākāṭakas. Mānāṅka is also described in the same record as the chastiser of the Kuntalas which shows that he also fought with the Kadambas of the Kanarese country.

Mānāṅka was succeeded by his son Devarāja, who, as we have already seen, cannot be identified with Mahāsudevarāja, son of Mānamātra, the Śarabhapurīya monarch. V.V. Mirashi thinks that he is identical with the king of the same name mentioned in the Siroda C.P. charter issued from Candrapura in the twelfth regnal year of the king.[2] The king of the Siroda charter is stated, however, to have belonged to the family of the Bhojas. Candrapura has been identified with modern Chandore in Goa. This shows that while the Vākāṭakas had been ruling in the Western Maharashtra region a minor local dynasty of the Bhoja stock had been ruling on the western sea-coast. It is not clear whether this Bhoja dynasty was independent or owed allegiance to the Kadambas.

After Devarāja three more kings sat on the throne. They are his two sons Bhaviṣya and Abhidheya and grandson Abhimanyu.

1. *ABORI*, xxv, 42
2. *Ep Ind*, xxiv, 143f; xxvi, 337f

It is difficult to determine their order of succession. The Undivatika grant of Abhimanyu states that the king granted the village Uṇḍikavāṭikā in presence of Jayasiṃha who was the commander of the fort of Harivatsakotta. G. J-Dubreuil raises the question, can this Jayasiṃha 'who overthrew the Rāṣṭrakūṭa (?) king Indra' be the founder of the Cālukya dynasty, for, in the Cālukya records Jayasiṃha of the *Mānavya gotra* is the first king of the dynasty ?[1]

Tīvaradeva

The Vākāṭaka supremacy in the north-east came under challenge from the Somavaṁśī king Tīvaradeva whose Rajim and Baloda plates were issued from Śrīpura.[2] The dynasty ruled in Bhandak at least for three generations before Tīvaradeva and it may be noted that all their plates have been found in the region. From these Bhandak records and the records of Tīvaradeva and his successors, the following genealogical table of the dynasty may be drawn up:

Udayana

Indrabala — Name not preserved

Nannadeva — Īśānadeva — (1) — (2) — (3) — Bhavadeva Raṇakeśarin

Mahāśiva Tīvaradeva — Candragupta

Harṣagupta = Vasatā (daughter of Sūryavarman, *mahārāja* of Magadha)

Mahāśivagupta Bālārjuna — Raṇakeśarin

The synchronism Harṣagupta = Vasatā, daughter of Sūryavarman, *mahārāja* of Magadha, helps us to fix the date of Tīvaradeva, who was assigned to 8th century by Kielhorn.[3] This Sūryavarman should be identified with the prince of the same name, son of Īśānavarman of the Haraha inscription of

1. *AHD*, 111
2. *Corpus*, iii, 291ff; *Ep Ind*, vii, 10ff
3. *Ep Ind*, iv, 258

554 A.D.[1] Harṣagupta's father Candragupta was thus a contemporary of Sūryavarman, and hence the latter's elder brother Mahāśiva Tīvaradeva probably flourished in the period 530-550 A.D. Tīvaradeva overthrew Mahāpravararāja, the Śarabhapurīya king, who acknowledged the suzerainty of the Vākāṭakas and occupied his capital (*supra*). In the Baloda plates he describes himself as the lord of entire Kośala[2] and this proves that he became a king of considerable importance. The Viṣṇukuṇḍin king Mādhavavarman I defeated Tīvaradeva and occupied his capital. The rule of the dynasty, however, continued for some time.

Kalacuris

While Tīvaradeva occupied a portion of the Vākāṭaka empire in the east, the Kalacuris appeared on the north. All their copper plate charters available to us were issued from their camps fixed at different places such as Ujjayinī, Vidiśā and Ānandapura. V.V. Mirashi thinks that their capital was Māhiṣmatī or Mandhata on the Narmada. The Abhona plates of the Kalacuri year 347 = 597 A.D. was issued by the illustrious Saṅkaragaṇa, son of the illustrious Kṛṣṇarāja. It records a grant of hundred *nivartanas* of land in the village of Vallisika which was situated in the *viṣaya* of Bhogavardhana. The donee was a brāhmaṇa residing at Kallivana and the grant was made at the request of Gogga, possibly the queen. The identification of the above places gives us interesting results. Mirashi says, 'Kallivana, where the donee was residing is modern Kalvan, the chief town of the Kalvan taluka of the Nasik district. It may be noted in this connection that the present plates were found at Abhona which lies only seven miles west of Kalvan. Bhogavardhana, the headquarter of the district in which the donated village was situated, is probably Bhokardhan in the Hyderabad State, where a large Brāhmaṇical cave temple of about 8th Century A.D. has been recently excavated. Vallisika is modern Valsa, 7 miles south of Bhokardhan.'[3]

1. *Ep Ind*, xiv, 115
2. *Ep Ind*, vii, 105
3. *Corpus*, iv, 40

It would thus appear that the kingdom of Saṅkaragaṇa extended from Malwa to Maharashtra and Andhra in the south. Kṛṣṇarāja, his father, is not credited with any conquest which seems to indicate that he was a petty local ruler of the Māhiṣmatī region and it was Saṅkaragaṇa who first really made extensive conquests. It is difficult to determine what the boundary of his empire in the east was though in the epigraph he claims that his empire was bounded by the eastern and the western oceans.

The western extension of the empire may be determined to some extent by the Sankheda plate of the same king. The plate was issued from the victorious camp at Nirgundipadraka by Śāntilla the *balādhikṛta* (military officer) of Nirihullaka who bore the titles of *bhogikapālaka* and *mahāpīlupati* and who is described as meditating on the feet of the illustrious Saṅkaragaṇa, the son of the illustrious Kṛṣṇarāja.[1] The find spot of the above epigraph shows that the Kalacuri dominion comprised Gujarat, in the west and thus it might have extended upto the sea.

V.V. Mirashi thinks that Saṅkaragaṇa ruled from 575 to 600 A.D. and that there were at least two kings in the dynasty ruling before him. We know Saṅkaragaṇa's father was Kṛṣṇarāja but his grandfather's name has not come down to us. 'Kṛṣṇarāja's father seems to have extended his power in the east, west and south. In the west he supplanted the Traikūṭakas and divided his extensive kingdom among his feudatories. The Mauryas were placed in charge of Aparānta or North Konkan, while Gujarat or at least the central part of it was given in charge of Saṅgamasiṃha. We do not know whether Maharashtra including ancient Vidarbha was annexed to the Kalacuri kingdom during his reign or during that of his son Kṛṣṇarāja.'[2]

1. *Ep Ind*, ii, 22ff; *Corpus*, iv, 44ff
2. *ib.*, xlvi

Appendix V

A NOTE ON THE FAR SOUTH

The history of Far South of India, i.e., India south of the Krishna, is somewhat obscure during the period with which we are dealing. We have already referred to the early history of Kāñcī which is also far from clear. Traditionally the region was divided into three kingdoms and a number of smaller states subordinate to them. Aśoka in his edicts, as we have seen, refers however to the four states lying outside his empire towards the south as Cola, Pāṇḍya, Satiyaputa and Keralaputa.

In any case, the region lying to the south of the hill of Tirupati formed a distinct unit known as Tamilakam, predominantly Dravidian or Tamil in culture and language, and the orthodox Tamils looked down with disfavour the crossing of the Tirupati belt. The significance was that the Aryan culture prevailed in the north and the Dravidians did not look upon it with favour.

The Kaliṅga king Khāravela who was a contemporary of the Sātavāhana monarch Śātakarṇi I and thus appears to have ruled in the beginning of the Christian era makes two interesting statements regarding the Far South in his Hathigumpha record :

1. 'and (*he*) thoroughly breaks up the confederacy of the T[r]amira (Dramira) countries of one hundred and thirteen years which has been a source of danger to (*his*) Country (Janapada)'.
2. 'and a wonderful and marvellous enclosure of stockade for driving in the elephants (*he*)....and horses, elephants, jewels and rubies as well as numerous pearls in hundreds (*he*) causes to be brought here from the Pāṇḍya king.'

It is difficult to determine exactly what is meant by the above passages. There is hardly any reference in Tamil literature to show that the three principal states or any three states of the Far South formed a confederacy lasting for one hundred and thirteen years and we have no means to determine how any of the Tamil states became a danger to the kingdom of

Kaliṅga. Similarly, the significance of the second statement is also not clear. It possibly alludes to some presents received by the Kaliṅga king from the Pāṇḍya monarch. In any case the mention of the pearls of the Pāṇḍya country is interesting, for the pearl fishery of the place is referred to in the foreign and the indigenous accounts. Thus we have not only the mention of *Pāṇḍya-Kavāṭaṃ ca mauktikam* (*Arthaśāstra*, ii. 11), but also the interesting statement of the *Periplus of the Erythraean Sea* that 'from Comari toward the south this region extends to Colchi (Korkai), where the pearl-fisheries are; (they are worked by condemned criminals); and it belongs to the Pandian kingdom.'

II. Foreign accounts

The foreign accounts constitute the most authentic source for studying the history of the Far South during the period with which we are dealing here. When the Sātavāhanas were busy in establishing their power in the upper Deccan and were facing opposition from North Indian dynasties, Kāñcī established commercial relations with China and 'from the first century B.C. the products of Southern India had begun to reach China by sea, and that at the beginning of the Christian era, under orders of the court, a Chinese mission traversed the entire Indian ocean'. As K.A.N. Sastri points out, 'One of the most surprising results of recent research is the discovery by Paul Pelliot of a passage (II) in Pan Kou, a very early Chinese writer, attesting the existence of an active intercourse between China and the states of Insulindia and Southern India in the Han period, beginning from the second century B.C. If the text of Pan Kou has been correctly interpreted, it would warrant a somewhat drastic revision of the notions now held regarding the age when the Hindu colonisation of the eastern lands began.' Such activities would presuppose a well-organized government in the region without which commercial activities can hardly prosper. This seems to show further that economically Cola and the Pāṇḍya kingdoms on the eastern side of the Peninsula were in a flourishing state, a fact indirectly proved by a reference to a Pāṇḍyan embassy being sent at the court of the Roman emperor Augustus in the work of Strabo.

It is stated that the embassy was accompanied by an Indian sophist who committed himself to the flames at Athens, like Kalanos, who had exhibited a similar spectacle in the presence of Alexander.

Curiously enough we hear nothing about the western side of the Far South till we come to the *Periplus of the Erythraean Sea*, composed by an anonymous sailor between 60 and 80 A.D. He possibly went up to Nelcynda and thus had a first-hand knowledge of the western sea-board of India. He divides the Peninsular India into two divisions, *Dachinabades* (Dakṣiṇāpatha) and *Damirika* or Tamilakam, i.e., the country of the Tamils. The statement is interesting showing that in the first century A.D., Tamil was the chief language of the region. Damirica on the other hand was parcelled into three kingdoms, Cerobothra, the Pandian kingdom and Coast Country. We are fortunate in having an account of each of them:

1. Cerobothra—The *Periplus* states, 'Then comes Naura (Cannanore) and Tyndis (Ponnāni), the first markets of Damirica and then Muziris (Cranganore) and Nelcynda (certainly very near the modern Kottayam), which are now of leading importance.

Tyndis is of the kingdom of Cerobothra ; it is a village in plain sight by the sea. Muziris, of the same kingdom, abounds in ships sent there with cargoes from Arabia, and by the Greeks; it is located on a river, distant from Tyndis by river and sea five hundred stadia, and up the river from the shore twenty stadia'.

Nelcynda is stated to be a part of the Pandian kingdom and so there is no confusion here. But nothing is said about Naura, which from the nature of the account quoted above seems to have been outside Cerobothra. Its political status cannot be precisely determined. Possibly it was a small independent unit.

The kingdom of Cerobothra carried on extensive trade with the west. The chief object of export was pepper and malabathrum. Though the account of the *Periplus* is somewhat confused it seems that the other objects of export from this kingdom were fine pearls, ivory, silk cloth and also spikenard from the

Ganges. The description shows that the Cera kingdom maintained inland trade with distant places like the Gangetic country.

The Cera kingdom—In this background we may note the Sangam account that the Cera ruler Imaiyavaramban Neduñjeral Ādan captured the Yavanas, poured oil on their heads, bound their hands behind them and did not release them until they paid him a huge ransom. Here evidently the Yavanas referred to the western sailors who possibly offended the king by some audacious acts. The date of the king has been fixed c. 155 A.D. This seems to show that the western trade of the Cera kingdom that had begun in the middle of the first century had been continuing till the middle of the next century at least. It must, however, be admitted that in view of the exaggerated nature of the indigenous accounts we are not always faced with sober history. Thus the title of the king Imaiyavaramban is explained as meaning that he conquered the whole of India from the Himalayas to Cape Comorin, an assertion which appears to be absurd on the very face of it. He might have entered into some diplomatic connections with the North Indian rulers and this has been exaggerated into conquests by the poets.

The Pandian kingdom—We have already noted reference to the *Pandian* kingdom in the *Periplus* and other earlier classical writers. It appears to have been a big territory extending in the west up to the modern Kottayam and in the south up to Cape Comorin. As already stated it was a centre of pearl trade centred at Korkai and worked by condemned criminals.

The Coast Country—According to the *Periplus* the *Coast Country* or the Cola kingdom stretched from Colchi or Korkai towards the north and had a region inland called Argaru (Uraiyur). The *Periplus* states that 'at this place, and nowhere else, are bought the pearls gathered on the coast thereabouts; and from there are exported muslins, those called Argaritic'. Aelian also refers to the pearl fishing of the kingdom of Soras (from Tamil Sola) who was a contemporary of the Bactrian king Eucratides. The Cola kingdom had three important ports Camara (Kaveripatnam or Puhar), Poduca (Pondicherry?) and Sopatma (Markanam). These ports carried on trade both with the western coast, on the one hand, and the Gangetic country and Chryse (Burma?) on the other. In this connection we may note that recent excavations at Arikamedu, near Pondicherry, have brought to light the remains of a Roman trading station and fragments of Roman pottery belonging to the first two centuries. The Śangam works mention colonies of Yavana merchants on the coastal districts which evidently refer to places like Arikamedu and others.

Ptolemy in his *Geography* mentions Limirica, identical with Damirica of the *Periplus*, and speaks of the following political units:

1. The kingdom of Karoura ruled by Kerobothra (Keralaputra).
2. Pounatta (S.W. Mysore).
3. The kingdom of Aioi, with capital at Kothiara, usually located at S. Travancore.
4. The kingdom of the Pandioi (Pāṇḍya) with capital at Madoura or Madura.
5. The kingdom of the Kareoi, possibly in the valley of the river Tamraparni.
6. The kingdom of the Batoi, with capital at Nikama.
7. The kingdom of Orthoura, ruled by the Soringoi, possibly representing the old Cola janapada.
8. The kingdom of Malanga ruled by Basaranagas.
9. The kingdom of Sora ruled by Arkatos.

From the above account it is clear that at the time of Ptolemy, the Far South was divided into at least eight smaller kingdoms, leaving out of course Pounatta the political status of which is not clearly stated. In this connection we may also note the following passage from the *Geography*:

68. 'Between Mount Bettigo and Adeisathros are the Sorai nomads, with these towns:—
Sangamarta
Sora, the capital of Arkatos.

The Mount Bettigo is the same as the Tamil Podigai, i.e., the Malaya ranges, while the Adeisthros refers to the Sahya or the Western Ghat ranges. The above description thus shows that the Sorai nomads lived somewhere in the South-West of the Deccan Peninsula. The name Sora, however, points to the Colas while Arkatos possibly refers to the Arkot region This shows that here we have really an account of the Arouarnoi or the Aruvanādu region, which really formed a part of the Cola janapada. This is one of the many instances where Ptolemy has located two different names of the same locality in two different places.

III. Indigenous accounts

Tamil Sangam literature is practically our only source for studying the history of the age. Judged in the background of chronology, Malayalam will be the youngest, while Telegu and the Kanarese had their beginning about the eighth century A.D. Though older in date the Sangam literature is full of fanciful stories no doubt mixed up with some historical facts and in the present stage of our knowledge it is very difficult for us to use this source without proper scrutiny. As K.A.N. Sastri puts it, 'we have the story of the three Tamil Sangams which is on the face of it a stupendous legend, but yet it has passed for history. And people insist again and again in South India in our talking only of the third Sangam'.

Tamil historians who have critically studied this literature have come tentatively to the conclusion that from the first century B.C. to the first century A.D. or a little later even, the Colas were the supreme power; then the supremacy passed on to the Pāṇḍyas while the Cera dynasties played a somewhat insignificant role compared to the Pāṇḍya ones. It must however be admitted that even such an assertion is only a tentative one and until fresh evidences are coming to the surface we have to abide by the same. Besides the above three monarchies there were many *vel* chieftains ruling in different parts of the land. These chieftains claim connection with Viṣṇu and Agastya and Ptolemy's kingdom of Aioi, referred to before, may be one such *vel* constituency.

Among the early Cola kings two names stand predominant, Karikāla and Kocceṅgaṇān. It is neither possible to determine the relationship between the two nor to fix their relative dates. From the preserved legends its appears that Karikāla possibly had no birthright to the throne but he somehow managed to become the king of the land. At the battle of Veṇṇi, identified with Kovil Veṇṇi, a village fifteen miles to the east of Tanjore, Karikāla defeated a confederacy of the Pāṇḍya and Cera kings aided by eleven minor chieftains. Puhar or Kaveripattinam was possibly his capital, while Kocceṅgaṇān, belonging to the rival Cola line, possibly ruled at Uraiyur or Uragapura and there were occasional civil strife between the two lines. Karikāla's rise pushed the Uraiyur line into the background, especially after the battle of Veṇṇi. In the Tamil works we meet with many legends regarding Karikāla's conquests but his victory at the battle of Vākaipparandalai in which he defeated a confederacy of nine chieftains is a memorable one. By his conquests the Cola king acquired some sort of control over the Cera and the Pāṇḍya kings and thus became in a way the *de facto* master of the region lying to the south of Kaveri. Later Ceylonese Chronicles credit him with the conquest of the island but it is difficult to determine how far the account is authentic as it is not mentioned in the *Mahāvaṃśa*.

The Cola monarch is said to have introduced a new system of irrigation in his kingdom. Thus he is credited with controlling the Kaveri and distributing its water through different channels. The Grand Anicut Srirangam is regarded as being Karikāla's creation, and if it be a fact then Karikāla certainly introduced a new chapter in the history of Cola agriculture. Tamil poems describe him as the promoter of art, trade and industry and as patronising brāhmaṇical religion and Tamil literature. But as numerous legends have cropped up round the name of the monarch it is not always possible for us to determine what he actually did. In any case, he is one of the early noted rulers of ancient Cola kingdom.

Among the Pāṇḍya kings, Neḍuñjeliyan is an important figure. He faced a joint attack of Cola, Cera and five other minor chieftains at the gates of Madura but drove them out beyond the frontier after a decisive encounter to the north-west of Tiruvalur. A patron of poets and follower of brāhmaṇical religion, Neḍuñjeliyan also defeated the chieftains of Nidur and Kongu and thus extended the boundaries of his kingdom. He possibly ruled about the beginning of the third century A.D.

As already stated, the Cera kings practically played a minor part in the politics of the period with which we are dealing here. Imaiyavaramban Neḍuñjeral Ādan, as noted before, defeated the Yavanas who are possibly to be identified with the

Greek and Arab sailors who came to the kingdom for purpose of trade. (*supra*) He is also said to have conquered Kadambu near the sea which several scholars identify with the Kadambas of Banavāsī or Vaijayantī. There is some controversy regarding the identification of the Cera capital Vañji. Some maintain that it is Karur near Trichinopoly while according to others it is Tiruvañjikulam on the west coast of Cochin.

We have already noted the history of Kāñcī during the early centuries of our era. Karikāla is said to have conquered the Oliyar who have been identified with the Kalabhras by T.V. Mahalingam, who further thinks that the latter were of Nāga lineage. This would seem to indicate that the predecessors of Sornagos had been ruling in the Kāñcī region which was occupied by the Oliyars from a very early period. It is however pointed out that Tondaimāṉ Ilandiraiyan who is said to have ruled at Kāñcī was possibly related to Karikāla and was latter's contemporary. It is really difficult to come to any definite conclusion regarding the status and lineage of Ilandiraiyan. In any case, the relation between Ilandiraiyan and the Pallavas or with the Oliyar remains somewhat vague and uncertain.

Appendix VI

THE MUḌĀNANDAS AND THE CUṬUS

It has already been shown that the Kuntala country was the citadel of the Sātavāhana power when the homeland of the dynasty passed under the heels of the Scythians, and it was the Vaijayantī army of Gautamīputra that freed the land from the hands of Nahapāna. Later on Vaijayantī or Banavāsī was placed under the rule of an *amātya* Śivagupta. We do not know exactly whether the successors of Yajñaśrī Śātakarṇi in the Western Maharashtra region had any hold over the Kanarese country once under the sway of the Sātavāhanas.

The Muḍānandas

Large lead coins bearing the legend *raño muḍānaṃdasa* have been found from the district of Karwar. *Muḍa* is evidently identical with *Muṇḍas*. The *Viṣṇu Purāṇa* maintains that thirteen Muṇḍa kings ruled after the Andhras, i.e., the Sātavāhanas. The coins signifying 'Joy of the Muṇḍas' evidently belong to one of the members of the dynasty. Some scholars have identified the Muḍānandas with the pirate kings mentioned in the *Geography* of Ptolemy.

The Cuṭus

From the same region as referred to above have been found lead coins bearing the legend *raño cuṭukulānaṃdasa*. We have at least two inscriptions referring to the Cuṭu kings. Thus a Banavāsī stone inscription mentions Hārītīputra Viṣṇukaḍa Cuṭukulānanda Śātakarṇi who in the twelfth year of his reign made a gift of a nāga, a tank and a *vihāra*. The Mallavalli inscription refers to the same king Mānavya-sagotra Hārītīputra Viṣṇukadda Cuṭukulananda Śātakarṇi who in the first year of his reign made the grant of a village. The king is described as the rājā of the city of Vaijayantī.

On the same pillar there is an inscription of an early Kadamba king referring to Mānavya-sagotra Hārītīputra

Vaijayantīpati Śivaskandavarman who is stated to have ruled previously in the same locality. This Śivaskandavarman has been supposed to be a member of the Cuṭu dynasty which however seems to be quite unconvincing since he does not adopt title like Cuṭukulānanda.

Thus in the present state of our knowledge we know of only one Muṇḍa king and one Cuṭu king. E. J. Rapson maintains that rājā Muḍānanda reigned after rājā Cuṭu-kulānanda. D. C. Sircar, however, holds exactly an opposite view. In the absence of more evidences it is not possible to come to a definite conclusion. Like the Kuras of Kolapur region, the Muḍānandas appear to have been local rulers of the North Kanara region possibly reigning contemporaneously with the Cuṭus who occupied Vaijayantī and the surrounding locality. Both of them appear to have been conquered by the Kadambas.

SELECT BIBLIOGRAPHY

(The list contains the names of a few books *only* bearing on the subject)

Aiyangar, S.K. — "The Vākāṭakas and their place in the History of India" *ABORI*, v, 31-54

Allan, J. — "The Vākāṭakas in Gupta History" *QIMS*, xv, 153-64

Catalogue of Ancient Indian coins in the British Museum, London, 1936

Altekar, A.S. — *Rāshṭrakūṭas and their times*, Poona, 1934

"Were the Vākāṭakas defeated by the Guptas in c. 350 A.D.?" *IC*, ix, 99-106

"Was there a Rāshṭrakūṭa Empire in the 6th century A.D.?" *ABORI*, xxiv, 149-55

Bhandarkar, D.R. — "Deccan of the Sātavāhana Period" *IA*, xlvii, 1918

Aśoka

Bhandarkar, R.G. — *The Early History of the Dekkan*, Bombay, 1895

Burgess, J. — *Buddhist Stūpas of Amarāvatī and Jayayyapeta*

Chanda, R.P. — *Indo-Aryan Races*

Chattopadhyaya, S. — *Social life in Ancient India*, Calcutta, 1965

Early History of North-India, Calcutta, 1968

The Śakas in India, Santiniketan, 1967

Chhabra, B. Ch. — "Kingdom of Mekala" *Bhārata Kaumudī*, i, 215-9

Cunningham, A. — *Coins of Ancient India*, London, 1891

Dubreuil, G.J. — *Ancient History of the Deccan*, Pondicherry, 1920

Gangoly, O.C. — "Who were the Sātavāhanas?" *JAHRS*, xi

Gopalachari, K. — *Early History of the Andhra Country*, Madras, 1941

Grierson, G.A. — *Linguistic Survey of India*, 1927

Jayaswal, K.P. — *History of India*, A.D. 150-350, Lahore, 1933

Keith, A.B. — *History of Sanskrit Literature*

Kirfel, W. — *Die kosmographic der Inder*

Kosambi, D.D. — *Ancient India*, London, 1965

Krishna, M.H. — "The Early Rāshṭrakūṭas of the Sixth century A.D." *PIHC*, vii, 70-7

Krishna Rao, B.V. — *Early Dynasties of the Andhradeśa*, Madras, 1942

Law, B.C. — *Historical Geography of Ancient India*, Paris, 1954

Macdonell, A. and Keith, A.B. — *Vedic Index*, 2 *vols*., London, 1912

Mahalingam, T.V. — *Kāñcīpuram*, Asia Publishing

Majumdar, R.C. — "Note on the Genealogy and Chronology of the Vākāṭakas" *JRASB* (*L*), xii, 1-5
"The Vākāṭaka Queen Prabhāvatīguptā" *POC*, xiii, 423-5
"Outline of the History of Kaliṅga" *Dacca University Studies*, ii. 2, 1ff

Majumdar, R.C. and Altekar, A.S. — *New History of Indian People, vol.* vi, Lahore, 1946
The Vedic Age
The Vākāṭaka-Gupta Age, Banaras, 1954
The Age of Imperial Unity, Bombay, 1960

Mandalik, V.N. — "Śālivāhana and the Śālivāhana Saptaśatī" *JBBRAS*, x

Marshall, J. — *A Guide to Taxila*

M'Crindle — *Ancient India as described by Megasthenes and Arrian*, Calcutta

Mirashi, V.V. — "An Ancient Dynasty of Khandesh" *PIHC*, 1944
Studies in Indology
"Historical Data in the Daśakumāracharita" *ABORI*, xxvi, 20-31
"Some Royal Poets of the Vākāṭaka Age" *IHQ*, xxi, 193-201
"The Vākāṭaka Chronology" *IHQ*, xxiv, 148-155

Mirashi, V.V. "The Vākāṭaka Dynasty of the Central Provinces and Berar" *Annual Bulletin of the Nagpur University Historical Society*, no.1, pp. 8-37

Inscriptions of the Kalachuri-Chedi Era, pt. i, Ootacamund, 1955

Mukherjee, B.N. *The Kushāṇas and the Deccan*, Calcutta, 1968

Pai, M.G. "Genealogy and Chronology of the Vākāṭakas" *JIH*, xiv, 1-26; 165-204

Pargiter, F.E. *Dynasties of the Kali Age*

Ancient Indian Historical Tradition, Motilal Banarsidass, 1962

Przyluski, J. "Hippokoura et Śātakarṇi" *JRAS*, 1929

Raghavan, V. "Kālidāsa's Kuntaleśvaradautya" B.C. Law volume ii, 191-7

Rao, B.V. Krishna *History of the Early Dynasties of Andhradeśa*, c. 200-625 A.D., Madras, 1942

Rao, M. Rama *Glimpses of Dakkan History*, Orient Longmans, 1951

Sātavāhana Coins in the Andhra Pradesh Govt. Museum, Hyderabad, 1961

Rapson, E.J. *British Museum Catalogue of the Coins of the Andhra Dynasty, Western Kshatrapa Dynasty, and the Bodhi Dynasty*, London, 1908

Raychaudhuri, H.C. *Political History of Ancient India*, Calcutta, 1938

Age of the Nandas and the Mauryas

Sastri, K.A.N. *A History of South India*, Oxford University Press, 1958

A Comprehensive History of India, Orient Longmans, 1957

Historical Method in Relation to Problems of South Indian History, Madras, 1941

Foreign Notices of South India, Madras, 1939

The Colas, Madras, 1935

Schoff, W.H. *The Periplus of the Erythraean Sea*, Longman Green & Co., 1912

Sircar, D.C. "A Note on the Vākāṭakas" *JRASB* (*L*), xii, 71-3

"Mahārājas Svāmidāsa, Bhuluṇḍa and Rudradāsa" *IHQ*, xxii

Select Inscriptions bearing on Indian History and Civilization, Calcutta, 1942

Successors of the Sātavāhanas, Calcutta, 1939

"Was Berar the Home Province of the Sātavāhanas?" *JNSI*, iii, 1941

"Further Notes on the Vākāṭakas" *JRASB* (*L*), xiii, 75-8

"Kuntala and Aśmaka" *IHQ*, xxiii

Smith, V.A. "The Vākāṭaka Dynasty of Berar in the 4th and 5th centuries" *JRAS*, 1914, 317-38

"Samudra Gupta" *JRAS*, 1897

"Andhra History and Coinage" *ZDMG*, 1902

Subba Rao, R. "Early History of North-East Deccan from Original Sources" *POC*, v, pt. 1, 492-524

Subramanian, K.R. *Buddhist Remains in Andhra and Andhra History, A.D.* 225-610, Madras, 1932

Tarn, W.W. *The Greeks in Bactria and India*, Cambridge, 1951

Venkataramayya, M. "Notes on the Ancient Political Geography of South India" *JOR*, xii

Yazdani, G. *The Early History of the Deccan*, Oxford University Press, 1960

Annals of the Bhandarkar Oriental Research Institute

Archaeological Survey of India Reports

Archaeological Survey of Western India

Bombay Gazetteer I. ii, Bombay, 1896

Corpus Inscriptionam Indicarum, II-IV

Epigraphia Indica

Indian Antiquary

Indian Historical Quarterly
Journal Asiatique
Journal of the Andhra Historical Research Society
Journal of the Bombay Branch of the Royal Asiatic Society
Journal of the Bihar and Orissa Research Society
Journal of Indian History
Journal of the Numismatic Society of India
Journal of the Royal Asiatic Society of Great Britain
Journal of the Royal Asiatic Society of Bengal
Mysore Archaeological Survey Report
Proceedings of the Indian History Congress
Proceedings of the All India Oriental Conference

INDEX

O

P

R

S

ERRATA

Page	*Line*	*Read*	*For*
6	21	Barbaricum	Barbarieum
17	22	*omit OHI*	
22	25	Tamilakam	Tamilacam
72	15	Hariṣena	Harisena
89	11	Siripolemaios	Siriptolemaios
94	13	Kukura	Kukara
98	13	G. V. Rao	G. B. Rao
101	1	Śakasena	Sakasena
117	31	Banavāsī	Vanavāsī
168	9	Citravarman	Chitravarman
171	20	*omit* III	
179	13	Podagarh	Podagadh